The Eventful History Of The Mutiny And Piratical Seizure Of H.M.S. Bounty: Its Cause And Consequences

Sir John Barrow

Contents

PREFACE 7
CHAPTER I OTAHEITE 9
CHAPTER II THE BREAD-FRUIT 34
CHAPTER III THE MUTINY 48
CHAPTER IV THE OPEN-BOAT NAVIGATION 71
CHAPTER V THE 'PANDORA' 102
CHAPTER VI THE COURT-MARTIAL 142
CHAPTER VII THE KING'S WARRANT 171
CHAPTER VIII THE LAST OF THE MUTINEERS 196
CONCLUSION 234
ADDITIONAL NOTE 239
NOTES: 245

THE EVENTFUL HISTORY OF THE MUTINY AND PIRATICAL SEIZURE OF H.M.S. BOUNTY: ITS CAUSE AND CONSEQUENCES

BY

Sir John Barrow

PREFACE

The Editor of this little volume (for he presumes not to write *Author*) has been induced to bring into one connected view what has hitherto appeared only as detached fragments (and some of these not generally accessible)--the historical narrative of an event which deeply interested the public at the time of its occurrence, and from which the naval service in particular, in all its ranks, may still draw instructive and useful lessons.

The story in itself is replete with interest. We are taught by ***The Book*** of sacred history that the disobedience of our first parents entailed on our globe of earth a sinful and a suffering race: in our time there has sprung up from the most abandoned of this sinful family--from pirates, mutineers, and murderers--a little society which, under the precepts of that sacred volume, is characterized by religion, morality, and innocence. The discovery of this happy people, as unexpected as it was accidental, and all that regards their condition and history, partake so much of the romantic as to render the story not ill adapted for an epic poem. Lord Byron, indeed, has partially treated the subject; but by blending two incongruous stories, and leaving both of them imperfect, and by mixing up fact with fiction, has been less felicitous than usual; for, beautiful as many passages in his *Island* are, in a region where every tree, and flower, and fountain breathe poetry, yet as a whole the poem is feeble and deficient in dramatic effect.

There still remains to us at least one poet, who, if he could be prevailed on to undertake it, would do justice to the story. To his suggestion the publication of the present narrative owes its appearance. But a higher object at present is engaging his attention, which, when completed, judging from that portion already before the public, will have raised a splendid and lasting monument to the name of William Sotheby, in his translation of the *Iliad* and the ***Odyssey***.

To the kindness of Mrs. Heywood, the relict of the late Captain Peter Heywood, the Editor is indebted for those beautiful and affectionate letters, written by a beloved sister to her unfortunate brother, while a prisoner and under sentence of death; as well as for some occasional poetry, which displays an intensity of feeling, a tenderness of expression, and a high tone of sentiment that do honour to the head and heart of this amiable and accomplished lady. Those letters also from the brother to his deeply afflicted family will be read with peculiar interest.

CHAPTER I
OTAHEITE

The gentle island, and the genial soil,
The friendly hearts, the feasts without a toil,
The courteous manners but from nature caught,
The wealth unhoarded, and the love unbougnt,

* * * * *

The bread-tree, which, without the ploughshare, yields
The unreap'd harvest of unfurrow'd fields,
And bakes its unadulterated loaves
Without a furnace in unpurchased groves,
And flings off famine from its fertile breast,
A priceless market for the gathering guest;--
These, etc.--
      BYRON.

The reign of George III will be distinguished in history by the great extension and improvement which geographical knowledge received under the immediate auspices of this sovereign. At a very early period, after his accession to the throne of these realms, expeditions of discovery were undertaken, 'not (as Dr. Hawkesworth observes) with a view to the acquisition of treasure, or the extent of dominion, but for the improvement of commerce, and the increase and diffusion of knowledge.' This excellent monarch was himself no mean proficient in the science of geography; and it may be doubted if any one of his subjects, at the period alluded to, was in possession of so extensive or so well-arranged a cabinet of maps and charts as his was, or who understood their merits or their defects so well as he did.

The first expeditions that were sent forth, after the conclusion of the war, were those of Byron, Wallis, and Carteret. In the instructions to the first of these commanders it is said, 'there is reason to believe that lands and islands of great extent, hitherto unvisited by any European power, may be found in the Atlantic Ocean, between the Cape of Good Hope and the Magellanic Strait, within the latitudes convenient for navigation, and in climates adapted to the produce of commodities useful in commerce.' It could not require much knowledge or consideration to be assured that, between the Cape and the Strait, climates producing commodities useful in commerce, with the exception of whales and seals, were likely to be found. The fact was that, among the real objects of this and other subsequent voyages, there was one which had engaged the attention of certain philosophers, from the time of the Spanish navigator, Quiros: this able navigator had maintained that a **Terra Australis incognita** must necessarily exist, somewhere in the high latitudes of the southern hemisphere, to counterbalance the great masses of land in those of the northern one, and thus maintain a just equipoise of the globe.

While these expeditions were in progress, the Royal Society, in 1768, addressed an application to the king, praying him to appoint a ship of war to convey to the South Seas Mr. Alexander Dalrymple (who had adopted the opinion of Quiros), and certain others, for the main purpose, however, of observing the transit of Venus over the sun's disc, which was to happen in the year 1769. By the king's command, a bark of three hundred and seventy tons was taken up by the Admiralty to perform this service, but, as Mr. Dalrymple was a civilian, he could not be entrusted with the command of the ship, and on that account declined going in her.

The command was therefore conferred on Lieutenant James Cook, an officer of undoubted ability, and well versed in astronomy and the theory and practice of navigation, with whom the Royal Society associated Mr. Charles Green, who had long been assistant to Dr. Bradley, the astronomer royal, to aid him in the observation of the transit. Mr. Banks, a private gentleman of good fortune, who afterwards became the valuable and distinguished President of the Royal Society, and Dr. Solander, a Swedish gentleman of great acquirements, particularly in natural history, accompanied Lieutenant Cook on this interesting voyage. The islands of Marquesas de Mendoza, or those of Rotterdam or Amsterdam, were proposed by the Royal Society as proper places for making the observation. While fitting out, however, Captain Wallis returned from his expedition, and strongly recommended as most suitable for the purpose, Port Royal Harbour, on an island he had discovered, to which he had given the name of 'King George's Island,' and which has since been known by its native name, *Otaheite* or *Tahite*.[1]

This lovely island is most intimately connected with the mutiny which took place on board the *Bounty*, and with the fate of the mutineers and their innocent offspring. Its many seducing temptations have been urged as one, if not the main, cause of the mutiny, which was supposed, at least by the commander of that ship, to have been excited by--

> Young hearts which languish'd for some sunny isle,
> Where summer years, and summer women smile,
> Men without country, who, too long estranged,
> Had found no native home, or found it changed,
> And, half uncivilized, preferr'd the cave
> Of some soft savage to the uncertain wave.

It may be proper, therefore, as introductory to the present narrative, to give a general description of the rich and spontaneous gifts which Nature has lavished on this once 'happy island;'--of the simple and ingenuous manners of its natives,--and of those allurements which were supposed, erroneously however, to have occasioned the unfortunate catastrophe alluded to;--to glance at

> The nymphs' seducements and the magic bower,

as they existed at the period of the first intercourse between the Otaheitans and the crews of those ships, which carried to their shores, in succession, Wallis, Bougainville, and Cook.

The first communication which Wallis had with these people was unfortunately of a hostile nature. Having approached with his ship close to the shore, the usual symbol of peace and friendship, a branch of the plantain tree, was held up by a native in one of the numerous canoes that surrounded the ship. Great numbers, on being invited, crowded on board the stranger ship, but one of them, being butted on the haunches by a goat, and turning hastily round, perceived it rearing on its hind legs, ready to repeat the blow, was so terrified at the appearance of this strange animal, so different from any he had ever seen, that, in the moment of terror, he jumped overboard, and all the rest followed his example with the utmost precipitation.

This little incident, however, produced no mischief; but as the boats were sounding in the bay, and several canoes crowding round them, Wallis suspected the islanders had a design to attack them, and, on this mere suspicion, ordered the boats by signal to come on board, 'and at the same time,' he says, 'to intimidate the Indians, I fired a nine-pounder over their heads.' This, as might have been imagined, startled the islanders, but did not prevent them from attempting immediately to cut off the cutter, as she was standing towards the ship. Several stones were thrown into this boat, on which the commanding officer fired a musket, loaded with buckshot, at the man who threw the first stone, and wounded him in the shoulder.

Finding no good anchorage at this place, the ship proceeded to another part of the island, where, on one of the boats being assailed by the Indians in two or three canoes, with their clubs and paddles in their hands, 'Our people,' says the commander, 'being much pressed, were obliged to fire, by which one of the assailants was killed, and another much wounded.' This unlucky rencontre did not, however, prevent, as soon as the ship was moored, a great number of canoes from coming off the next morning, with hogs, fowls, and fruit. A brisk traffic soon commenced, our people exchanging knives, nails, and trinkets, for more substantial articles of food, of which they were in want. Among the canoes that came out last were some double ones of very large size, with twelve or fifteen stout men in each, and it was observed that they had little on board except a quantity of round pebble stones. Other canoes came off along with them, having only women on board; and while these females were assiduously practising their allurements, by attitudes that could not be misunderstood, with the view, as it would seem, to distract the attention of the crew, the large double canoes closed round the ship; and as these advanced, some of the men began singing, some blowing conchs, and others playing on flutes. One of them, with a person sitting under a canopy, approached the ship so close, as to allow this person to hand up a bunch of red and yellow feathers, making signs it was for the captain. He then put off to a little distance, and, on holding up the branch of a cocoa-nut tree, there was an universal shout from all the canoes, which at the same moment moved towards the ship, and a shower of stones was poured into her on every side. The guard was now ordered to fire, and two of the quarter-deck guns, loaded with small shot, were fired among them at the same time, which created great terror and confusion, and caused them to retreat to a short distance. In a few minutes, however, they renewed the attack. The great guns were now ordered to be discharged among them, and also into a mass of canoes that were putting off from the shore. It is stated that, at this time, there could not be less than three hundred canoes about the ship, having on board at least two thousand men. Again they dispersed, but having soon collected into something like order, they hoisted white streamers, and pulled towards the ship's stern, when they again began to throw stones with great force and dexterity, by the help of slings, each of the stones weighing about two pounds, and many of them wounded the people on board. At length a shot hit the canoe that apparently had the chief on board, and cut it asunder. This was no sooner observed by the rest, than they all dispersed in such haste, that in half an hour there was not a single canoe to be seen; and all the people who had crowded the shore fled over the hills with the utmost precipitation. What was to happen on the following day was matter of conjecture, but this point was soon decided.

The white man landed;--need the rest be told?
The new world stretch'd its dusk hand to the old.

Lieutenant Furneaux, on the next morning, landed, without opposition, close to a fine river that fell into the bay--stuck up a staff on which was hoisted a pendant,--turned a turf,--and by this process took possession of the island in the name of his Majesty, and called it **King George the Third's Island**. Just as he was embarking, an old man, to whom the Lieutenant had given a few trifles, brought some green boughs, which he threw down at the foot of the staff, then retiring, brought about a dozen of his countrymen, who approached the staff in a supplicating posture, then retired and brought two live hogs, which they laid down at the foot of the staff, and then began to dance. After this ceremony the hogs were put into a canoe and the old man carried them on board, handing up several green plantain leaves, and uttering a sentence on the delivery of each. Some presents were offered him in return, but he would accept of none.

Concluding that peace was now established, and that no further attack would be made, the boats were sent on shore the following day to get water. While the casks were filling, several natives were perceived coming from behind the hills and through the woods, and at the same time a multitude of canoes from behind a projecting point of the bay. As these were discovered to be laden with stones, and were making towards the ship, it was concluded their intention was to try their fortune in a second grand attack. 'As to shorten the contest would certainly lessen the mischief, I determined,' says Captain Wallis, 'to make this action decisive, and put an end to hostilities at once.' Accordingly a tremendous fire was opened at once on all the groups of canoes, which had the effect of immediately dispersing them. The fire was then directed into the wood, to drive out the islanders, who had assembled in large numbers, on which they all fled to the hill, where the women and children had seated themselves. Here they collected to the amount of several thousands, imagining themselves at that distance to be perfectly safe. The captain, however, ordered four shot to be fired over them, but two of the balls, having fallen close to a tree where a number of them were sitting, they were so struck with terror and consternation, that, in less than two minutes, not a creature was to be seen. The coast being cleared, the boats were manned and armed, and all the carpenters with their axes were sent on shore, with directions to destroy every canoe they could find; and we are told this service was effectually performed, and that more than fifty canoes, many of which were sixty feet long, and three broad, and lashed together, were cut to pieces.

This act of severity must have been cruelly felt by these poor people, who, without iron or any kind of tools, but such as stones, shells, teeth, and bones supplied them with, must have spent months and probably years in the construction of one of these extraordinary double boats.

Such was the inauspicious commencement of our acquaintance with the natives of Otaheite. Their determined hostility and perseverance in an unequal combat could only have arisen from one of two motives--either from an opinion that a ship of such magnitude, as they had never before beheld, could only be come to their coast to take their country from them; or an irresistible temptation to endeavour, at all hazards, to possess themselves of so valuable a prize. Be that as it may, the dread inspired by the effects of the cannon, and perhaps a conviction of the truth of what had been explained to them, that the 'strangers wanted only provisions and water,' had the effect of allaying all jealousy; for from the day of the last action, the most friendly and uninterrupted intercourse was established, and continued to the day of the *Dolphin's* departure; and provisions of all kinds, hogs, dogs, fruit, and vegetables, were supplied in the greatest abundance, in exchange for pieces of iron, nails, and trinkets.

As a proof of the readiness of these simple people to forgive injuries, a poor woman, accompanied by a young man bearing a branch of the plantain tree, and another man with two hogs, approached the gunner, whom Captain Wallis had appointed to regulate the market, and looking round on the strangers with great attention, fixing her eyes sometimes on one and sometimes on another, at length burst into tears. It appeared that her husband and three of her sons had been killed in the attack on the ship. While this was under explanation, the poor creature was so affected as to require the support of the two young men, who from their weeping were probably two more of her sons. When somewhat composed, she ordered the two hogs to be delivered to the gunner, and gave him her hand in token of friendship, but would accept nothing in return.

Captain Wallis was now so well satisfied that there was nothing further to apprehend from the hostility of the natives, that he sent a party up the country to cut wood, who were treated with great kindness and hospitality by all they met, and the ship was visited by persons of both sexes, who by their dress and behaviour appeared to be of a superior rank. Among others was a tall lady about five and forty years of age, of a pleasing countenance and majestic deportment. She was under no restraint, either from diffidence or fear, and conducted herself with that easy freedom which generally distinguishes conscious superiority and habitual command. She accepted some small present which the captain gave her, with a good grace and much pleasure; and having observed that he was weak and suffering from ill health, she pointed to the shore, which he understood to be an invitation, and made signs that he would go thither the next morning. His visit to this lady displays so much character and good feeling, that it will best be described in the captain's own words.

'The next morning I went on shore for the first time, and my princess or rather queen, for such by her authority she appeared to be, soon after came to me, followed by many of her attendants. As she perceived that my disorder had left me very weak, she ordered her people to take me in their arms, and carry me not only over the river, but all the way to her house; and observing that some of the people who were with me, particularly the first lieutenant and purser, had also been sick, she caused them also to be carried in the same manner, and a guard, which I had ordered out upon the occasion, followed. In our way, a vast multitude crowded about us, but upon her waving her hand, without speaking a word, they withdrew, and left us a free passage. When we approached near her house, a great number of both sexes came out to meet her; these she presented to me, after having intimated by signs that they were her relations, and taking hold of my hand she made them kiss it.

'We then entered the house, which covered a piece of ground three hundred and twenty-seven feet long, and forty-two feet broad. It consisted of a roof thatched with palm leaves, and raised upon thirty-nine pillars on each side, and fourteen in the middle. The ridge of the thatch, on the inside, was thirty feet high, and the sides of the house, to the edge of the roof, were twelve feet high; all below the roof being open. As soon as we entered the house, she made us sit down, and then calling four young girls, she assisted them to take off my shoes, draw down my stockings, and pull off my coat, and then directed them to smooth down the skin, and gently chafe it with their hands. The same operation was also performed on the first lieutenant and the purser, but upon none of those who appeared to be in health. While this was doing, our surgeon, who had walked till he was very warm, took off his wig to cool and refresh himself: a sudden exclamation of one of the Indians, who saw it, drew the attention of the rest, and in a moment every eye was fixed upon the prodigy, and every operation was suspended. The whole assembly stood some time motionless, in silent astonishment, which could not have been more strongly expressed, if they had discovered that our friend's limbs had been screwed on to the trunk. In a short time, however, the young women who were chafing us, resumed their employment, and having continued for about half an hour, they dressed us again, but in this they were, as may easily be imagined, very awkward; I found great benefit, however, from the chafing, and so did the lieutenant and the purser.

'After a little time our generous benefactress ordered some bales of Indian cloth to be brought out, with which she clothed me, and all that were with me, according to the fashion of the country. At first I declined the acceptance of this favour, but being unwilling not to seem pleased with what was intended to please me, I acquiesced. When we went away, she ordered a very large sow, big with young, to be taken down to the boat, and accompanied us thither herself. She had given directions to her people to carry me, as they had done when I came, but as I chose rather to walk, she took me by the arm, and whenever we came to a plash of water or dirt, she lifted me over with as little trouble as it would have cost me to have lifted over a child, if I had been well.'

The following morning Captain Wallis sent her a present by the gunner, who found her in the midst of an entertainment given to at least a thousand people. The messes were put into shells of cocoa-nuts, and the shells into wooden trays, like those used by our butchers, and she distributed them with her own hands to the guests, who were seated in rows in the open air, round the great house. When this was done, she sat down herself upon a place somewhat elevated above the rest, and two women, placing themselves, one on each side of her, fed her, she opening her mouth as they brought their hands up with the food. From this time, provisions were sent to market in the greatest abundance. The queen frequently visited the captain on board, and always with a present, but she never condescended to barter, nor would she accept of any return.

One day, after visiting her at her house, the captain at parting made her comprehend by signs, that he intended to quit the island in seven days: she immediately understood his meaning, and by similar signs, expressed her wish that he should stay twenty days; that he should go with her a couple of days' journey into the country, stay there a few days, return with plenty of hogs and poultry, and then go away; but on persisting in his first intention, she burst into tears, and it was not without great difficulty that she could be pacified. The next time that she went on board, Captain Wallis ordered a good dinner for her entertainment and those chiefs who were of her party; but the queen would neither eat nor drink. As she was going over the ship's side, she asked, by signs, whether he still persisted in leaving the island at the time he had fixed, and on receiving an answer in the affirmative, she expressed her regret by a flood of tears; and as soon as her passion subsided, she told the captain that she would come on board again the following day.

Accordingly, the next day she again visited the ship twice, bringing each time large presents of hogs, fowls, and fruits. The captain, after expressing his sense of her kindness and bounty, announced his intention of sailing the following morning. This, as usual, threw her into tears, and after recovering herself, she made anxious inquiry when he should return; he said in fifty days, with which she seemed to be satisfied. 'She stayed on board,' says Captain Wallis, 'till night, and it was then with the greatest difficulty that she could be prevailed upon to go on shore. When she was told that the boat was ready, she threw herself down upon the arm-chest, and wept a long time, with an excess of passion that could not be pacified; at last, however, with the greatest reluctance, she was prevailed upon to go into the boat, and was followed by her attendants.'

The next day, while the ship was unmooring, the whole beach was covered with the inhabitants. The queen came down, and having ordered a double canoe to be launched, was rowed off by her own people, followed by fifteen or sixteen other canoes. She soon made her appearance on board, but, not being able to speak, she sat down and gave vent to her passion by weeping. Shortly after a breeze springing up, the ship made sail; and finding it now necessary to return into her canoe, 'she embraced us all,' says Captain Wallis, 'in the most affectionate manner, and with many tears; all her attendants also expressed great sorrow at our departure. In a few minutes she came into the bow of her canoe, where she sat weeping with inconsolable sorrow. I gave her many things which I thought would be of great use to her, and some for ornament; she silently accepted of all, but took little notice of any thing. About ten o'clock we had got without the reef, and a fresh breeze springing up, our Indian friends, and particularly the queen, once more bade us farewell, with such tenderness of affection and grief, as filled both my heart and my eyes.'

The tender passion had certainly caught hold of one or both of these worthies; and if her Majesty's language had been as well understood by Captain Wallis, as that of Dido was to AEneas, when pressing him to stay with her, there is no doubt it would have been found not less pathetic--

Nec te noster amor, nec te data dextera quondam,
Nec moritura tenet crudeli funere Dido?

This lady, however, did not sink, like the 'miserrima Dido,' under her griefs; on the contrary, we find her in full activity and animation, and equally generous, to Lieut. Cook and his party, under the name of **Oberea**, who, it now appeared, was no queen, but whose husband they discovered was uncle to the young king, then a minor, but from whom she was separated. She soon evinced a partiality for Mr. Banks, though not quite so strong as that for Wallis, but it appears to have been mutual, until an unlucky discovery took place, that she had, at her command, a stout strong-boned ***cavaliere servente***; added to which, a theft, rather of an amusing nature, contributed for a time to create a coolness, and somewhat to disturb the good understanding that had subsisted between them. It happened that a party, consisting of Cook, Banks, Solander, and three or four others, were benighted at a distance from the anchorage. Mr. Banks, says Lieut. Cook, thought himself fortunate in being offered a place by Oberea, in her own canoe, and wishing his friends a good night, took his leave. He went to rest early, according to the custom of the country; and taking off his clothes, as was his constant practice, the nights being hot, Oberea kindly insisted upon taking them into her own custody, for otherwise, she said, they would certainly be stolen. Mr. Banks having, as he thought, so good a safeguard, resigned himself to sleep with all imaginable tranquillity; but awakening about eleven o'clock, and wanting to get up, he searched for his clothes where he had seen them carefully deposited by Oberea, when he lay down to sleep, and perceived to his sorrow and surprise, that they were missing. He immediately awakened Oberea, who, starting up and hearing his complaint, ordered lights, and prepared in great haste to recover what had been lost. Tootahah (the regent) slept in the next canoe, and being soon alarmed, he came to them and set out with Oberea in search of the thief. Mr. Banks was not in a condition to go with them, as of his apparel scarcely any thing was left him but his breeches. In about half an hour his two noble friends returned, but without having obtained any intelligence of his clothes or of the thief. Where Cook and Solander had disposed of themselves he did not know; but hearing music, which was sure to bring a crowd together, in which there was a chance of his associates being among them, he rose, and made the best of his way towards it, and joined his party, as Cook says, 'more than half naked, and told us his melancholy story.'

It was some consolation to find that his friends were fellow-sufferers, Cook having lost his stockings, that had been stolen from under his head, though he had never been asleep, and his associates their jackets. At day-break Oberea brought to Mr. Banks some of her country clothes; 'so that when he came to us,' says Cook, 'he made a most motley appearance, half Indian and half English.' Such an adventure must have been highly amusing to him who was the object of it, when the inconvenience had been removed, as every one will admit who knew the late venerable President of the Royal Society. He never doubted, however, that Oberea was privy to the theft, and there was strong suspicion of her having some of the articles in her custody. Being aware that this feeling existed, she absented herself for some time, and when she again appeared, she said a favourite of hers had taken them away, whom she had beaten and dismissed; 'but she seemed conscious,' says Cook, 'that she had no right to be believed; she discovered the strongest signs of fear, yet she surmounted it with astonishing resolution, and was very pressing to be allowed to sleep with her attendants in Mr. Banks's tent; in this, however, she was not gratified.' Sir Joseph might have thought that, if he complied with her request, his breeches might be in danger of following the other articles of his dress.

The Otaheitans cannot resist pilfering. 'I must bear my testimony,' says Cook, 'that the people of this country, of all ranks, men and women, are the arrantest thieves upon the face of the earth; but,' he adds, 'we must not hastily conclude that theft is a testimony of the same depravity in them that it is in us, in the instances in which our people were sufferers by their dishonesty; for their temptation was such, as to surmount what would be considered as a proof of uncommon integrity among those who have more knowledge, better principles, and stronger motives to resist the temptations of illicit advantage; an Indian among penny knives and beads, and even nails and broken glass, is in the same state of mind with the meanest servant in Europe among unlocked coffers of jewels and gold.' Captain Wallis has illustrated the truth of this position by an experiment he made on some persons, whose dress and behaviour indicated that they were of a superior cast. 'To discover what present,' he says, 'would most gratify them, I laid down before them a Johannes, a guinea, a crown piece, a Spanish dollar, a few shillings, some new halfpence, and two large nails, making signs that they should take what they liked best. The nails were first seized with great eagerness, and then a few of the halfpence, but the silver and gold lay neglected.' Here then it might with truth be said was discovered

The goldless age, where gold disturbs no dreams.

But their thirst after iron was irresistible; Wallis's ship was stripped of all the nails in her by the seamen to purchase the good graces of the women, who assembled in crowds on the shore. The men even drew out of different parts of the ship those nails that fastened the cleats to her side. This commerce established with the women rendered the men, as might readily be expected, less obedient to command, and made it necessary to punish some of them by flogging. The Otaheitans regarded this punishment with horror. One of Cook's men having insulted a chief's wife, he was ordered to be flogged in their presence. The Indians saw him stripped and tied up to the rigging with a fixed attention, waiting in silent suspense for the event; but as soon as the first stroke was given, they interfered with great agitation, earnestly entreating that the rest of the punishment might be remitted; and when they found they were unable to prevail, they gave vent to their pity by tears. 'But their tears,' as Cook observes, 'like those of children, were always ready to express any passion that was strongly excited, and like those of children, they also appeared to be forgotten as soon as shed.' And he instances this by the following incident:-- Mr. Banks seeing a young woman in great affliction, the tears streaming from her eyes, inquired earnestly the cause; but instead of answering, she took from under her garment a shark's tooth, and struck it six or seven times into her head with great force; a profusion of blood followed, and disregarding his inquiries, she continued to talk loud in a melancholy tone, while those around were laughing and talking without taking the least notice of her distress. The bleeding having ceased, she looked up with a smile, and collecting the pieces of cloth which she had used to stanch the blood, threw them into the sea; then plunging into the river, and washing her whole body, she returned to the tents with the same gaiety and cheerfulness as if nothing had happened. The same thing occurred in the case of a chief, who had given great offence to Mr. Banks, when he and all his followers were overwhelmed with grief and dejection; but one of his women, having struck a shark's tooth into her head several times, till it was covered with blood, the scene was immediately changed, and laughing and good humour took place. Wallis witnessed the same kind of conduct. This, therefore, and the tears, are probably considered a sort of expiation or doing penance for a fault.

But the sorrows of these simple and artless people are transient. Cook justly observes, that what they feel they have never been taught either to disguise or suppress; and having no habits of thinking, which perpetually recall the past and anticipate the future, they are affected by all the changes of the passing hour, and reflect the colour of the time, however frequently it may vary. They grieve for the death of a relation, and place the body on a stage erected on piles and covered with a roof of thatch, for they never bury the dead, and never approach one of these *morais* without great solemnity; but theirs is no lasting grief.

An old woman having died, Mr. Banks, whose pursuit was knowledge of every kind, and to gain it made himself one of the people, requested he might attend the ceremony and witness all the mysteries of the solemnity of depositing the body in the morai. The request was complied with, but on no other condition than his taking a part in it. This was just what he wished. In the evening he repaired to the house of mourning, where he was received by the daughter of the deceased and several others, among whom was a boy about fourteen years old. One of the chiefs of the district was the principal mourner, wearing a fantastical dress. Mr. Banks was stripped entirely of his European clothes, and a small piece of cloth was tied round his middle. His face and body were then smeared with charcoal and water, as low as the shoulders, till they were as black as those of a negro: the same operation was performed on the rest, among whom were some women, who were reduced to a state as near to nakedness as himself; the boy was blacked all over, after which the procession set forward, the chief mourner having mumbled something like a prayer over the body. It is the custom of the Indians to fly from these processions with the utmost precipitation. On the present occasion several large bodies of the natives were put to flight, all the houses were deserted, and not an Otaheitan was to be seen. The body being deposited on the stage, the mourners were dismissed to wash themselves in the river, and to resume their customary dresses and their usual gaiety.

They are, however, so jealous of any one approaching these abodes of the dead, that one of Cook's party, happening one day to pull a flower from a tree which grew in one of these sepulchral inclosures, was struck by a native who saw it, and came suddenly behind him. The morai of Oberea was a pile of stone-work raised pyramidically, two hundred and sixty-seven feet long, eighty-seven feet wide, and forty-four feet high, terminating in a ridge like the roof of a house, and ascended by steps of white coral stone neatly squared and polished, some of them not less than three feet and a half by two feet and a half. Such a structure, observes Cook, raised without the assistance of iron tools, or mortar to join them, struck us with astonishment, as a work of considerable skill and incredible labour.

On the same principle of making himself acquainted with every novelty that presented itself, Captain Cook states that 'Mr. Banks saw the operation of ***tattooing*** performed upon the back of a girl about thirteen years old. The instrument used upon this occasion had thirty teeth, and every stroke, of which at least a hundred were made in a minute, drew an ichor or serum a little tinged with blood. The girl bore it with most stoical resolution for about a quarter of an hour; but the pain of so many hundred punctures as she had received in that time then became intolerable: she first complained in murmurs, then wept, and at last burst into loud lamentations, earnestly imploring the operator to desist. He was however inexorable; and when she began to struggle, she was held down by two women, who sometimes soothed and sometimes chid her, and now and then, when she was most unruly, gave her a smart blow. Mr. Banks stayed in the neighbouring house an hour, and the operation was not over when he went away.'

The sufferings of this young lady did not however deter the late President of the Royal Society from undergoing the operation on his own person.

The skill and labour which the Otaheitans bestow on their large double boats is not less wonderful than their stone morais, from the felling of the tree and splitting it into plank, to the minutest carved ornaments that decorate the head and the stern. The whole operation is performed without the use of any metallic instrument. 'To fabricate one of their principal vessels with their tools is,' says Cook, 'as great a work as to build a British man of war with ours.' The fighting boats are sometimes more than seventy feet long, but not above three broad; but they are fastened in pairs, side by side, at the distance of about three feet; the head and stern rise in a semi-circular form, the latter to the height of seventeen or eighteen feet. To build these boats, and the smaller kinds of canoes;--to build their houses, and finish the slight furniture they contain;--to fell, cleave, carve, and polish timber for various purposes;--and, in short, for every conversion of wood--the tools they make use of are the following: an adze of stone; a chisel or gouge of bone, generally that of a man's arm between the wrist and elbow; a rasp of coral; and the skin of a sting-ray, with coral sand as a file or polisher.

The persons of the Otaheitan men are in general tall, strong, well-limbed and finely shaped; equal in size to the largest of Europeans. The women of superior rank are also above the middle stature of Europeans, but the inferior class are rather below it. The complexion of the former class is that which we call a brunette, and the skin is most delicately smooth and soft. The shape of the face is comely, the cheek bones are not high, neither are the eyes hollow, nor the brow prominent; the nose is a little, but not much, flattened; but their eyes, and more particularly those of the women, are full of expression, sometimes sparkling with fire, and sometimes melting with softness; their teeth also are, almost without exception, most beautifully even and white, and their breath perfectly without taint. In their motions there is at once vigour as well as ease; their walk is graceful, their deportment liberal, and their behaviour to strangers and to each other, affable and courteous. In their dispositions they appear to be brave, open, and candid, without suspicion or treachery, cruelty or revenge. Mr. Banks had such confidence in them, as to sleep frequently in their houses in the woods, without a companion, and consequently wholly in their power. They are delicate and cleanly, almost wholly without example.

'The natives of Otaheite,' says Cook, 'both men and women, constantly wash their whole bodies in running water three times every day; once as soon as they rise in the morning, once at noon, and again before they sleep at night, whether the sea or river be near them or at a distance. They wash not only the mouth, but the hands at their meals, almost between every morsel; and their clothes, as well as their persons, are kept without spot or stain.'

If any one should think this picture somewhat overcharged, he will find it fully confirmed in an account of them made by a description of men who are not much disposed to represent worldly objects in the most favourable light. In the first missionary voyage, in the year 1797, the natives of Otaheite are thus described:

'Natural colour olive, inclining to copper; the women, who carefully clothe themselves, and avoid the sun-beams, are but a shade or two darker than an European brunette; their eyes are black and sparkling; their teeth white and even; their skin soft and delicate; their limbs finely turned; their hair jetty, perfumed and ornamented with flowers; they are in general large and wide over the shoulders; we were therefore disappointed in the judgement we had formed from the report of preceding visitors; and though here and there was to be seen a young person who might be esteemed comely, we saw few who, in fact, could be called beauties; yet they possess eminent feminine graces: their faces are never darkened with a scowl, or covered with a cloud of sullenness or suspicion. Their manners are affable and engaging; their step easy, firm, and graceful; their behaviour free and unguarded; always boundless in generosity to each other, and to strangers; their tempers mild, gentle, and unaffected; slow to take offence, easily pacified, and seldom retaining resentment or revenge, whatever provocation they may have received. Their arms and hands are very delicately formed; and though they go barefoot, their feet are not coarse and spreading.

'As wives in private life, they are affectionate, tender and obedient to their husbands, and uncommonly fond of their children: they nurse them with the utmost care, and are particularly attentive to keep the infant's limbs supple and straight. A cripple is hardly ever seen among them in early life. A rickety child is never known; anything resembling it would reflect the highest disgrace on the mother.

'The Otaheitans have no partitions in their houses; but, it may be affirmed, they have in many instances more refined ideas of decency than ourselves; and one, long a resident, scruples not to declare, that he never saw any appetite, hunger and thirst excepted, gratified in public. It is too true that, for the sake of gaining our extraordinary curiosities, and to please our brutes, they have appeared immodest in the extreme. Yet they lay this charge wholly at our door, and say that Englishmen are ashamed of nothing, and that we have led them to public acts of indecency never before practised among themselves. Iron here, more precious than gold, bears down every barrier of restraint; honesty and modesty yield to the force of temptation.'[2]

Such are the females and the mothers here described, whose interesting offspring are now peopling Pitcairn's Island, and who, while they inherit their mothers' virtues, have hitherto kept themselves free from their vices.

The greater part of the food of Otaheitans is vegetable. Hogs, dogs, and poultry are their only animals, and all of them serve for food. 'We all agreed,' says Cook, 'that a South-Sea dog was little inferior to an English lamb,' which he ascribes to its being kept up and fed wholly on vegetables. Broiling and baking are the only two modes of applying fire to their cookery. Captain Wallis observes, that having no vessel in which water could be subjected to the action of fire, they had no more idea that it could be made ***hot***, than that it could be made ***solid***; and he mentions that one of the attendants of the supposed queen, having observed the surgeon fill the tea-pot from an urn, turned the cock himself, and received the water in his hand; and that as soon as he felt himself scalded, he roared out and began to dance about the cabin with the most extravagant and ridiculous expressions of pain and astonishment; his companions, unable to conceive what was the matter, staring at him in amaze, and not without some mixture of terror.

One of Oberea's peace-offerings to Mr. Banks, for the robbery of his clothes committed in her boat, was a fine fat dog, and the way in which it was prepared and baked was as follows. Tupei, the high priest, undertook to perform the double office of butcher and cook. He first killed him by holding his hands close over his mouth and nose for the space of a quarter of an hour. A hole was then made in the ground about a foot deep, in which a fire was kindled, and some small stones placed in layers, alternately with the wood, to be heated. The dog was then singed, scraped with a shell, and the hair taken off as clean as if he had been scalded in hot water. He was then cut up with the same instrument, and his entrails carefully washed. When the hole was sufficiently heated, the fire was taken out, and some of the stones, being placed at the bottom, were covered with green leaves. The dog, with the entrails, was then placed upon the leaves, and other leaves being laid upon them, the whole was covered with the rest of the hot stones, and the mouth of the hole close stopped with mould. In somewhat less than four hours, it was again opened, and the dog taken out excellently baked, and the party all agreed that he made a very good dish. These dogs it seems are bred to be eaten, and live wholly on bread-fruit, cocoa-nuts, yams, and other vegetables of the like kind.

The food of the natives, being chiefly vegetable, consists of the various preparations of the bread-fruit, of cocoa-nuts, bananas, plantains, and a great variety of other fruit, the spontaneous products of a rich soil and genial climate. The bread-fruit, when baked in the same manner as the dog was, is rendered soft, and not unlike a boiled potato; not quite so farinaceous as a good one, but more so than those of the middling sort. Much of this fruit is gathered before it is ripe, and by a certain process is made to undergo the two states of fermentation, the saccharine and acetous, in the latter of which it is moulded into balls, and called ***Mahie***. The natives seldom make a meal without this sour paste. Salt water is the universal sauce, without which no meal is eaten. Their drink in general consists of water, or the juice of the cocoa-nut; the art of producing liquors that intoxicate by fermentation being at this time happily unknown among them; neither did they make use of any narcotic, as the natives of some other countries do opium, beetel-nut, and tobacco. One day the wife of one of the chiefs came running to Mr. Banks, who was always applied to in every emergency and distress, and with a mixture of grief and terror in her countenance, made him understand that her husband was dying, in consequence of something the strangers had given him to eat. Mr. Banks found his friend leaning his head against a post, in an attitude of the utmost languor and despondency. His attendants brought out a leaf folded up with great care, containing part of the poison of the effects of which their master was now dying. On opening the leaf Mr. Banks found in it a chew of tobacco, which the chief had asked from some of the seamen, and imitating them, as he thought, he had rolled it about in his mouth, grinding it to powder with his teeth, and ultimately swallowing it. During the examination of the leaf he looked up at Mr. Banks with the most piteous countenance, and intimated that he had but a very short time to live. A copious draught of cocoa-nut milk, however, set all to rights, and the chief and his attendants were at once restored to that flow of cheerfulness and good-humour, which is the characteristic of these single-minded people.

There is, however, one plant from the root of which they extract a juice of an intoxicating quality, called ***Ava***, but Cook's party saw nothing of its effects, probably owing to their considering drunkenness as a disgrace. This vice of drinking ava is said to be peculiar almost to the chiefs, who vie with each other in drinking the greatest number of draughts, each draught being about a pint. They keep this intoxicating juice with great care from the women.

As eating is one of the most important concerns of life, here as well as elsewhere, Captain Cook's description of a meal made by one of the chiefs of the island cannot be considered as uninteresting, and is here given in his own words.

'He sits down under the shade of the next tree, or on the shady side of his house, and a large quantity of leaves, either of the bread-fruit or bananas, are neatly spread before him upon the ground as a table-cloth; a basket is then set by him that contains his provision, which, if fish or flesh, is ready dressed, and wrapped up in leaves, and two cocoa-nut shells, one full of salt water and one of fresh. His attendants, which are not few, seat themselves round him, and when all is ready, he begins by washing his hands and his mouth thoroughly with the fresh water, and this he repeats almost continually throughout the whole meal. He then takes part of his provision out of the basket, which generally consists of a small fish or two, two or three bread-fruits, fourteen or fifteen ripe bananas, or six or seven apples. He first takes half a bread-fruit, peels off the rind, and takes out the core with his nails; of this he puts as much into his mouth as it can hold, and while he chews it, takes the fish out of the leaves and breaks one of them into the salt water, placing the other, and what remains of the bread-fruit, upon the leaves that have been spread before him. When this is done, he takes up a small piece of the fish that has been broken into the salt-water, with all the fingers of one hand, and sucks it into his mouth, so as to get with it as much of the salt-water as possible. In the same manner he takes the rest by different morsels, and between each, at least very frequently, takes a small sup of the salt-water, either out of the cocoa-nut shell, or the palm of his hand. In the meantime one of his attendants has prepared a young cocoa-nut, by peeling off the outer rind with his teeth, an operation which to an European appears very surprising; but it depends so much upon sleight, that many of us were able to do it before we left the island, and some that could scarcely crack a filbert. The master when he chooses to drink takes the cocoa-nut thus prepared, and boring a hole through the shell with his fingers, or breaking it with a stone, he sucks out the liquor. When he has eaten his bread-fruit and fish, he begins with his plantains, one of which makes but a mouthful, though it be as big as a black-pudding; if instead of plantains he has apples, he never tastes them till they have been pared; to do this a shell is picked up from the ground, where they are always in plenty, and tossed to him by an attendant. He immediately begins to cut or scrape off the rind, but so awkwardly that great part of the fruit is wasted. If, instead of fish, he has flesh, he must have some succedaneum for a knife to divide it; and for this purpose a piece of bamboo is tossed to him, of which he makes the necessary implement by splitting it transversely with his nail. While all this has been doing, some of his attendants have been employed in beating bread-fruit with a stone pestle upon a block of wood; by being beaten in this manner, and sprinkled from time to time with water, it is reduced to the consistence of a soft paste, and is then put into a vessel somewhat like a butcher's tray, and either made up alone, or mixed with banana or *mahie*, according to the taste of the master, by pouring water upon it by degrees and squeezing it often through the hand. Under this operation it acquires the consistence of a thick custard, and a large cocoa-nut shell full of it being set before him, he sips it as we should do a jelly if we had no spoon to take it from the glass. The meal is then finished by again washing his hands and his mouth. After which the cocoa-nut shells are cleaned, and everything that is left is replaced in the basket.'

Captain Cook adds, 'the quantity of food which these people eat at a meal is prodigious. I have seen one man devour two or three fishes as big as a perch; three bread-fruits, each bigger than two fists; fourteen or fifteen plantains or bananas, each of them six or seven inches long, and four or five round; and near a quart of the pounded bread-fruit, which is as substantial as the thickest unbaked custard. This is so extraordinary that I scarcely expect to be believed; and I would not have related it upon my own single testimony, but Mr. Banks, Dr. Solander, and most of the other gentlemen have had ocular demonstration of its truth, and know that I mention them on the occasion.'

The women, who, on other occasions, always mix in the amusements of the men, who are particularly fond of their society, are wholly excluded from their meals; nor could the latter be prevailed on to partake of anything when dining in company on board ship; they said it was not right: even brothers and sisters have each their separate baskets, and their provisions are separately prepared; but the English officers and men, when visiting the young ones at their own houses, frequently ate out of the same basket and drank out of the same cup, to the horror and dismay of the older ladies, who were always offended at this liberty; and if by chance any of the victuals were touched, or even the basket that contained them, they would throw them away.

In this fine climate houses are almost unnecessary. The minimum range of the thermometer is about 63 deg., the maximum 85 deg., giving an average of 74 deg.. Their sheds or houses consist generally of a thatched roof raised on posts, the eaves reaching to within three or four feet of the ground; the floor is covered with soft hay, over which are laid mats, so that the whole is one cushion, on which they sit by day and sleep by night. They eat in the open air, under the shade of the nearest tree. In each district there is a house erected for general use, much larger than common, some of them exceeding two hundred feet in length, thirty broad, and twenty high. The dwelling-houses all stand in the woody belt which surrounds the island, between the feet of the central mountains and the sea, each having a very small piece of ground cleared, just enough to keep the dropping of the trees from the thatch. An Otaheitan wood consists chiefly of groves of bread-fruit and cocoa-nuts, without underwood, and intersected in all directions by the paths that lead from one house to another. 'Nothing,' says Cook, 'can be more grateful than this shade, in so warm a climate, nor anything more beautiful than these walks,'

With all the activity they are capable of displaying, and the sprightliness of their disposition, they are fond of indulging in ease and indolence. The trees that produce their food are mostly of spontaneous growth--the bread-fruit, cocoa-nut, bananas of thirteen sorts, besides plantains; a fruit not unlike an apple, which, when ripe, is very pleasant; sweet potatoes, yams, and a species of *arum*; the pandanus, the jambu and the sugar-cane; a variety of plants whose roots are esculent--these, with many others, are produced with so little culture, that, as Cook observes, they seem to be exempted from the first general curse that 'man should eat his bread in the sweat of his brow.' Then for clothing they have the bark of three different trees, the paper mulberry, the bread-fruit tree, and a tree which resembles the wild fig-tree of the West Indies; of these the mulberry only requires to be cultivated.

In preparing the cloth they display a very considerable degree of ingenuity. Red and yellow are the two colours most in use for dyeing their cloth; the red is stated to be exceedingly brilliant and beautiful, approaching nearest to our full scarlet; it is produced by the mixture of the juices of two vegetables, neither of which separately has the least tendency to that hue: one is the ***Cordia Sebestina***, the other a species of ***Ficus***; of the former the leaves, of the latter the fruits yield the juices. The yellow dye is extracted from the bark of the root of the ***Morinda citrifolia***, by scraping and infusing it in water.

Their matting is exceedingly beautiful, particularly that which is made from the bark of the ***Hibiscus tiliaceus***, and of a species of ***Pandanus***. Others are made of rushes and grass with amazing facility and dispatch. In the same manner their basket and wicker work are most ingeniously made; the former in patterns of a thousand different kinds. Their nets and fishing-lines are strong and neatly made, so are their fish-hooks of pearl-shell; and their clubs are admirable specimens of wood-carving.

A people so lively, sprightly, and good-humoured as the Otaheitans are, must necessarily have their amusements. They are fond of music, such as is derived from a rude flute and a drum; of dancing, wrestling, shooting with the bow, and throwing the lance. They exhibit frequent trials of skill and strength in wrestling; and Cook says it is scarcely possible for those who are acquainted with the athletic sports of very remote antiquity, not to remark a rude resemblance of them in a wrestling-match (which he describes) among the natives of a little island in the midst of the Pacific Ocean.

But these simple-minded people have their vices, and great ones too. Chastity is almost unknown among a certain description of women: there is a detestable society called **Arreoy**, composed, it would seem, of a particular class, who are supposed to be the chief warriors of the island. In this society the men and women live in common; and on the birth of a child it is immediately smothered, that its bringing up may not interfere with the brutal pleasures of either father or mother. Another savage practice is that of immolating human beings at the **Morais**, which serve as temples as well as sepulchres, and yet, by the report of the missionaries, they entertain a due sense and reverential awe of the Deity. 'With regard to their worship,' Captain Cook does the Otaheitans but justice in saying, 'they reproach many who bear the name of Christians. You see no instances of an Otaheitan drawing near the Eatooa with carelessness and inattention; he is all devotion; he approaches the place of worship with reverential awe; uncovers when he treads on sacred ground; and prays with a fervour that would do honour to a better profession. He firmly credits the traditions of his ancestors. None dares dispute the existence of the Deity.' Thieving may also be reckoned as one of their vices; this, however, is common to all uncivilized nations, and, it may be added, civilized too. But to judge them fairly in this respect, we should compare their situation with that of a more civilized people. A native of Otaheite goes on board a ship and finds himself in the midst of iron bolts, nails, knives, scattered about, and is tempted to carry off a few of them. If we could suppose a ship from El Dorado to arrive in the Thames, and that the custom-house officers, on boarding her, found themselves in the midst of bolts, hatchets, chisels, all of solid gold, scattered about the deck, one need scarcely say what would be likely to happen. If the former found the temptation irresistible to supply himself with what was essentially useful--the latter would be as little able to resist that which would contribute to the indulgence of his avarice or the gratification of his pleasures, or of both.

Such was the state of this beautiful island and its interesting and fascinating natives at the time when Captain Wallis first discovered and Lieutenant Cook shortly afterwards visited it. What they now are, as described by Captain Beechey, it is lamentable to reflect. All their usual and innocent amusements have been denounced by the missionaries, and, in lieu of them, these poor people have been driven to seek for resources in habits of indolence and apathy: that simplicity of character, which atoned for many of their faults, has been converted into cunning and hypocrisy; and drunkenness, poverty, and disease have thinned the island of its former population to a frightful degree. By a survey of the first missionaries, and a census of the inhabitants, taken in 1797, the population was estimated at 16,050 souls; Captain Waldegrave, in 1830, states it, on the authority of a census also taken by the missionaries, to amount only to 5000--and there is but too much reason to ascribe this diminution to praying, psalm-singing, and dram-drinking.[3]

The island of Otaheite is in shape two circles united by a low and narrow isthmus. The larger circle is named Otaheite Mooe, and is about thirty miles in diameter; the lesser, named Tiaraboo, about ten miles in diameter. A belt of low land, terminating in numerous valleys, ascending by gentle slopes to the central mountain, which is about seven thousand feet high, surrounds the larger circle, and the same is the case with the smaller circle on a proportionate scale. Down these valleys flow streams and rivulets of clear water, and the most luxuriant and verdant foliage fills their sides and the hilly ridges that separate them, among which were once scattered the smiling cottages and little plantations of the natives. All these are now destroyed, and the remnant of the population has crept down to the flats and swampy ground on the sea shore, completely subservient to the seven establishments of missionaries, who have taken from them what little trade they used to carry on, to possess themselves of it; who have their warehouses, act as agents, and monopolize all the cattle on the island--but, in return, they have given them a new religion and a parliament (risum teneatis?) and reduced them to a state of complete pauperism--and all, as they say, and probably have so persuaded themselves, for the honour of God, and the salvation of their souls! How much is such a change brought about by such conduct to be deprecated! how lamentable is it to reflect, that an island on which Nature has lavished so many of her bounteous gifts, with which neither Cyprus nor Cythera, nor the fanciful island of Calypso, can compete in splendid and luxuriant beauties, should be doomed to such a fate,--in an enlightened age, and by a people that call themselves civilized!

CHAPTER II
THE BREAD-FRUIT

--The happy shores without a law,

    *   *   *   *   *

Where all partake the earth without dispute,
And bread itself is gather'd as a fruit;
Where none contest the fields, the woods, the streams:--
The goldless age, where gold disturbs no dreams,
Inhabits or inhabited the shore,
Till Europe taught them better than before,
Bestow'd her customs, and amended theirs,
But left her vices also to their heirs.
                      BYRON.

In the year 1787, being seventeen years after Cook's return from his first voyage, the merchants and planters resident in London, and interested in the West India possessions, having represented to his Majesty, that the introduction of the bread-fruit tree into the islands of those seas, to constitute an article of food, would be of very essential benefit to the inhabitants, the king was graciously pleased to comply with their request; and a vessel was accordingly purchased, and fitted at Deptford with the necessary fixtures and preparations, for carrying into effect the benevolent object of the voyage. The arrangements for disposing the plants were undertaken, and completed in a most ingenious and effective manner, by Sir Joseph Banks, who superintended the whole equipment of the ship with the greatest attention and assiduity till she was in all respects ready for sea. He named the ship the **Bounty**, and recommended Lieutenant Bligh, who had been with Captain Cook, to command her. Her burden was about two hundred and fifteen tons; and her establishment consisted of one lieutenant, who was commanding officer, one master, three warrant officers, one surgeon, two master's mates, two midshipmen, and thirty-four petty officers and seamen, making in all forty-four; to which were added two skilful and careful men, recommended by Sir Joseph Banks, to have the management of the plants intended to be carried to the West Indies, and others to be brought home for his Majesty's garden at Kew: one was David Nelson, who had served in a similar situation in Captain Cook's last voyage; the other William Brown, as an assistant to him.

The object of all the former voyages to the South Seas, undertaken by command of his Majesty George III, was the increase of knowledge by new discoveries, and the advancement of science, more particularly of natural history and geography: the intention of the present voyage was to derive some practical benefit from the distant discoveries that had already been made; and no object was deemed more likely to realise the expectation of benefit than the bread-fruit, which afforded to the natives of Otaheite so very considerable a portion of their food, and which it was hoped it might also do for the black population of the West India Islands. The bread-fruit plant was no new discovery of either Wallis or Cook. So early as the year 1688, that excellent old navigator, Dampier, thus describes it:--'The bread-fruit, as we call it, grows on a large tree, as big and high as our largest apple-trees; it hath a spreading head, full of branches and dark leaves. The fruit grows on the boughs like apples; it is as big as a penny-loaf, when wheat is at five shillings the bushel; it is of a round shape, and hath a thick tough rind; when the fruit is ripe it is yellow and soft, and the taste is sweet and pleasant. The natives of Guam use it for bread. They gather it, when full grown, while it is green and hard; then they bake it in an oven, which scorcheth the rind and makes it black, but they scrape off the outside black crust, and there remains a tender thin crust; and the inside is soft, tender, and white, like the crumb of a penny-loaf. There is neither seed nor stone in the inside, but all is of a pure substance like bread. It must be eaten new; for if it is kept above twenty-four hours, it grows harsh and choaky; but it is very pleasant before it is too stale. This fruit lasts in season eight months in the year, during which the natives eat no other sort of food of bread kind. I did never see of this fruit anywhere but here. The natives told us that there is plenty of this fruit growing on the rest of the Ladrone Islands; and I did never hear of it anywhere else.'

Lord Anson corroborates this account of the bread-fruit, and says that, while at Tinian, it was constantly eaten by his officers and ship's company during their two months' stay, instead of bread; and so universally preferred, that no ship's bread was expended in that whole interval. The only essential difference between Dampier's and Cook's description is, where the latter says, which is true, that this fruit has a *core*, and that the eatable part lies between the skin and the core. Cook says also that its taste is insipid, with a slight sweetness, somewhat resembling that of the crumb of wheaten bread mixed with a Jerusalem artichoke. From such a description, it is not surprising that the West India planters should have felt desirous of introducing it into those islands; and accordingly the introduction of it was subsequently accomplished, notwithstanding the failure of the present voyage; it has not, however, been found to answer the expectation that had reasonably been entertained. The climate, as to latitude, ought to be the same, or nearly so, as that of Otaheite, but there would appear to be some difference in the situation or nature of the soil, that prevents it from thriving in the West India Islands. At Otaheite and on several of the Pacific Islands,

> The bread-tree, which, without the ploughshare yields,
> The unreap'd harvest of unfurrow'd fields,
> And bakes its unadulterated loaves
> Without a furnace in unpurchased groves,
> And flings off famine from its fertile breast,
> A priceless market for the gathering guest--

is to the natives of those islands a most invaluable gift, but it has not been found to yield similar benefits to the West India Islands.

On the 23rd December, 1787, the ***Bounty*** sailed from Spithead, and on the 26th it blew a severe storm of wind from the eastward, which continued to the 29th, in the course of which the ship suffered greatly. One sea broke away the spare-yards and spars out of the starboard main-chains. Another heavy sea broke into the ship and stove all the boats. Several casks of beer that had been lashed upon deck, were broke loose and washed overboard; and it was not without great difficulty and risk that they were able to secure the boats from being washed away entirely. Besides other mischief done to them in this storm, a large quantity of bread was damaged and rendered useless, for the sea had stove in the stern and filled the cabin with water.

This made it desirable to touch at Teneriffe to put the ship to rights, where they arrived on the 5th January, 1788, and having refitted and refreshed, they sailed again on the 10th.

'I now,' says Bligh, 'divided the people into three watches, and gave the charge of the third watch to Mr. Fletcher Christian, one of the mates. I have always considered this a desirable regulation when circumstances will admit of it, and I am persuaded that unbroken rest not only contributes much towards the health of the ship's company, but enables them more readily to exert themselves in cases of sudden emergency.'

Wishing to proceed to Otaheite without stopping, and the late storm having diminished their supply of provisions, it was deemed expedient to put all hands on an allowance of two-thirds of bread. It was also decided that water for drinking should be passed through filtering stones that had been procured at Teneriffe. 'I now,' says Bligh, 'made the ship's company acquainted with the object of the voyage, and gave assurances of the certainty of promotion to every one whose endeavours should merit it.' Nothing, indeed, seemed to be neglected on the part of the commander to make his officers and men comfortable and happy. He was himself a thorough-bred sailor, and availed himself of every possible means of preserving the health of his crew. Continued rain and a close atmosphere had covered everything in the ship with mildew. She was therefore aired below with fires, and frequently sprinkled with vinegar, and every interval of dry weather was taken advantage of to open all the hatchways, and clean the ship, and to have all the people's wet things washed and dried. With these precautions to secure health, they passed the hazy and sultry atmosphere of the low latitudes without a single complaint.

On Sunday, the 2nd of March, Lieutenant Bligh observes, 'after seeing that every person was clean, Divine service was performed, according to my usual custom. On this day I gave to Mr. Fletcher Christian, whom I had before desired to take charge of the third watch, a written order to act as lieutenant.'

Having reached as far as the latitude of 36 degrees south, on the 9th March, 'the change of temperature,' he observes, 'began now to be sensibly felt, there being a variation in the thermometer, since yesterday, of eight degrees. That the people might not suffer by their own negligence, I gave orders for their light tropical clothing to be put by, and made them dress in a manner more suited to a cold climate. I had provided for this before I left England, by giving directions for such clothes to be purchased as would be found necessary. On this day, on a complaint of the master, I found it necessary to punish Matthew Quintal, one of the seamen, with two dozen lashes, for insolence and mutinous behaviour. Before this I had not had occasion to punish any person on board.'

The sight of New Year's Harbour, in Staaten Land, almost tempted him, he says, to put in; but the lateness of the season, and the people being in good health, determined him to lay aside all thoughts of refreshment until they should reach Otaheite. Indeed the extraordinary care he had taken to preserve the health of the ship's company rendered any delay in this cold and inhospitable region unnecessary.

They soon after this had to encounter tremendous weather off Cape Horn, storms of wind, with hail and sleet, which made it necessary to keep a constant fire night and day; and one of the watch always attended to dry the people's wet clothes. This stormy weather continued for nine days; the ship began to complain, and required pumping every hour; the decks became so leaky that the commander was obliged to allot the great cabin to those who had wet berths, to hang their hammocks in. Finding they were losing ground every day, and that it was hopeless to persist in attempting a passage by this route, at this season of the year, to the Society Islands, and after struggling for thirty days in this tempestuous ocean, it was determined to bear away for the Cape of Good Hope. The helm was accordingly put a-weather, to the great joy of every person on board.

They arrived at the Cape on the 23rd of May, and having remained there thirty-eight days to refit the ship, replenish provisions, and refresh the crew, they sailed again on the 1st July, and anchored in Adventure Bay, in Van Diemen's Land, on the 20th August. Here they remained taking in wood and water till the 4th September, and on the evening of the 25th October they saw Otaheite; and the next day came to anchor in Matavai Bay, after a distance which the ship had run over, by the log, since leaving England, of twenty-seven thousand and eighty-six miles, being on an average one hundred and eight miles each twenty-four hours. Of their proceedings in Otaheite a short abstract from Bligh's Journal will suffice.

Many inquiries were made by the natives after Captain Cook, Sir Joseph Banks, and others of their former friends. 'One of my first questions,' says Bligh, 'was after our friend Omai; and it was a sensible mortification and disappointment to me to hear, that not only Omai, but both the New Zealand boys who had been left with him, were dead. There appeared among the natives in general great good-will towards us, and they seemed to be much rejoiced at our arrival. The whole day we experienced no instance of dishonesty; and we were so much crowded, that I could not undertake to remove to a more proper station, without danger of disobliging our visitors, by desiring them to leave the ship.'

Otoo, the chief of the district, on hearing of the arrival of the *Bounty*, sent a small pig and a young plantain tree, as a token of friendship. The ship was now plentifully supplied with provisions; every man on board having as much as he could consume.

As soon as the ship was secured, Lieutenant Bligh went on shore with the chief, Poeeno, passing through a walk delightfully shaded with bread-fruit trees, to his own house, where his wife and her sister were busily employed staining a piece of cloth red. They desired him to sit down on a mat, and with great kindness offered him refreshments. Several strangers were now introduced, who came to offer their congratulations, and behaved with great decorum and attention. On taking leave, he says, 'the ladies, for they deserve to be called such from their natural and unaffected manners, and elegance of deportment, got up, and taking some of their finest cloth and a mat, clothed me in the Otaheitan fashion, and then said, "We will go with you to your boat;" and each taking me by the hand, amidst a great crowd, led me to the water side, and then took their leave.' In this day's walk, Bligh had the satisfaction to see that the island had received some benefit from the former visits of Captain Cook. Two shaddocks were brought to him, a fruit which they had not till Cook introduced it; and among the articles which they brought off to the ship, and offered for sale, were capsicums, pumpkins, and two young goats. In the course of two or three days,' says he, 'an intimacy between the natives and the ship's company was become so general, that there was scarcely a man in the ship who had not already his *tayo* or friend.'

Nelson, the gardener, and his assistant, being sent out to look for young plants, it was no small degree of pleasure to find them report on their return, that, according to appearances, the object of the voyage would probably be accomplished with ease; the plants were plentiful, and no apparent objection on the part of the natives to collect as many as might be wanted. Nelson had the gratification to meet with two fine shaddock trees which he had planted in 1777, and which were now full of fruit, but not ripe.

Presents were now given to Otoo, the Chief of Matavai, who had changed his name to Tinah. He was told that, on account of the kindness of his people to Captain Cook, and from a desire to serve him and his country; King George had sent out those valuable presents to him; and 'will you not, Tinah,' said Bligh, 'send something to King George in return?' 'Yes,' he said, 'I will send him anything I have;' and then began to enumerate the different articles in his power, among which he mentioned the bread-fruit. This was the exact point to which Bligh was endeavouring to lead him, and he was immediately told that the bread-fruit trees were what King George would like very much, on which he promised that a great many should be put on board.

Hitherto no thefts had been committed, and Bligh was congratulating himself on the improvement of the Otaheitans in this respect, as the same facilities and the same temptations were open to them as before. The ship, as on former occasions, was constantly crowded with visitors. One day, however, the gudgeon of the rudder belonging to the large cutter was drawn out and stolen, without being perceived by the man who was stationed to take care of her; and as this and some other petty thefts, mostly owing to the negligence of the men, were commencing, and would have a tendency to interrupt the good terms on which they were with the chiefs, 'I thought,' says Bligh, 'it would have a good effect to punish the boat-keeper in their presence, and accordingly I ordered him a dozen lashes. All who attended the punishment interceded very earnestly to get it mitigated: the women shewed great sympathy, and that degree of feeling which characterizes the amiable part of their sex.'

The longer they remained on the island, the more they had occasion to be pleased with the conduct of the islanders, and the less incommoded either on board or when on shore, by the natives following them as at first. Into every house they wished to enter, they always experienced a kind reception. The Otaheitans, we are told, have the most perfect easiness of manner, equally free from forwardness and formality; and that 'there is a candour and sincerity about them that is quite delightful.' When they offer refreshments, for instance, if they are not accepted, they do not think of offering them a second time; for they have not the least idea of that ceremonious kind of refusal which expects a second invitation. 'Having one day,' says Bligh, 'exposed myself too much in the sun, I was taken ill, on which all the powerful people, both men and women, collected round me, offering their assistance. For this short illness I was made ample amends by the pleasure I received from the attention and appearance of affection in these kind people.'

On one occasion the *Bounty* had nearly gone ashore in a tremendous gale of wind, and on another did actually get aground; on both which accidents, these kind-hearted people came in crowds to congratulate the captain on her escape; and many of them are stated to have been affected in the most lively manner, shedding tears while the danger in which the ship was placed continued.

On the 9th December, the surgeon of the *Bounty* died from the effects of intemperance and indolence. This unfortunate man is represented to have been in a constant state of intoxication, and was so averse from any kind of exercise, that he never could be prevailed on to take half a dozen hours upon deck at a time in the whole course of the voyage. Lieutenant Bligh had obtained permission to bury him on shore; and on going with the chief Tinah to the spot intended for his burial place, 'I found,' says he, 'the natives had already begun to dig his grave.' Tinah asked if they were doing it right? 'There,' says he, 'the sun rises, and there it sets.' Whether the idea of making the grave east and west is their own, or whether they learnt it from the Spaniards, who buried the captain of their ship on the island in 1774, there were no means of ascertaining; but it was certain they had no intimation of that kind from anybody belonging to the *Bounty.* When the funeral took place, the chiefs and many of the natives attended the ceremony, and shewed great attention during the service. Many of the principal natives attended divine service on Sundays, and behaved with great decency. Some of the women at one time betrayed an inclination to laugh at the general responses; but, the captain says, on looking at them they appeared much ashamed.

The border of low land, which is of the breadth of about three miles, between the sea-coast and the foot of the hills, consists of a very delightful country, well covered with bread-fruit and cocoa-trees, and strewed with houses in which are swarms of children playing about. 'It is delightful,' Bligh observes, 'to see the swarms of little children that are every where to be seen employed at their several amusements; some flying kites, some swinging in ropes suspended from the boughs of trees, others walking on stilts, some wrestling, and others playing all manner of antic tricks such as are common to boys in England. The little girls have also their amusements, consisting generally of heivahs or dances. On an evening, just before sunset the whole beach abreast the ship is described as being like a parade, crowded with men, women, and children, who go on with their sports and amusements till nearly dark, when every one peaceably returns to his home. At such times, we are told, from three to four hundred people are assembled together, and all happily diverted, good humoured, and affectionate to one another, without a single quarrel having ever happened to disturb the harmony that existed among these amiable people. Both boys and girls are said to be handsome and very sprightly.

It did not appear that much pains were taken in their plantations, except those of the ava and the cloth-plant; many of the latter are fenced with stone, and surrounded with a ditch. In fact, Nature has done so much for them, that they have no great occasion to use exertion in obtaining a sufficient supply of either food or raiment. Yet when Bligh commenced taking up the bread-fruit plants, he derived much assistance from the natives in collecting and pruning them, which they understood perfectly well.

The behaviour of these people on all occasions was highly deserving of praise. One morning, at the relief of the watch, the small cutter was missing. The ship's company were immediately mustered, when it appeared that three men were absent. They had taken with them eight stand of arms and ammunition; but what their plan was, or which way they had gone, no one on board seemed to have the least knowledge. Information being given of the route they had taken, the master was dispatched to search for the cutter, and one of the chiefs went with him; but before they had got half way, they met the boat with five of the natives, who were bringing her back to the ship. For this service they were handsomely rewarded. The chiefs promised to use every possible means to detect and bring back the deserters, which, in a few days, some of the islanders had so far accomplished as to seize and bind them, but let them loose again on a promise that they would return to their ship, which they did not exactly fulfil, but gave themselves up soon after on a search being made for them.

A few days after this, a much more serious occurrence happened, that was calculated to give to the commander great concern. The wind had blown fresh in the night, and at daylight it was discovered that the cable, by which the ship rode, had been cut near the water's edge, in such a manner, that only one strand remained whole. While they were securing the ship, Tinah came on board; and though there was no reason whatever to suppose otherwise than that he was perfectly innocent of the transaction, nevertheless, says the commander, 'I spoke to him in a very peremptory manner, and insisted upon his discovering and bringing to me the offender. He promised to use his utmost endeavours to discover the guilty person. The next morning he and his wife came to me, and assured me that they had made the strictest inquiries without success. This was not at all satisfactory, and I behaved towards them with great coolness, at which they were much distressed; and the lady at length gave vent to her sorrow by tears. I could no longer keep up the appearance of mistrusting them, but I earnestly recommended to them, as they valued the King of England's friendship, that they would exert their utmost endeavours to find out the offenders, which they faithfully promised to do.'

Here Bligh observes, it had since occurred to him, that this attempt to cut the ship adrift was most probably the act of some of his own people; whose purpose of remaining at Otaheite might have been effectually answered without danger, if the ship had been driven on shore. At the time it occurred, he says, he entertained not the least thought of this kind, nor did the possibility of it enter into his ideas, having no suspicion that so general an indication, or so strong an attachment to these islands, could prevail among his people, as to induce them to abandon every prospect of returning to their native country.

This after-thought of Bligh will appear in the sequel to be wholly gratuitous, and yet he might naturally enough have concluded that so long and unrestrained an intercourse with a people among whom every man had his *tayo* or friend; among whom every man was free to indulge every wish of his heart; where, from the moment he set his foot on shore, he found himself surrounded by female allurements in the midst of ease and indolence, and living in a state of luxury without submitting to any kind of labour--such enticements to a common sailor might naturally enough be supposed to create a desire for a longer residence in such a country; but this supposition is not borne out by subsequent events. The damage done to the cable was, in all probability, owing to its chafing over the rocky bottom.

The ***Bounty*** arrived on the 26th October, 1788, and remained till the 4th April, 1789. On the 31st March, the Commander says, 'To-day, all the plants were on board, being in seven hundred and seventy-four pots, thirty-nine tubs, and twenty-four boxes. The number of bread-fruit plants were one thousand and fifteen; besides which, we had collected a number of other plants: the ***avee***, which is one of the finest flavoured fruits in the world; the ***ayyah***, which is a fruit not so rich, but of a fine flavour and very refreshing; the ***rattah***, not much unlike a chestnut, which grows on a large tree in great quantities; they are singly in large pods, from one to two inches broad, and may be eaten raw, or boiled in the same manner as Windsor beans, and so dressed are equally good; the ***orai-ab***, which is a very superior kind of plantain. All these I was particularly recommended to collect, by my worthy friend Sir Joseph Banks.'

While these active preparations for departure were going on, the good chief Tinah, on bringing a present for King George, could not refrain from shedding tears. During the remainder of their stay, there appeared among the natives an evident degree of sorrow that they were so soon to leave them, which they showed by a more than usual degree of kindness and attention. The above-mentioned excellent chief, with his wife, brothers, and sister, requested permission to remain on board for the night previous to the sailing of the ***Bounty***. The ship was crowded the whole day with the natives, and she was loaded with presents of cocoa-nuts, plantains, bread-fruits, hogs, and goats. Contrary to what had been the usual practice, there was this evening no dancing or mirth on the beach, such as they had long been accustomed to, but all was silent.

At sunset, the boat returned from landing Tinah and his wife, and the ship made sail, bidding farewell to Otaheite, where, Bligh observes, 'for twenty-three weeks we had been treated with the utmost affection and regard, and which seemed to increase in proportion to our stay. That we were not insensible to their kindness, the events which followed more than sufficiently prove; for to the friendly and endearing behaviour of these people, may be ascribed the motives for that event which effected the ruin of an expedition, that there was every reason to hope would have been completed in the most fortunate manner.'

The morning after their departure, they got sight of Huaheine; and a double canoe soon coming alongside, containing ten natives, among them was a young man who recollected Captain Bligh, and called him by name; having known him when here in the year 1780, with Captain Cook in the ***Resolution***. Several other canoes arrived with hogs, yams, and other provisions, which they purchased. This person confirmed, the account that had already been received of Omai, and said that, of all the animals which had been left with Omai, the mare only remained alive; that the seeds and plants had been all destroyed, except one tree: but of what kind that was, he could not satisfactorily explain. A few days after sailing from this island, the weather became squally, and a thick body of black clouds collected in the east. A water-spout was in a short time seen at no great distance from the ship, which appeared to great advantage from the darkness of the clouds behind it. The upper part is described as being about two feet in diameter; and the lower about eight inches. It advanced rapidly towards the ship, when it was deemed expedient to alter the course, and to take in all the sails, except the foresail; soon after which it passed within ten yards of the stern, making a rustling noise, but without their feeling the least effect from its being so near. The rate at which it travelled was judged to be about ten miles per hour, going towards the west, in the direction of the wind; and in a quarter of an hour after passing the ship, it dispersed. As they passed several low islands, the natives of one of them came out in their canoes, and it was observed that they all spoke the language of Otaheite. Presents of iron, beads, and a looking-glass were given to them; but it was observed that the chief, on leaving the ship, took possession of everything that had been distributed. One of them showed some signs of dissatisfaction; but after a little altercation they joined noses and were reconciled.

The ***Bounty*** anchored at Anamooka on the 23rd April; and an old lame man, named Tepa, whom Bligh had known here in 1777, and immediately recollected, came on board along with others from different islands in the vicinity. This man having formerly been accustomed to the English manner of speaking their language, the Commander found he could converse with him tolerably well. He told him that the cattle which had been left at Tongataboo had all bred, and that the old ones were yet living. Being desirous of seeing the ship, he and his companions were taken below, and the bread-fruit and other plants were shown to them, on seeing which they were greatly surprised.

'I landed,' says Bligh, 'in order to procure some bread-fruit plants to supply the place of one that was dead, and two or three others that were a little sickly. I walked to the west part of the bay, where some plants and seeds had been sown by Captain Cook; and had the satisfaction to see, in a plantation close by, about twenty fine pineapple plants, but no fruit, this not being the proper season. They told me that they had eaten many of them, that they were very fine and large, and that at Tongataboo there were great numbers.'

Numerous were the marks of mourning with which these people disfigure themselves, such as bloody temples, their heads deprived of most of the hair, and, which was worse, almost all of them with the loss of some of their fingers. Several fine boys, not above six years of age, had lost both their little fingers; and some of the men had parted with the middle finger of the right hand.

A brisk trade soon began to be carried on for yams; some plantains and bread-fruit were likewise brought on board, but no hogs. Some of the sailing canoes, which arrived in the course of the day, were large enough to contain not less than ninety passengers. From these the officers and crew purchased hogs, dogs, fowls, and shaddocks; yams, very fine and large; one of them actually weighed above forty-five pounds. The crowd of natives had become so great the next day, Sunday 26th, that it became impossible to do anything. The watering party were therefore ordered to go on board, and it was determined to sail; the ship was accordingly unmoored and got under weigh. A grapnel, however, had been stolen, and Bligh informed the chiefs that were still on board, that unless it was returned, they must remain in the ship, at which they were surprised and not a little alarmed. 'I detained them,' he says, 'till sunset, when their uneasiness and impatience increased to such a degree, that they began to beat themselves about the face and eyes, and some of them cried bitterly. As this distress was more than the grapnel was worth, I could not think of detaining them longer, and called their canoes alongside. I told them they were at liberty to go, and made each of them a present of a hatchet, a saw, with some knives, gimlets, and nails. This unexpected present, and the sudden change in their situation, affected them not less with joy than they had before been with apprehension. They were unbounded in their acknowledgements; and I have little doubt but that we parted better friends than if the affair had never happened.'

From this island the ship stood to the northward all night, with light winds; and on the next day, the 27th, at noon, they were between the islands Tofoa and Kotoo.

'Thus far,' says Bligh, 'the voyage had advanced in a course of uninterrupted prosperity, and had been attended with many circumstances equally pleasing and satisfactory. A very different scene was now to be experienced. A conspiracy had been formed, which was to render all our past labour productive only of extreme misery and distress. The means had been concerted and prepared with so much secrecy and circumspection, that no one circumstance appeared to occasion the smallest suspicion of the impending calamity, the result of an act of piracy the most consummate and atrocious that was probably ever committed.'

How far Bligh was justified in ascribing the calamity to a conspiracy will be seen hereafter. The following chapter will detail the facts of the mutinous proceedings as stated by the Lieutenant, in his own words.

CHAPTER III
THE MUTINY

That,--Captain Bligh,--that is the thing;--I am in hell!--I am in hell!--FLETCHER CHRISTIAN.

--Horror and doubt distract
His troubled thoughts, and from the bottom stir
The hell within him; for within him hell
He brings, and round about him, nor from hell
One step no more than from himself can fly
By change of place; now conscience wakes despair
That slumber'd, wakes the bitter memory
Of what he was, what is, and what must be
Worse; of worse deeds worse sufferings must ensue.

In the morning of the 28th April, the north-westernmost of the Friendly Islands, called Tofoa, bearing north-east, I was steering to the westward with a ship in most perfect order, all my plants in a most flourishing condition, all my men and officers in good health, and in short, everything to flatter and insure my most sanguine expectations. On leaving the deck I gave directions for the course to be steered during the night. The master had the first watch; the gunner, the middle watch; and Mr. Christian, the morning watch. This was the turn of duty for the night.

'Just before sun-rising on Tuesday the 28th, while I was yet asleep, Mr. Christian, officer of the watch, Charles Churchill, ship's corporal, John Mills, gunner's mate, and Thomas Burkitt, seaman, came into my cabin, and seizing me, tied my hands with a cord behind my back, threatening me with instant death if I spoke or made the least noise. I called, however, as loud as I could in hopes of assistance; but they had already secured the officers who were not of their party, by placing sentinels at their doors. There were three men at my cabin door, besides the four within; Christian had only a cutlass in his hand, the others had muskets and bayonets. I was hauled out of bed, and forced on deck in my shirt, suffering great pain from the tightness with which they had tied my hands[4] [behind my back, held by Fletcher Christian, and Charles Churchill, with a bayonet at my breast, and two men, Alexander Smith and Thomas Burkitt behind me, with loaded muskets cocked and bayonets fixed]. I demanded the reason of such violence, but received no other answer than abuse, for not holding my tongue. The master, the gunner, Mr. Elphinstone, the master's mate, and Nelson, were kept confined below; and the fore-hatchway was guarded by sentinels. The boatswain and carpenter, and also Mr. Samuel the clerk, were allowed to come upon deck, where they saw me standing abaft the mizen-mast, with my hands tied behind my back, under a guard, with Christian at their head. The boatswain was ordered to hoist the launch out, with a threat, if he did not do it instantly, to take care of himself.

'When the boat was out, Mr. Hayward and Mr. Hallet, two of the midshipmen, and Mr. Samuel, were ordered into it. I demanded what their intention Was in giving this order, and endeavoured to persuade the people near me not to persist in such acts of violence; but it was to no effect--"Hold your tongue, Sir, or you are dead this instant," was constantly repeated to me.

'The master by this time had sent to request that he might come on deck, which was permitted; but he was soon ordered back again to his cabin.

'[When I exerted myself in speaking loud, to try if I could rally any with a sense of duty in them, I was saluted with--"d--n his eyes, the----, blow his brains out"; while Christian was threatening me with instant death, if I did not hold my tongue.]

'I continued my endeavours to turn the tide of affairs, when Christian changed the cutlass which he had in his hand for a bayonet that was brought to him, and holding me with a strong grip by the cord that tied my hands, he threatened, with many oaths, to kill me immediately, if I would not be quiet; the villains round me had their pieces cocked and bayonets fixed. Particular persons were called on to go into the boat and were hurried over the side; whence I concluded that with these people I was to be set adrift. I therefore made another effort to bring about a change, but with no other effect than to be threatened with having my brains blown out.

The boatswain and seamen who were to go in the boat, were allowed to collect twine, canvas, lines, sails, cordage, an eight-and-twenty gallon cask of water; and Mr. Samuel got one hundred and fifty pounds of bread, with a small quantity of rum and wine, also a quadrant and compass; but he was forbidden, on pain of death, to touch either map, ephemeris, book of astronomical observations, sextant, timekeeper, or any of my surveys or drawings.

'The mutineers having forced those of the seamen whom they meant to get rid of into the boat, Christian directed a dram to be served to each of his own crew. I then unhappily saw that nothing could be done to effect the recovery of the ship: there was no one to assist me, and every endeavour on my part was answered with threats of death.

'The officers were next called upon deck, and forced over the side into the boat, while I was kept apart from every one, abaft the mizen-mast; Christian, armed with a bayonet, holding me by the bandage that secured my hands. The guard round me had their pieces cocked, but on my daring the ungrateful wretches to fire, they uncocked them.

'Isaac Martin, one of the guard over me, I saw had an inclination to assist me, and as he fed me with shaddock (my lips being quite parched) we explained our wishes to each other by our looks; but this being observed, Martin was removed from me. He then attempted to leave the ship, for which purpose he got into the boat; but with many threats they obliged him to return.

'The armourer, Joseph Coleman, and two of the carpenters, M'Intosh and Norman, were also kept, contrary to their inclination; and they begged of me, after I was astern in the boat, to remember that they declared they had no hand in the transaction. Michael Byrne, I am told, likewise wanted to leave the ship.

'It is of no moment for me to recount my endeavours to bring back the offenders to a sense of their duty; all I could do was by speaking to them in general; but it was to no purpose, for I was kept securely bound, and no one except the guard suffered to come near me.

'To Mr. Samuel (clerk) I am indebted for securing my journals and commission, with some material ship papers. Without these I had nothing to certify what I had done, and my honour and character might have been suspected, without my possessing a proper document to have defended them. All this he did with great resolution, though guarded and strictly watched. He attempted to save the timekeeper, and a box with my surveys, drawings, and remarks, for fifteen years past, which were numerous; when he was hurried away with "D--n your eyes, you are well off to get what you have."

It appeared to me that Christian was some time in doubt whether he should keep the carpenter, or his mates; at length he determined on the latter, and the carpenter was ordered into the boat. He was permitted, but not without some opposition, to take his tool-chest.

'Much altercation took place among the mutinous crew during the whole business: some swore "I'll be d---- d if he does not find his way home, if he gets anything with him"; and when the carpenter's chest was carrying away, "D---- n my eyes, he will have a vessel built in a month"; while others laughed at the helpless situation of the boat, being very deep, and so little room for those who were in her. As for Christian, he seemed as if meditating destruction on himself and every one else.

'I asked for arms, but they laughed at me, and said I was well acquainted with the people among whom I was going, and therefore did not want them; four cutlasses, however, were thrown into the boat, after we were veered astern.

'The officers and men being in the boat, they only waited for me, of which the master-at-arms informed Christian; who then said--"Come, Captain Bligh, your officers and men are now in the boat, and you must go with them; if you attempt to make the least resistance, you will instantly be put to death"; and without further ceremony, with a tribe of armed ruffians about me, I was forced over the side, when they untied my hands. Being in the boat, we were veered astern by a rope, a few pieces of pork were thrown to us, and some clothes, also the cutlasses I have already mentioned; and it was then that the armourer and carpenters called out to me to remember that they had no hand in the transaction. After having undergone a great deal of ridicule, and been kept for some time to make sport for these unfeeling wretches, we were at length cast adrift in the open ocean.

'I had with me in the boat the following persons:

Names.   Stations.

JOHN FRYER   Master.
THOMAS LEDWAKD   Acting Surgeon.
DAVID NELSON   Botanist.
WILLIAM PECKOVER   Gunner.
WILLIAM COLE   Boatswain.
WILLIAM PURCELL   Carpenter.
WILLIAM ELPHINSTONE   Master's Mate.
THOMAS HAYWARD   }   Midshipman.
JOHN HALLET   }   do.
JOHN NORTON   }   Quarter-Master.
PETER LENKLETTER   }   do.
LAWRENCE LEBOGUE   Sailmaker.
JOHN SMITH   }   Cook.
THOMAS HALL   }   do.
GEORGE SIMPSON   Quarter-Master's Mate.
ROBERT TINKLER   A boy.
ROBERT LAMB   Butcher.
MR. SAMUEL   Clerk.

In all eighteen.

'There remained in the *Bounty*:

Names.   Stations.

FLETCHER CHRISTIAN   Master's Mate.
PETER HEYWOOD   }   Midshipman.
EDWARD YOUNG   }   Midshipman.
GEORGE STEWART   }   Midshipman.
CHARLES CHURCHILL   Master-at-Arms.
JOHN MILLS   Gunner's Mate.

JAMES MORRISON	Boatswain's Mate.
THOMAS BURKITT }	Able Seaman.
MATTHEW QUINTAL }	do.
JOHN SUMNER }	do.
JOHN MILLWARD }	do.
WILLIAM M'KOY }	do.
HENRY HILLBRANT }	do.
MICHAEL BYRNE }	do.
WILLIAM MUSPRATT }	do.
ALEXANDER SMITH }	do.
JOHN WILLIAMS }	do.
THOMAS ELLISON }	do.
ISAAC MARTIN }	do.
RICHARD SKINNER }	do.
MATTHEW THOMPSON }	do.
WILLIAM BROWN	Gardener.
JOSEPH COLEMAN	Armourer.
CHARLES NORMAN	Carpenter's Mate.
THOMAS M'INTOSH	Carpenter's Crew.

In all twenty-five--and the most able of the ship's company.

'Christian, the chief of the mutineers, is of a respectable family in the North of England. This was the third voyage he had made with me; and as I found it necessary to keep my ship's company at three watches, I had given him an order to take charge of the third, his abilities being thoroughly equal to the task; and by this means the master and gunner were not at watch and watch.

'Heywood is also of a respectable family in the North of England,[5] and a young man of abilities as well as Christian. These two had been objects of my particular regard and attention, and I had taken great pains to instruct them, having entertained hopes that, as professional men, they would have become a credit to their country.

'Young was well recommended, and had the look of an able, stout seaman; he, however, fell short of what his appearance promised. [In the account sent home he is thus described: Edward Young, midshipman, aged twenty-two years. Dark complexion and rather a bad look--strong made--has lost several of his fore teeth, and those that remain are all rotten.]

'Stewart was a young man of creditable parents in the Orkneys; at which place, on the return of the ***Resolution*** from the South Seas, in 1780, we received so many civilities that, on that account only, I should gladly have taken him with me: but, independent of this recommendation, he was a seaman, and had always borne a good character.

'Notwithstanding the roughness with which I was treated, the remembrance of past kindnesses produced some signs of remorse in Christian. When they were forcing me out of the ship, I asked him if this treatment was a proper return for the many instances he had received of my friendship? he appeared disturbed at my question, and answered with much emotion, "That,--Captain Bligh,--that is the thing;--I am in hell,--I am in hell!"

'As soon as I had time to reflect, I felt an inward satisfaction, which prevented any depression of my spirits: conscious of my integrity, and anxious solicitude for the good of the service in which I had been engaged, I found my mind wonderfully supported, and I began to conceive hopes, notwithstanding so heavy a calamity, that I should one day be able to account to my king and country for the misfortune. A few hours before my situation had been peculiarly flattering. I had a ship in the most perfect order, and well stored with every necessary both for service and health; by early attention to those particulars I had, as much as lay in my power, provided against any accident in case I could not get through Endeavour Straits, as well as against what might befall me in them; add to this, the plants had been successfully preserved in the most flourishing state: so that, upon the whole, the voyage was two-thirds completed, and the remaining part, to all appearance, in a very promising way; every person on board being in perfect health, to establish which was ever amongst the principal objects of my attention.

'It will very naturally be asked, what could be the reason for such a revolt? In answer to which I can only conjecture that the mutineers had flattered themselves with the hopes of a more happy life among the Otaheitans than they could possibly enjoy in England; and this, joined to some female connexions, most probably occasioned the whole transaction. The ship, indeed, while within our sight, steered to the W.N.W., but I considered this only as a feint; for when we were sent away,--"Huzza for Otaheite!"--was frequently heard among the mutineers.

'The women of Otaheite are handsome, mild, and cheerful in their manners and conversation, possessed of great sensibility, and have sufficient delicacy to make them admired and beloved. The chiefs were so much attached to our people, that they rather encouraged their stay among them than otherwise, and even made them promises of large possessions. Under these and many other attendant circumstances, equally desirable, it is now perhaps not so much to be wondered at, though scarcely possible to have been foreseen, that a set of sailors, most of them void of connexions, should be led away; especially when, in addition to such powerful inducements, they imagined it in their power to fix themselves in the midst of plenty, on one of the finest islands in the world, where they need hot labour, and where the allurements of dissipation are beyond anything that can be conceived. The utmost, however, that any commander could have supposed to have happened is, that some of the people would have been tempted to desert. But if it should be asserted that a commander is to guard against an act of mutiny and piracy in his own ship, more than by the common rules of service, it is as much as to say that he must sleep locked up, and when awake, be girded with pistols.

'Desertions have happened, more or less, from most of the ships that have been at the Society Islands; but it has always been in the commander's power to make the chiefs return their people; the knowledge, therefore, that it was unsafe to desert, perhaps first led mine to consider with what ease so small a ship might be surprised, and that so favourable an opportunity would never offer to them again.

'The secrecy of this mutiny is beyond all conception. Thirteen of the party, who were with me, had always lived forward among the seamen; yet neither they, nor the messmates of Christian, Stewart, Heywood, and Young, had ever observed any circumstance that made them in the least suspect what was going on. To such a close-planned act of villainy, my mind being entirely free from any suspicion, it is not wonderful that I fell a sacrifice. Perhaps, if there had been marines on board, a sentinel at my cabin-door might have prevented it; for I slept with the door always open, that the officer of the watch might have access to me on all occasions, the possibility of such a conspiracy being ever the farthest from my thoughts. Had their mutiny been occasioned by any grievances, either real or imaginary, I must have discovered symptoms of their discontent, which would have put me on my guard; but the ease was far otherwise. Christian, in particular, I was on the most friendly terms with: that very day he was engaged to have dined with me; and the preceding night he excused himself from supping with me, on pretence of being unwell; for which I felt concerned, having no suspicions of his integrity and honour.'

Such is the story published by Lieutenant Bligh immediately on his return to England, after one of the most distressing and perilous passages over nearly four thousand miles of the wide ocean, with eighteen persons, in an open boat. The story obtained implicit credit; and though Lieutenant Bligh's character never stood high in the navy for suavity of manners or mildness of temper, he was always considered as an excellent seaman, and his veracity stood unimpeached. But in this age of refined liberality, when the most atrocious criminals find their apologists, it is not surprising it should now be discovered, when all are dead that could either prove or disprove it, that it was the tyranny of the commander alone, and not the wickedness of the ringleader of the mutineers of the *Bounty*, that caused that event. 'We all know,' it is said, 'that mutiny can arise but from one of these two sources, excessive folly or excessive tyranny; therefore'--the logic is admirable--'as it is admitted that Bligh was no idiot, the inference is obvious.'[6] If this be so, it may be asked to which of the two causes must be ascribed the mutiny at the Nore, etc.? The true answer will be, to neither. 'Not only,' continues the writer, 'was the *narrative* which he published proved to be false in many material bearings, by evidence before a court-martial, but every act of his public life after this event, from his successive command of the *Director*, the *Glatton*, and the *Warrior*, to his disgraceful expulsion from New South Wales,--was stamped with an insolence, an inhumanity, and coarseness, which fully developed his character.'

There is no intention, in narrating this eventful history, to accuse or defend either the character or the conduct of the late Admiral Bligh; it is well known his temper was irritable in the extreme; but the circumstance of his having been the friend of Captain Cook, with whom he sailed as his master,--of his ever afterwards being patronized by Sir Joseph Banks,--of the Admiralty promoting him to the rank of commander, appointing him immediately to the *Providence*, to proceed on the same expedition to Otaheite,--and of his returning in a very short time to England with complete success, and recommending all his officers for promotion on account of their exemplary conduct;--of his holding several subsequent employments in the service,--of his having commanded ships of the line in the battles of Copenhagen and Camperdown,--and risen to the rank of a flag-officer,--these may perhaps be considered to speak something in his favour, and be allowed to stand as some proof that, with all his failings, he had his merits. That he was a man of coarse habits, and entertained very mistaken notions with regard to discipline, is quite true: yet he had many redeeming qualities. The accusation, by the writer in question, of Bligh having falsified his 'narrative,' is a very heavy charge, and, it is to be feared, is not wholly without foundation; though it would perhaps be more correct to say, that in the printed narrative of his voyage, and the narrative on which the mutineers were tried, there are many important omissions from his original manuscript journal, some of which it will be necessary to notice presently.

The same writer further says, 'We know that the officers fared in every way worse than the men, and that even young Heywood was kept at the mast head no less than eight hours at one spell, in the worst weather which they encountered off Cape Horn.'

Perhaps Heywood may himself be brought forward as authority, if not to disprove, at least to render highly improbable, his experiencing any such treatment on the part of his captain. This young officer, in his defence, says, 'Captain Bligh, in his narrative, acknowledges that he had left some friends on board the ***Bounty***, and no part of my conduct could have induced him to believe that I ought not to be reckoned of the number. Indeed, from his attention to, ***and very kind treatment of me personally***, I should have been a monster of depravity to have betrayed him. The idea alone is sufficient to disturb a mind, where humanity and gratitude have, I hope, ever been noticed as its characteristic features.' Bligh, too, has declared in a letter to Heywood's uncle, Holwell, after accusing him of ingratitude, that 'he never once had an angry word from me during the whole course of the voyage, as his conduct always gave me much pleasure and satisfaction.'

In looking over a manuscript journal, kept by Morrison, the boatswain's mate, who was tried and convicted as one of the mutineers, but received the king's pardon, the conduct of Bligh appears in a very unfavourable point of view. This Morrison was a person, from talent and education, far above the situation he held in the ***Bounty***; he had previously served in the navy as midshipman, and, after his pardon, was appointed gunner of the ***Blenheim***, in which he perished with Sir Thomas Troubridge. In comparing this journal with other documents, the dates and transactions appear to be correctly stated, though the latter may occasionally be somewhat too highly coloured. How he contrived to preserve this journal, in the wreck of the ***Pandora***, does not appear; but there can be no doubt of its authenticity, having been kept among the late Captain Heywood's papers; various passages in it have been corrected either by this officer or some other person, but without altering their sense.

It would appear from this important document that the seeds of discord, in the unfortunate ship ***Bounty***, were sown at a very early period of the voyage. It happened, as was the case in all small vessels, that the duties of commander and purser were united in the person of Lieutenant Bligh; and it would seem that this proved the cause of very serious discontent among the officers and crew; of the mischief arising out of this union, the following statement of Mr. Morrison may serve as a specimen. At Teneriffe, Lieutenant Bligh ordered the cheese to be hoisted up and exposed to the air; which was no sooner done, than he pretended to miss a certain quantity, and declared that it had been stolen. The cooper, Henry Hillbrant, informed him that the cask in question had been opened by the orders of Mr. Samuel, his clerk, who acted also as steward, and the cheese sent on shore to his own house, previous to the ***Bounty*** leaving the river on her way to Portsmouth. Lieutenant Bligh, without making any further inquiry, immediately ordered the allowance of that article to be stopped, both from ***officers*** and ***men***, until the deficiency should be made good, and told the cooper he would give him a d--d good flogging if he said another word on the subject. It can hardly be supposed that a man of Bligh's shrewdness, if disposed to play the rogue, would have placed himself so completely in the hands of the cooper, in a transaction which, if revealed, must have cost him his commission.

Again, on approaching the equator, some decayed pumpkins, purchased at Teneriffe, were ordered to be issued to the crew, at the rate of ***one*** pound of pumpkin for ***two*** pounds of biscuit. The reluctance of the men to accept this proposed substitute, ***on such terms***, being reported to Lieutenant Bligh, he flew upon deck in a violent rage, turned the hands up, and ordered the first man on the list of each mess to be called by name; at the same time saying, 'I'll see who will dare to refuse the pumpkin, or any thing else I may order to be served out;' to which he added, 'You d--d infernal scoundrels, I'll make you eat grass, or any thing you can catch, before I have done with you.' This speech had the desired effect, every one receiving the pumpkins, even the *officers*.

Next comes a complaint respecting the mode of issuing beef and pork: but when a representation was made to Lieutenant Bligh in the quiet and orderly manner prescribed by the twenty-first article of war, he called the crew aft, told them that every thing relative to the provisions was transacted by his orders; that it was therefore needless for them to complain, as they would get no redress, he being the fittest judge of what was right or wrong, and that he would flog the first man who should dare attempt to make any complaint in future. To this imperious menace they bowed in silence, and not another murmur was heard from them during the remainder of the voyage to Otaheite, it being their determination to seek legal redress on the ***Bounty's*** return to England. Happy would it have been had they kept their resolution. By so doing, if the story be true, they would amply have been avenged, a vast number of human lives spared, and a world of misery avoided.

According to this Journalist, 'the seeds of eternal discord were sown between Lieutenant Bligh and some of his officers,' while in Adventure Bay, Van Diemen's Land; and on arriving at Matavai Bay, in Otaheite, he is accused of taking the officers' hogs and bread-fruit, and serving them to the ship's company; and when the master remonstrated with him on the subject, he replied that 'he would convince him that every thing became ***his*** as soon as it was brought on board; that he would take nine-tenths of every man's property, and let him see who dared to say anything to the contrary.' The sailors' pigs were seized without ceremony, and it became a favour for a man to obtain an extra pound of his own meat.

The writer then says, 'the object of our visit to the Society Islands being at length accomplished, we weighed on the 4th April, 1789. Every one seemed in high spirits, and began to talk of home, as though they had just left Jamaica instead of Otaheite, so far onward did their flattering fancies waft them. On the 23rd, we anchored off Anamooka, the inhabitants of which island were very rude, and attempted to take the casks and axes from the parties sent to fill water and cut wood. A musket pointed at them produced no other effect than a return of the compliment, by poising their clubs or spears with menacing looks; and, as it was Lieutenant Bligh's orders, that no person should affront them on any occasion, they were emboldened by meeting with no check to their insolence. They at length became so troublesome, that Mr. Christian, who commanded the watering party, found it difficult to carry on his duty; but on acquainting Lieutenant Bligh with their behaviour, he received a volley of abuse, was d--d as a cowardly rascal, and asked if he were afraid of naked savages whilst he had weapons in his hand? To this he replied in a respectful manner, "The arms are of no effect, Sir, while your orders prohibit their use."'

This happened but three days before the mutiny, and the same circumstance is noticed, but somewhat differently, in Bligh's MS. Journal, where he says, 'the men cleared themselves, and they therefore merit no punishment. As to the officers I have no resource, nor do I ever feel myself safe in the few instances I trust to them.' A perusal of all the documents certainly leads to the conclusion that all his officers were of a very inferior description; they had no proper feeling of their own situation; and this, together with the contempt in which they were held by Bligh, and which he could not disguise, may account for that perfect indifference, with regard both to the captain and the ship, which was manifested on the day of the mutiny.

That sad catastrophe, if the writer of the Journal be correct, was hastened, if not brought about by, the following circumstance, of which Bligh takes no notice.

'In the afternoon of the 27th, Lieutenant Bligh came upon deck, and missing some of the cocoa-nuts, which had been piled up between the guns, said they had been stolen, and could not have been taken away without the knowledge of the officers, all of whom were sent for and questioned on the subject. On their declaring that they had not seen any of the people touch them, he exclaimed, "Then you must have taken them yourselves"; and proceeded to inquire of them separately, how many they had purchased. On coming to Mr. Christian, that gentleman answered, "I do not know, Sir, but I hope you do not think me so mean as to be guilty of stealing yours." Mr. Bligh replied, "Yes, you d---- d hound, I do--you must have stolen them from me, or you would be able to give a better account of them;" then turning to the other officers, he said, "God d---- n you, you scoundrels, you are all thieves alike, and combine with the men to rob me: I suppose you will steal my yams next; but I'll sweat you for it, you rascals--I'll make half of you jump overboard, before you get through Endeavour Straits." This threat was followed by an order to the clerk "to stop the villains' grog, and give them but half a pound of yams to-morrow; if they steal them, I'll reduce them to a quarter."'

It is difficult to believe that an officer in his Majesty's service could condescend to make use of such language to the meanest of the crew, much less to gentlemen: it is to be feared, however, that there is sufficient ground for the truth of these statements: with regard to the last, it is borne out by the evidence of Mr. Fryer, the master, on the court-martial. This officer, being asked, 'what did you suppose to be Mr. Christian's meaning, when he said he had been in hell for a fortnight?' answered, 'From the frequent quarrels they had had, and the abuse which he had received from Mr. Bligh.'--'Had there been any very recent quarrel?'--'The day before Mr. Bligh challenged all the young gentlemen and people with stealing his cocoa-nuts.' It was on the evening of this day that Lieutenant Bligh, according to his printed narrative, says Christian was to have supped with him; but excused himself on account of being unwell; and that he was invited to dine with him on the day of the mutiny.

Every one of these circumstances, and many others, which might be stated from Mr. Morrison's Journal, are omitted in Bligh's published narrative; but many of them are alluded to in his original Journal, and others that prove distinctly the constant reproofs to which his officers were subject, and the bad terms on which they stood with their commander. A few extracts from this Journal will sufficiently establish this point.

In so early a part of the voyage as their arrival in Adventure Bay, he found fault with his officers, and put the carpenter into confinement. Again, at Matavai Bay, on the 5th December, Bligh says, 'I ordered the carpenter to cut a large stone that was brought off by one of the natives, requesting me to get it made fit for them to grind their hatchets on, but to my astonishment he refused, in direct terms, to comply, saying, "I will not cut the stone, for it will spoil my chisel; and though there may be law to take away my clothes, there is none to take away my tools." This man having before shown his mutinous and insolent behaviour, I was under the necessity of confining him to his cabin.'

On the 5th January three men deserted in the cutter, on which occasion Bligh says, 'Had the mate of the watch been awake, no trouble of this kind would have happened. I have therefore disrated and turned him before the mast; such neglectful and worthless petty officers, I believe, never were in a ship as are in this. No orders for a few hours together are obeyed by them, and their conduct in general is so bad, that no confidence or trust can be reposed in them; in short, they have driven me to every thing but corporal punishment, and that must follow if they do not improve.'

By Morrison's Journal it would appear that 'corporal punishment' was not long delayed; for, on the very day, he says, the midshipman was put in irons, and confined from the 5th January to the 23rd March--eleven weeks!

On the 17th January, orders being given to clear out the sail-room and to air the sails, many of them were found very much mildewed and rotten in many places, on which he observes, 'If I had any officers to supersede the master and boatswain, or was capable of doing without them, considering them as common seamen, they should no longer occupy their respective stations; scarcely any neglect of duty can equal the criminality of this.'

On the 24th January, the three deserters were brought back and flogged, then put in irons for further punishment. 'As this affair,' he says, 'was solely caused by the neglect of the officers who had the watch, I was induced to give them all a lecture on this occasion, and endeavour to show them that, however exempt they were at present from the like punishment, yet they were equally subject, by the articles of war, to a condign one.' He then tells them, that it is only necessity that makes him have recourse to reprimand, because there are no means of trying them by court-martial; and adds a remark, not very intelligible, but what he calls an unpleasant one, about *such* offenders having no feelings of honour or sense of shame.

On the 7th March, a native Otaheitan, whom Bligh had confined in irons, contrived to break the lock of the bilboa-bolt and make his escape. 'I had given,' says Bligh, 'a written order that the mate of the watch was to be answerable for the prisoners, and to visit and see that they were safe in his watch, but I have such a neglectful set about me, that I believe nothing but condign punishment can alter their conduct. Verbal orders, in the course of a month, were so forgotten, that they would impudently assert no such thing or directions were given, and I have been at last under the necessity to trouble myself with writing, what, by decent young officers, would be complied with as the common rules of the service. Sir. Stewart was the mate of the watch.'

These extracts show the terms on which Bligh was with his officers; and these few instances, with others from Morrison's Journal, make it pretty clear, that though Christian, as fiery and passionate a youth as his commander could well be, and with feelings too acute to bear the foul and opprobious language constantly addressed to him, was the sole instigator of the mutiny;--the captain had no support to expect, and certainly received none, from the rest of his officers. That Christian was the sole author appears still more strongly from the following passage in Morrison's Journal. 'When Mr. Bligh found he must go into the boat, he begged of Mr. Christian to desist, saying "I'll pawn my honour, I'll give my bond, Mr. Christian, never to think of this, if you'll desist," and urged his wife and family; to which Mr. Christian replied, "No, Captain Bligh, if you had any honour, things had not come to this; and if you had any regard for your wife and family, you should have thought on them before, and not behaved so much like a villain." Lieutenant Bligh again attempted to speak, but was ordered to be silent. The boatswain also tried to pacify Mr. Christian, to whom he replied, "It is too late, I have been in hell for this fortnight past, and am determined to bear it no longer; and you know, Mr. Cole, that I have been used like a dog all the voyage."'

It is pretty evident, therefore, that the mutiny was not, as Bligh in his narrative states it to have been, the result of a conspiracy. It will be seen by the minutes of the court-martial, that the whole affair was planned and executed between the hours of four and eight o'clock, on the morning of the 28th April, when Christian had the watch upon deck; that Christian, unable longer to bear the abusive and insulting language, had meditated his own escape from the ship the day before, choosing to trust himself to fate, rather than submit to the constant upbraiding to which he had been subject; but the unfortunate business of the cocoa-nuts drove him to the commission of the rash and felonious act, which ended, as such criminal acts usually do, in his own destruction, and that of a great number of others, many of whom were wholly innocent.

Lieutenant Bligh, like most passionate men, whose unruly tempers get the better of their reason, having vented his rage about the cocoa-nuts, became immediately calm, and by inviting Christian to sup with him the same evening, evidently wished to renew their friendly intercourse; and happy would it have been for all parties had he accepted the invitation. On the same night, towards ten o'clock, when the master had the watch, Bligh came on deck, as was his custom, before retiring to sleep. It was one of those calm and beautiful nights, so frequent in tropical regions, whose soothing influence can be appreciated only by those who have felt it, when, after a scorching day, the air breathes a most refreshing coolness,--it was an evening of this sort, when Bligh for the last time came upon deck, in the capacity of commander; a gentle breeze scarcely rippled the water, and the moon, then in its first quarter, shed its soft light along the surface of the sea. The short and quiet conversation that took place between Bligh and the master on this evening, after the irritation of the morning had subsided, only to burst forth again in all the horrors of mutiny and piracy, recalls to one's recollection that beautiful passage of Shakespeare, where, on the evening of the murder, Duncan, on approaching the castle of Macbeth, observes to Banquo--

--'The air
Nimbly and sweetly recommends itself
Unto our gentle senses,' etc.--

a passage which Sir Joshua Reynolds considers as a striking instance of what in painting is termed *repose*. 'The subject,' he says, 'of this quiet and easy conversation, gives that repose so necessary to the mind, after the tumultuous bustle of the preceding scenes, and beautifully contrasts the scene of terror that immediately succeeds.' While, on this lovely night, Bligh and his master were congratulating themselves on the pleasing prospect of fine weather and a full moon, to light them through Endeavour's dangerous straits, the unhappy and deluded Christian was, in all probability, brooding over his wrongs, and meditating on the criminal act he was to perpetrate the following morning; for he has himself stated, that he had just fallen asleep about half after three in the morning, and was much out of order.

The evidence on the court-martial is sufficiently explicit as to the mode in which this act of piracy was committed. By the Journal of James Morrison, the following is the account of the transaction, as given by Christian himself to the two midshipmen, Heywood and Stewart (both of whom had been kept below), the moment they were allowed to come upon deck, after the boat, in which were Bligh and his companions, had been turned adrift.

He said, that, 'finding himself much hurt by the treatment he had received from Lieutenant Bligh, he had determined to quit the ship the preceding evening, and had informed the boatswain, carpenter, and two midshipmen (Stewart and Hayward), of his intention to do so; that by them he was supplied with part of a roasted pig, some nails, beads, and other articles of trade, which he put into a bag that was given him by the last-named gentleman; that he put this bag into the clue of Robert Tinkler's hammock, where it was discovered by that young gentleman when going to bed at night, but the business was smothered, and passed off without any further notice. He said he had fastened some staves to a stout plank, with which he intended to make his escape; but finding he could not effect it during the first and middle watches, as the ship had no way through the water, and the people were all moving about, he laid down to rest about half-past three in the morning; that when Mr. Stewart called him to relieve the deck at four o'clock, he had but just fallen asleep, and was much out of order; upon observing which, Mr. Stewart strenuously advised him to abandon his intention; that as soon as he had taken charge of the deck, he saw Mr. Hayward, the mate of his watch, lie down on the arm-chest to take a nap; and finding that Mr. Hallet, the other midshipman, did not make his appearance, he suddenly formed the resolution of seizing the ship. Disclosing his intention to Matthew Quintal and Isaac Martin, both of whom had been flogged by Lieutenant Bligh, they called up Charles Churchill, who had also tasted the cat, and Matthew Thompson, both of whom readily joined in the plot. That Alexander Smith (*alias* John Adams), John Williams, and William M'Koy, evinced equal willingness, and went with Churchill to the armourer, of whom they obtained the keys of the arm-chest, under pretence of wanting a musket to fire at a shark, then alongside; that finding Mr. Hallet asleep on an arm-chest in the main-hatchway, they roused and sent him on deck. Charles Norman, unconscious of their proceedings, had in the meantime awaked Mr. Hayward, and directed his attention to the shark, whose movements he was watching at the moment that Mr. Christian and his confederates came up the fore-hatchway, after having placed arms in the hands of several men who were not aware of their design. One man, Matthew Thompson, was left in charge of the chest, and he served out arms to Thomas Burkitt and Robert Lamb. Mr. Christian said he then proceeded to secure Lieutenant Bligh, the master, gunner, and botanist.'

'When Mr. Christian,' observes Morrison in his Journal, 'related the above circumstances, I recollected having seen him fasten some staves to a plank lying on the larboard gangway, as also having heard the boatswain say to the carpenter, "it will not do to-night." I likewise remembered that; Mr. Christian had visited the forecockpit several times that evening, although he had very seldom, if ever, frequented the warrant-officers' cabins before.'

If this be a correct statement, and the greater part of it is borne out by evidence on the court-martial, it removes every doubt of Christian being the sole instigator of the mutiny, and that no conspiracy nor pre-concerted measures had any existence, but that it was suddenly conceived by a hot-headed young man, in a state of great excitement of mind, amounting to a temporary aberration of intellect, caused by the frequent abusive and insulting language of his commanding officer. Waking out of a short half hour's disturbed sleep, to take the command of the deck--finding the two mates of the watch, Hayward and Hallet, asleep (for which they ought to have been dismissed the service instead of being, as they were, promoted)--the opportunity tempting, and the ship completely in his power, with a momentary impulse he darted down the fore-hatchway, got possession of the keys of the arm-chest, and made the hazardous experiment of arming such of the men as he thought he could trust, and effected his purpose.

There is a passage in Captain Beechey's account of Pitcairn Island, which, if correct, would cast a stain on the memory of the unfortunate Stewart--who, if there was one innocent man in the ship, was that man. Captain Beechey says (speaking of Christian), 'His plan, strange as it must appear for a young officer to adopt, who was fairly advanced in an honourable profession, was to set himself adrift upon a raft, and make his way to the island (Tofoa) then in sight. As quick in the execution as in the design, the raft was soon constructed, various useful articles were got together, and he was on the point of launching it, when a young officer, **who afterwards perished in the Pandora**, to whom Christian communicated his intention, recommended him, rather than risk his life on so hazardous an expedition, **to endeavour to take possession of the ship**, which he thought would not be very difficult, as many of the ship's company were not well disposed towards the commander, and would all be very glad to return to Otaheite, and reside among their friends in that island. This daring proposition is even more extraordinary than the premeditated scheme of his companion, and, if true, certainly relieves Christian from part of the odium which has hitherto attached to him as the sole instigator of the mutiny.' Relieve him?--not a jot--but on the best authority it may boldly be stated, that it is ***not*** true--the authority of Stewart's friend and messmate, the late Captain Heywood.

Captain Beechey, desirous of being correct in his statement, very properly sent his chapter on Pitcairn's Island for any observations Captain Heywood might have to make on what was said therein regarding the mutiny; observing in his note which accompanied it, that this account, received from Adams, differed materially from a footnote in Marshall's ***Naval Biography***; to which Captain Heywood returned the following reply.

'*5th April*, 1830.

'DEAR SIR,--I have perused the account you received from Adams of the mutiny in the ***Bounty***, which does indeed differ very materially from a footnote in Marshall's ***Naval Biography***, by the editor, to whom I verbally detailed the facts, which are strictly true.

'That Christian informed the boatswain and the carpenter, Messrs. Hayward and Stewart, of his determination to leave the ship upon a raft, on the night preceding the mutiny, is certain; but that any one of them (Stewart in particular) should have "recommended, rather than risk his life on so hazardous an expedition, that he should try the expedient of taking the ship from the captain, etc.," is entirely at variance with the whole character and conduct of the latter, both before and after the mutiny; as well as with the assurance of Christian himself, the very night he quitted Taheite, that the idea of attempting to take the ship had never entered his distracted mind, until the moment he relieved the deck, and found his mate and midshipman asleep.[7]

'At that last interview with Christian he also communicated to me, for the satisfaction of his relations, other circumstances connected with that unfortunate disaster, which, after their deaths, may or may not be laid before the public. And although they can implicate none but himself, either living or dead, they may extenuate but will contain not a word of his in defence of the crime he committed against the laws of his country.--I am, etc.,

'P. HEYWOOD.'

Captain Beechey stated only what he had heard from old Adams, who was not always correct in the information he gave to the visitors of his island; but this part of his statement gave great pain to Heywood, who adverted to it on his death-bed, wishing, out of regard for Stewart's memory and his surviving friends, that it should be publicly contradicted; and with this view the above reply of Captain Heywood is here inserted.

The temptations, therefore, which it was supposed Otaheite held out to the deluded men of the ***Bounty***, had no more share in the transaction than the supposed conspiracy; it does not appear, indeed, that the cry of 'Huzza for Otaheite!' was ever uttered; if this island had been the object of either Christian or the crew, they would not have left it three hundred miles behind them, before they perpetrated the act of piracy; but after the deed had been committed, it would be natural enough that they should turn their minds to the lovely island and its fascinating inhabitants, which they had but just quitted, and that in the moment of excitement some of them should have so called out; but Bligh is the only person who has said they did so.

If, however, the recollection of the 'sunny isle' and its 'smiling women' had really tempted the men to mutiny, Bligh would himself not be free from blame, for having allowed them to indulge for six whole months among this voluptuous and fascinating people; for though he was one of the most active and anxious commanders of his time, 'the service,' as is observed by a naval officer, 'was carried on in those days in a very different spirit from that which regulates its movements now, otherwise the ***Bounty*** would never have passed six whole months at one island "stowing away the fruit," during which time the officers and seamen had free access to the shore. Under similar circumstances nowadays, if the fruit happened not to be ready, the ship would have been off, after ten days' relaxation, to survey other islands, or speculate on coral reefs, or make astronomical observations; in short, to do something or other to keep the devil out of the heads of the crew.'[8] Bligh would appear to have been sensible of this on his next expedition in the ***Providence***, for on that occasion he collected more bread-fruit plants than on the former, and spent only half the time in doing so.

Be that as it may, Bligh might naturally enough conclude that the seamen were casting 'a lingering look behind' towards Otaheite. 'If,' says Forster (who accompanied Cook), 'we fairly consider the different situations of a common sailor on board the ***Resolution***, and of a Taheitan on his island, we cannot blame the former if he attempt to rid himself of the numberless discomforts of a voyage round the world, and prefer an easy life, free from cares, in the happiest climate of the world, to the frequent vicissitudes which are entailed upon the mariner. The most favourable prospects of future success in England, which he might form in idea, could never be so flattering to his senses as the lowly hope of living like the meanest Taheitan. And supposing him to escape the misfortunes incident to seamen, still he must earn his subsistence in England at the expense of labour, and "in the sweat of his brow," when this oldest curse on mankind is scarcely felt at Taheite. Two or three bread-fruit trees, which grow almost without any culture, and which flourish as long as he himself can expect to live, supply him with abundant food during three-fourths of the year. The cloth-trees and eddo-roots are cultivated with much less trouble than our cabbages and kitchen-herbs. The banana, the royal palm, the golden apple, all thrive with such luxuriance, and require so little trouble, that I may venture to call them spontaneous. Most of their days are therefore spent in a round of various enjoyments, where Nature has lavished many a pleasing landscape; where the temperature of the air is warm, but continually refreshed by a wholesome breeze from the sea; and where the sky is almost constantly serene. A kind of happy uniformity runs through the whole life of the Taheitans. They rise with the sun, and hasten to rivers and fountains to perform an ablution equally reviving and cleanly. They pass the morning at work, or walk about till the heat of the day increases, when they retreat to their dwellings, or repose under some tufted tree. There they amuse themselves with smoothing their hair, and anoint it with fragrant oils; or they blow the flute, and sing to it, or listen to the songs of the birds. At the hour of noon, or a little later, they go to dinner. After their meals they resume their domestic amusements, during which the flame of mutual affection spreads in every heart, and unites the rising generation with new and tender ties. The lively jest, without any ill-nature, the artless tale, the jocund dance and frugal supper, bring on the evening; and another visit to the river concludes the actions of the day. Thus contented with their simple way of life, and placed in a delightful country, they are free from cares, and happy in their ignorance.'

Such is the picture drawn of the happy people of Otaheite by a cold, philosophical, German doctor, and such, with very little change, Bligh found them. As far, however, as the mutiny of his people was concerned, we must wholly discard the idea thrown out by him, that the seductions of Otaheite had any share in producing it. It could not have escaped a person of Christian's sagacity, that certain interrogatories would unquestionably be put by the natives of Otaheite, on finding the ship return so soon without her commander, without the bread-fruit plants, and with only about half her crew; questions he knew to which no satisfactory answer could be made; and though, at subsequent periods, he twice visited that island, it was some time afterwards, and not from choice but necessity; his object was to find a place of concealment, where he might pass the remainder of his days, unheard of and unknown, and where it is to be hoped he had time for sincere repentance, the only atonement he could make for the commission of a crime, which involved so many human beings in misery, and brought others to an untimely end--but of this hereafter.

CHAPTER IV
THE OPEN-BOAT NAVIGATION

The boat is lower'd with all the haste of hate,
With its slight plank between thee and thy fate;
Her only cargo such a scant supply
As promises the death their hands deny;
And just enough of water and of bread
To keep, some days, the dying from the dead:
Some cordage, canvas, sails, and lines, and twine.
But treasures all to hermits of the brine,
Were added after, to the earnest prayer
Of those who saw no hope save sea and air;
And last, that trembling vassal of the Pole,
The feeling compass, Navigation's soul.

* * * * *

The launch is crowded with the faithful few
Who wait their Chief--a melancholy crew:
But some remained reluctant on the deck
Of that proud vessel, now a moral wreck--And
view'd their Captain's fate with piteous eyes;
While others scoff'd his augur'd miseries,
Sneer'd at the prospect of his pigmy sail,
And the slight bark so laden and so frail.

Christian had intended to send away his captain and associates in the cutter, and ordered that it should be hoisted out for that purpose, which was done--a small wretched boat, that could hold but eight or ten men at the most, with a very small additional weight; and, what was still worse, she was so worm-eaten and decayed, especially in the bottom planks, that the probability was, she would have gone down before she had proceeded a mile from the ship. In this 'rotten carcass of a boat,' not unlike that into which Prospero and his lovely daughter were 'hoist,'

> not rigg'd,
> Nor tackle, sail, nor mast; the very rats
> Instinctively had quit it,

did Christian intend to cast adrift his late commander and his eighteen innocent companions, or as many of them as she would stow, to find, as they inevitably must have found, a watery grave. But the remonstrances of the master, boatswain, and carpenter prevailed on him to let those unfortunate men have the launch, into which nineteen persons were thrust, whose weight, together with that of the few articles they were permitted to take, brought down the boat so near to the water, as to endanger her sinking with but a moderate swell of the sea--and to all human appearance, in no state to survive the length of voyage they were destined to perform over the wide ocean, but which they did most miraculously survive.

The first consideration of Lieutenant Bligh and his eighteen unfortunate companions, on being cast adrift in their open boat, was to examine the state of their resources. The quantity of provisions which they found to have been thrown into the boat, by some few kind-hearted messmates, amounted to one hundred and fifty pounds of bread, sixteen pieces of pork, each weighing two pounds, six quarts of rum, six bottles of wine, with twenty-eight gallons of water, and four empty barricoes. Being so near to the island of Tofoa, it was resolved to seek there a supply of bread-fruit and water, to preserve if possible the above-mentioned stock entire; but after rowing along the coast, they discovered only some cocoa-nut trees, on the top of high precipices, from which, with much danger owing to the surf, and great difficulty in climbing the cliffs, they succeeded in obtaining about twenty nuts. The second day they made excursions into the island, but without success. They met however with a few natives, who came down with them to the cove where the boat was lying; and others presently followed. They made inquiries after the ship, and Bligh unfortunately advised they should say that the ship had overset and sunk, and that they only were saved. The story might be innocent, but it was certainly indiscreet to put the people in possession of their defenceless situation; however, they brought in small quantities of bread-fruit, plantains, and cocoa-nuts, but little or no water could be procured. These supplies, scanty as they were, served to keep up the spirits of the men; 'They no longer, says Bligh, 'regarded me with those anxious looks, which had constantly been directed towards me, since we lost sight of the ship: every countenance appeared to have a degree of cheerfulness, and they all seemed determined to do their best.'

The numbers of the natives having so much increased as to line the whole beach, they began knocking stones together, which was known to be the preparatory signal for an attack. With some difficulty on account of the surf, our seamen succeeded in getting the things that were on shore into the boat, together with all the men, except John Norton, quarter-master, who was casting off the stern-fast. The natives immediately rushed upon this poor man, and actually stoned him to death. A volley of stones was also discharged at the boat, and every one in it was more or less hurt. This induced the people to push out to sea with all the speed they were able to give to the launch, but to their surprise and alarm, several canoes, filled with stones, followed close after them and renewed the attack; against which, the only return the unfortunate men in the boat could make, was with the stones of the assailants that lodged in her, a species of warfare in which they were very inferior to the Indians. The only expedient left was to tempt the enemy to desist from the pursuit, by throwing overboard some clothes, which fortunately induced the canoes to stop and pick them up; and night coming on, they returned to the shore, leaving the party in the boat to reflect on their unhappy situation.

The men now intreated their commander to take them towards home; and on being told that no hope of relief could be entertained till they reached Timor, a distance of full twelve hundred leagues, they all readily agreed to be content with an allowance, which, on calculation of their resources, the commander informed them would not exceed one ounce of bread, and a quarter of a pint of water, per day. Recommending them, therefore, in the most solemn manner, not to depart from their promise in this respect, 'we bore away,' says Bligh, 'across a sea where the navigation is but little known, in a small boat twenty-three feet long from stem to stern, deeply laden with eighteen men. I was happy, however, to see that every one seemed better satisfied with our situation than myself. It was about eight o'clock at night on the 2nd May, when we bore away under a reefed lug-foresail; and having divided the people into watches, and got the boat into a little order, we returned thanks to God for our miraculous preservation, and, in full confidence of His gracious support, I found my mind more at ease than it had been for some time past.'

At day-break on the 3rd, the forlorn and almost hopeless navigators saw with alarm the sun to rise fiery and red,--a sure indication of a severe gale of wind; and accordingly, at eight o'clock it blew a violent storm, and the sea ran so very high, that the sail was becalmed when between the seas, and too much to have set when on the top of the sea; yet it is stated that they could not venture to take it in, as they were in very imminent danger and distress, the sea curling over the stern of the boat, and obliging them to bale with all their might. 'A situation,' observes the commander, 'more distressing has, perhaps, seldom been experienced.'

The bread, being in bags, was in the greatest danger of being spoiled by the wet, the consequence of which, if not prevented, must have been fatal, as the whole party would inevitably be starved to death, if they should fortunately escape the fury of the waves. It was determined, therefore, that all superfluous clothes, with some rope and spare sails, should be thrown overboard, by which the boat was considerably lightened. The carpenter's tool-chest was cleared, and the tools stowed in the bottom of the boat, and the bread secured in the chest. All the people being thoroughly wet and cold, a teaspoonful of rum was served out to each person, with a quarter of a bread-fruit, which is stated to have been scarcely eatable, for dinner; Bligh having determined to preserve sacredly, and at the peril of his life, the engagement they entered into, and to make their small stock of provisions last eight weeks, let the daily proportion be ever so small.

The sea continuing to run even higher than in the morning, the fatigue of baling became very great; the boat was necessarily kept before the sea. The men were constantly wet, the night very cold, and at daylight their limbs were so benumbed, that they could scarcely find the use of them. At this time a teaspoonful of rum served out to each person was found of great benefit to all. Five small cocoa-nuts were distributed for dinner, and every one was satisfied; and in the evening, a few broken pieces of bread-fruit were served for supper, after which prayers were performed.

On the night of the 4th and morning of the 5th, the gale had abated; the first step to be taken was to examine the state of the bread, a great part of which was found to be damaged and rotten--but even this was carefully preserved for use. The boat was now running among some islands, but after their reception at Tofoa, they did not venture to land. On the 6th, they still continued to see islands at a distance; and this day, for the first time, they hooked a fish, to their great joy; 'but,' says the commander, 'we were miserably disappointed by its being lost in trying to get it into the boat.' In the evening, each person had an ounce of the damaged bread, and a quarter of a pint of water for supper.

Lieutenant Bligh observes, 'it will readily be supposed our lodgings were very miserable, and confined for want of room'; but he endeavoured to remedy the latter defect, by putting themselves at watch and watch; so that one half always sat up, while the other lay down on the boat's bottom, or upon a chest, but with nothing to cover them except the heavens. Their limbs, he says, were dreadfully cramped, for they could not stretch them out; and the nights were so cold, and they were so constantly wet, that, after a few hours' sleep, they were scarcely able to move. At dawn of day on the 7th, being very wet and cold, he says, 'I served a spoonful of rum and a morsel of bread for breakfast.'

In the course of this day they passed close to some rocky isles, from which two large sailing-canoes came swiftly after them, but in the afternoon gave over the chase. They were of the same construction as those of the Friendly Islands, and the land seen for the last two days was supposed to be the Fiji Islands. But being constantly wet, Bligh says, 'it is with the utmost difficulty I can open a book to write, and I feel truly sensible I can do no more than point out where these lands are to be found, and give some idea of their extent.' Heavy rain came on in the afternoon, when every person in the boat did his utmost to catch some water, and thus succeeded in increasing their stock to thirty-four gallons, besides quenching their thirst for the first time they had been able to do so since they had been at sea: but it seems an attendant consequence of the heavy rain caused them to pass the night very miserably; for being extremely wet, and having no dry things to shift or cover themselves, they experienced cold and shiverings scarcely to be conceived.

On the 8th, the allowance issued was an ounce and a half of pork, a teaspoonful of rum, half a pint of cocoa-nut milk, and an ounce of bread. The rum, though so small in quantity, is stated to have been of the greatest service. In the afternoon they were employed in cleaning out the boat, which occupied them until sunset before they got every thing dry and in order. 'Hitherto,' Bligh says, 'I had issued the allowance by guess, but I now made a pair of scales with two cocoa-nut shells; and having accidentally some pistol-balls in the boat, twenty-five of which weighed one pound or sixteen ounces, I adopted one of these balls as the proportion of weight that each person should receive of bread at the times I served it. I also amused all hands with describing the situations of New Guinea and New Holland, and gave them every information in my power, that in case any accident should happen to me, those who survived might have some idea of what they were about, and be able to find their way to Timor, which at present they knew nothing of more than the name, and some not even that. At night I served a quarter of a pint of water and half an ounce of bread for supper.

On the morning of the 9th, a quarter of a pint of cocoa-nut milk and some of the decayed bread were served for breakfast; and for dinner, the kernels of four cocoa-nuts, with the remainder of the rotten bread, which, he says, was eatable only by such distressed people as themselves. A storm of thunder and lightning gave them about twenty gallons of water. 'Being miserably wet and cold, I served to the people a teaspoonful of rum each, to enable them to bear with their distressing situation. The weather continued extremely bad, and the wind increased; we spent a very miserable night, without sleep, except such as could be got in the midst of rain.'

The following day, the 10th, brought no relief, except that of its light. The sea broke over the boat so much, that two men were kept constantly baling; and it was necessary to keep the boat before the waves for fear of its filling. The allowance now served regularly to each person was one twenty-fifth part of a pound of bread and a quarter of a pint of water, at eight in the morning, at noon, and at sunset. To-day was added about half an ounce of pork for dinner, which, though any moderate person would have considered only as a mouthful, was divided into three or four.

The morning of the 11th did not improve. 'At day-break I served to every person a teaspoonful of rum, our limbs being so much cramped that we could scarcely move them. Our situation was now extremely dangerous, the sea frequently running over our stern, which kept us baling with all our strength. At noon the sun appeared, which gave us as much pleasure as is felt when it shows itself on a winter's day in England.

'In the evening of the 12th it still rained hard, and we again experienced a dreadful night. At length the day came, and showed a miserable set of beings, full of wants, without any thing to relieve them. Some complained of great pain in their bowels, and every one of having almost lost the use of his limbs. The little sleep we got was in no way refreshing, as we were constantly covered with the sea and rain. The weather continuing, and no sun affording the least prospect of getting our clothes dried, I recommended to every one to strip and wring them through the sea-water, by which means they received a warmth that, while wet with rain-water, they could not have.' The shipping of seas and constant baling continued; and though the men were shivering with wet and cold, the commander was under the necessity of informing them, that he could no longer afford them the comfort they had derived from the teaspoonful of rum.

On the 13th and 14th the stormy weather and heavy sea continued unabated, and on these days they saw distant land, and passed several islands. The sight of these islands, it may well be supposed, served only to increase the misery of their situation. They were as men very little better than starving with plenty in their view; yet, to attempt procuring any relief was considered to be attended with so much danger, that the prolongation of life, even in the midst of misery, was thought preferable, while there remained hopes of being able to surmount their hardships.

The whole day and night of the 15th were still rainy; the latter was dark, not a star to be seen by which the steerage could be directed, and the sea was continually breaking over the boat. On the next day, the 16th, was issued for dinner an ounce of salt pork, in addition to their miserable allowance of one twenty-fifth part of a pound of bread. The night was again truly horrible, with storms of thunder, lightning, and rain; not a star visible, so that the steerage was quite uncertain.

On the morning of the 17th, at dawn of day, 'I found,' says the commander, 'every person complaining, and some of them solicited extra allowance, which I positively refused. Our situation was miserable; always wet, and suffering extreme cold in the night, without the least shelter from the weather. The little rum we had was of the greatest service: when our nights were particularly distressing, I generally served a teaspoonful or two to each person, and it was always joyful tidings when they heard of my intentions. The night was again a dark and dismal one, the sea constantly breaking over us, and nothing but the wind and waves to direct our steerage. It was my intention, if possible, to make the coast of New Holland to the southward of Endeavour Straits, being sensible that it was necessary to preserve such a situation as would make a southerly wind a fair one; that we might range along the reefs till an opening should be found into smooth water, and we the sooner be able to pick up some refreshments.'

On the 18th the rain abated, when, at their commander's recommendation, they all stripped and wrung their clothes through the sea-water, from which, as usual, they derived much warmth and refreshment; but every one complained of violent pains in their bones. At night the heavy rain recommenced, with severe lightning, which obliged them to keep baling without intermission. The same weather continued through the 19th and 20th; the rain constant--at times a deluge--the men always baling; the commander, too, found it necessary to issue for dinner only half an ounce of pork.

At dawn of day, Lieutenant Bligh states, that some of his people seemed half dead; that their appearances were horrible; 'and I could look,' says he, 'no way, but I caught the eye of some one in distress. Extreme hunger was now too evident, but no one suffered from thirst, nor had we much inclination to drink, that desire perhaps being satisfied through the skin. The little sleep we got was in the midst of water, and we constantly awoke with severe cramps and pains in our bones. At noon the sun broke out and revived every one.

'During the whole of the afternoon of the 21st we were so covered with rain and salt water, that we could scarcely see. We suffered extreme cold, and every one dreaded the approach of night. Sleep, though we longed for it, afforded no comfort; for my own part, I almost lived without it. On the 22nd, our situation was extremely calamitous. We were obliged to take the course of the sea, running right before it, and watching with the utmost care, as the least error in the helm would in a moment have been our destruction. It continued through the day to blow hard, and the foam of the sea kept running over our stern and quarters.

'The misery we suffered this night exceeded the preceding. The sea flew over us with great force, and kept us baling with horror and anxiety. At dawn of day I found every one in a most distressed condition, and I began to fear that another such night would put an end to the lives of several, who seemed no longer able to support their sufferings. I served an allowance of *two* teaspoonfuls of rum; after drinking which, and having wrung our clothes and taken our breakfast of bread and water, we became a little refreshed.

On the evening of the 24th, the wind moderated and the weather looked much better, which rejoiced all hands, so that they ate their scanty allowance with more satisfaction than for some time past. The night also was fair; but being always wet with the sea, we suffered much from the cold. I had the pleasure to see a fine morning produce some cheerful countenances; and for the first time, during the last fifteen days, we experienced comfort from the warmth of the sun. We stripped and hung up our clothes to dry, which were by this time become so thread-bare, that they could not keep out either wet or cold. In the afternoon we had many birds about us, which are never seen far from land, such as boobies and noddies.'

As the sea now began to run fair, and the boat shipped but little water, Lieutenant Bligh took the opportunity to examine into the state of their bread; and it was found that, according to the present mode of living, there was a sufficient quantity remaining for twenty-nine days' allowance, by which time there was every reason to expect they would be able to reach Timor. But as this was still uncertain, and it was possible that, after all, they might be obliged to go to Java, it was determined to proportion the allowance, so as to make the stock hold out six weeks. 'I was apprehensive,' he says, 'that this would be ill received, and that it would require my utmost resolution to enforce it; for, small as the quantity was which I intended to take away for our future good, yet it might appear to my people like robbing them of life; and some who were less patient than their companions, I expected would very ill brook it. However, on my representing the necessity of guarding against delays that might be occasioned by contrary winds, or other causes, and promising to enlarge upon the allowance as we got on, they cheerfully agreed to my proposal.' It was accordingly settled that every person should receive one twenty-fifth part of a pound of bread for breakfast, and the same quantity for dinner as usual, but that the proportion for supper should be discontinued; this arrangement left them forty-three days' consumption.

On the 25th about noon, some noddies came so near to the boat, that one of them was caught by hand. This bird was about the size of a small pigeon. 'I divided it,' says Bligh, 'with its entrails, into eighteen portions, and by a well-known method at sea, of " ***Who shall have this?***"[9] it was distributed, with the allowance of bread and water for dinner, and eaten up, bones and all, with salt water for sauce. In the evening, several boobies flying very near to us, we had the good fortune to catch one of them. This bird is as large as a duck. They are the most presumptive proof of being near land, of any sea-fowl we are acquainted with. I directed the bird to be killed for supper, and the blood to be given to three of the people who were the most distressed for want of food. The body, with the entrails, beak, and feet, I divided into eighteen shares, and with the allowance of bread, which I made a merit of granting, we made a good supper compared with our usual fare.

'On the next day, the 26th, we caught another booby, so that Providence appeared to be relieving our wants in an extraordinary manner. The people were overjoyed at this addition to their dinner, which was distributed in the same manner as on the preceding evening; giving the blood to those who were the most in want of food. To make the bread a little savoury, most of the men frequently dipped it in salt water, but I generally broke mine into small pieces, and ate it in my allowance of water, out of a cocoa-nut shell, with a spoon; economically avoiding to take too large a piece at a time, so that I was as long at dinner as if it had been a much more plentiful meal.'

The weather was now serene, which, nevertheless, was not without its inconveniences, for, it appears, they began to feel distress of a different kind from that which they had hitherto been accustomed to suffer. The heat of the sun was now so powerful, that several of the people were seized with a languor and faintness, which made life indifferent. But the little circumstance of catching two boobies in the evening, trifling as it may appear, had the effect of raising their spirits. The stomachs of these birds contained several flying-fish, and small cuttle-fish, all of which were carefully saved to be divided for dinner the next day; which were accordingly divided with their entrails, and the contents of their maws, into eighteen portions, and, as the prize was a very valuable one, it was distributed as before, by calling out, '***Who shall have this?***'--'so that to-day,' says the lieutenant, 'with the usual allowance of bread at breakfast and at dinner, I was happy to see that every person thought he had feasted.' From the appearance of the clouds in the evening, Mr. Bligh had no doubt they were then near the land, and the people amused themselves with conversing on the probability of what they would meet with on it.

Accordingly, at one in the morning of the 28th, the person at the helm heard the sound of breakers. It was the 'barrier reef' which runs along the eastern coast of New Holland, through which it now became the anxious object to discover a passage; Mr. Bligh says this was now become absolutely necessary, without a moment's loss of time. The idea of getting into smooth water and finding refreshments kept up the people's spirits. The sea broke furiously over the reef in every part; within, the water was so smooth and calm, that every man already anticipated the heartfelt satisfaction he was about to receive, as soon as he should have passed the barrier. At length a break in the reef was discovered, a quarter of a mile in width, and through this the boat rapidly passed with a strong stream running to the westward, and came immediately into smooth water, and all the past hardships seemed at once to be forgotten.

They now returned thanks to God for His generous protection, and with much content took their miserable allowance of the twenty-fifth part of a pound of bread, and a quarter of a pint of water, for dinner.

The coast now began to show itself very distinctly, and in the evening they landed on the sandy point of an island, when it was soon discovered there were oysters on the rocks, it being low water. The party sent out to reconnoitre returned highly rejoiced at having found plenty of oysters and fresh water. By help of a small magnifying--glass a fire was made, and among the things that had been thrown into the boat was a tinder-box and a piece of brimstone, so that in future they had the ready means of making a fire. One of the men too had been so provident as to bring away with him from the ship a copper pot; and thus with a mixture of oysters, bread, and pork, a stew was made, of which each person received a full pint. It is remarked that the oysters grew so fast to the rocks, that it was with great difficulty they could be broken off; but they at length discovered it to be the most expeditious way to open them where they were fixed.

The general complaints among the people were a dizziness in the head, great weakness in the joints, and violent tenesmus, but none of them are stated to have been alarming; and notwithstanding their sufferings from cold and hunger, all of them retained marks of strength. Mr. Bligh had cautioned them not to touch any kind of berry or fruit that they might find; yet it appears they were no sooner out of sight, than they began to make free with three different kinds that grew all over the island, eating without any reserve. The symptoms of having eaten too much began at last to frighten some of them; they fancied they were all poisoned, and regarded each other with the strongest marks of apprehension, uncertain what might be the issue of their imprudence: fortunately the fruit proved to be wholesome and good.

'This day (29th May) being,' says Lieutenant Bligh, 'the anniversary of the restoration of King Charles II, and the name not being inapplicable to our present situation (for we were ***restored*** to fresh life and strength), I named this "Restoration Island"; for I thought it probable that Captain Cook might not have taken notice of it.'

With oysters and palm-tops stewed together the people now made excellent meals, without consuming any of their bread. In the morning of the 30th, Mr. Bligh saw with great delight a visible alteration in the men for the better, and he sent them away to gather oysters, in order to carry a stock of them to sea, for he determined to put off again that evening. They also procured fresh water, and filled all their vessels to the amount of nearly sixty gallons. On examining the bread, it was found there still remained about thirty-eight days' allowance.

Being now ready for sea, every person was ordered to attend prayers; but just as they were embarking, about twenty naked savages made their appearance, running and hallooing, and beckoning the strangers to come to them; but, as each was armed with a spear or lance, it was thought prudent to hold no communication with them. They now proceeded to the northward, having the continent on their left, and several islands and reefs on their right.

On the 31st they landed on one of these islands, to which was given the name of 'Sunday.' 'I sent out two parties (says Bligh), one to the northward and the other to the southward, to seek for supplies, and others I ordered to stay by the boat. On this occasion, fatigue and weakness so far got the better of their sense of duty, that some of the people expressed their discontent at having worked harder than their companions, and declared that they would rather be without their dinner than go in search of it. One person, in particular, went so far as to tell me, with a mutinous look, that he was as good a man as myself. It was not possible for one to judge where this might have an end, if not stopped in time; to prevent therefore such disputes in future, I determined either to preserve my command or die in the attempt; and seizing a cutlass, I ordered him to lay hold of another and defend himself; on which he called out that I was going to kill him, and immediately made concessions. I did not allow this to interfere further with the harmony of the boat's crew, and every thing soon became quiet.'

On this island they obtained oysters, and clams, and dog-fish; also a small bean, which Nelson, the botanist, pronounced to be a species of dolichos. On the 1st of June, they stopped in the midst of some sandy islands, such as are known by the name of *keys*, where they procured a few clams and beams. Here Nelson was taken very ill with a violent heat in his bowels, a loss of sight, great thirst, and an inability to walk. A little wine, which had carefully been saved, with some pieces of bread soaked in it, was given to him in small quantities, and he soon began to recover. The boatswain and carpenter were also ill, and complained of headache and sickness of the stomach. Others became shockingly distressed with tenesmus; in fact, there were few without complaints.

A party was sent out by night to catch birds; they returned with only twelve noddies, but it is stated, that, had it not been for the folly and obstinacy of one of the party, who separated from the others and disturbed the birds, a great many more might have been taken. The offender was Robert Lamb, who acknowledged, when he got to Java, that he had that night eaten *nine* raw birds, after he separated from his two companions. The birds, with a few clams, were the whole of the supplies afforded at these small islands.

On the 3rd of June, after passing several keys and islands, and doubling Cape York, the north-easternmost point of New Holland, at eight in the evening the little boat and her brave crew once more launched into the open ocean. 'Miserable,' says Lieutenant Bligh, 'as our situation was in every respect, I was secretly surprised to see that it did not appear to affect any one so strongly as myself; on the contrary, it seemed as if they had embarked on a voyage to Timor in a vessel sufficiently calculated for safety and convenience. So much confidence gave me great pleasure, and I may venture to assert that to this cause our preservation is chiefly to be attributed. I encouraged every one with hopes that eight or ten days would bring us to a land of safety; and, after praying to God for a continuance of His most gracious protection, I served out an allowance of water for supper, and directed our course to the west south-west.

'We had been just six days on the coast of New Holland, in the course of which we found oysters, a few clams, some birds and water. But a benefit, probably not less than this, was that of being relieved from the fatigue of sitting constantly in the boat, and enjoying good rest at night. These advantages certainly preserved our lives; and small as the supply was, I am very sensible how much it alleviated our distresses. Before this time nature must have sunk under the extremes of hunger and fatigue. Even in our present situation, we were most deplorable objects, but the hopes of a speedy relief kept up our spirits. For my own part, incredible as it may appear, I felt neither extreme hunger nor thirst. My allowance contented me, knowing that I could have no more.' In his manuscript journal, he adds, 'This, perhaps, does not permit me to be a proper judge on a story of miserable people like us being at last driven to the necessity of destroying one another for food--but, if I may be allowed, I deny the fact in its greatest extent. I say, I do not believe that, among us, such a thing could happen, but death through famine would be received in the same way as any mortal disease.'[10]

On the 5th a booby was caught by the hand, the blood of which was divided among three of the men who were weakest, and the bird kept for next day's dinner; and on the evening of the 6th the allowance for supper was recommenced, according to a promise made when it had been discontinued. On the 7th, after a miserably wet and cold night, nothing more could be afforded than the usual allowance for breakfast; but at dinner each person had the luxury of an ounce of dried clams, which consumed all that remained. The sea was running high and breaking over the boat the whole of this day. Mr. Ledward, the surgeon, and Lawrence Lebogue, an old hardy seaman, appeared to be giving way very fast. No other assistance could be given to them than a teaspoonful or two of wine, that had been carefully saved for such a melancholy occasion, which was not at all unexpected.

On the 8th the weather was more moderate, and a small dolphin was caught, which gave about two ounces to each man: in the night it again blew strong, the boat shipped much water, and they all suffered greatly from wet and cold. The surgeon and Lebogue still continued very ill, and the only relief that could be afforded them was a small quantity of wine, and encouraging them with the hope that a very few days more, at the rate they were then sailing, would bring them to Timor.

'In the morning of the 10th, after a very comfortless night, there was a visible alteration for the worse,' says Mr. Bligh, 'in many of the people, which gave me great apprehensions. An extreme weakness, swelled legs, hollow and ghastly countenances, a more than common inclination to sleep, with an apparent debility of understanding, seemed to me the melancholy presages of an approaching dissolution. The surgeon and Lebogue, in particular, were most miserable objects. I occasionally gave them a few teaspoonfuls of wine, out of the little that remained, which greatly assisted them. The hope of being able to accomplish the voyage was our principal support. The boatswain very innocently told me that he really thought I looked worse than any in the boat. The simplicity with which he uttered such an opinion amused me, and I returned him a better compliment.'

On the 11th Lieutenant Bligh announced to his wretched companions that he had no doubt they had now passed the meridian of the eastern part of Timor, a piece of intelligence that diffused universal joy and satisfaction. Accordingly at three in the morning of the following day Timor was discovered at the distance only of two leagues from the shore.

'It is not possible for me,' says this experienced navigator, 'to describe the pleasure which the blessing of the sight of this land diffused among us. It appeared scarcely credible to ourselves that, in an open boat, and so poorly provided, we should have been able to reach the coast of Timor in forty-one days after leaving Tofoa, having in that time run, by our log, a distance of three thousand six hundred and eighteen nautical miles; and that, notwithstanding our extreme distress, no one should have perished in the voyage.'

On Sunday the 14th they came safely to anchor in Coupang Bay, where they were received with every mark of kindness, hospitality, and humanity. The houses of the principal people were thrown open for their reception. The poor sufferers when landed were scarcely able to walk; their condition is described as most deplorable. 'The abilities of a painter could rarely, perhaps, have been displayed to more advantage than in the delineation of the two groups of figures which at this time presented themselves to each other. An indifferent spectator (if such could be found) would have been at a loss which most to admire, the eyes of famine sparkling at immediate relief, or the horror of their preservers at the sight of so many spectres, whose ghastly countenances, if the cause had been unknown, would rather have excited terror than pity. Our bodies were nothing but skin and bones, our limbs were full of sores, and we were clothed in rags, in this condition, with the tears of joy and gratitude flowing down our cheeks, the people of Timor beheld us with a mixture of horror, surprise, and pity.

'When,' continues the commander, 'I reflect how providentially our lives were saved at Tofoa, by the Indians delaying their attack? and that, with scarcely anything to support life, we crossed a sea of more than twelve hundred leagues, without shelter from the inclemency of the weather; when I reflect that in an open boat, with so much stormy weather, we escaped foundering, that not any of us were taken off by disease, that we had the great good fortune to pass the unfriendly natives of other countries without accident, and at last to meet with the most friendly and best of people to relieve our distresses--I say, when I reflect on all these wonderful escapes, the remembrance of such great mercies enables me to bear with resignation and cheerfulness the failure of an expedition, the success of which I had so much at heart, and which was frustrated at a time when I was congratulating myself on the fairest prospect of being able to complete it in a manner that would fully have answered the intention of his Majesty, and the humane promoters of so benevolent a plan.'

Having recruited their strength by a residence of two months among the friendly inhabitants of Coupang, they proceeded to the westward on the 20th August in a small schooner, which was purchased and armed for the purpose, and arrived on the 1st October in Batavia Road, where Mr. Bligh embarked in a Dutch packet, and was landed on the Isle of Wight on the 14th March, 1790. The rest of the people had passages provided for them in ships of the Dutch East India Company, then about to sail for Europe. All of them, however, did not survive to reach England. Nelson, the botanist, died at Coupang; Mr. Elphinstone, master's-mate, Peter Linkletter and Thomas Hall, seamen, died at Batavia; Robert Lamb, seaman (the booby-eater), died on the passage; and Mr. Ledward, the surgeon, was left behind, and not afterwards heard of. These six, with John Norton, who was stoned to death, left twelve of the nineteen, forced by the mutineers into the launch, to survive the difficulties and dangers of this unparalleled voyage, and to revisit their native country. With great truth might Bligh exclaim with the poet,

> --'Tis mine to tell their tale of grief,
> Their constant peril and their scant relief;
> Their days of danger, and their nights of pain;
> Their manly courage, even when deem'd in vain;
> The sapping famine, rendering scarce a son
> Known to his mother in the skeleton;
> The ills that lessen'd still their little store,
> And starved even Hunger till he wrung no more;
> The varying frowns and favours of the deep,
> That now almost engulphs, then leaves to creep
> With crazy oar and shatter'd strength along
> The tide, that yields reluctant to the strong;
> Th' incessant fever of that arid thirst
> Which welcomes, as a well, the clouds that burst
> Above their naked bones, and feels delight
> In the cold drenching of the stormy night,
> And from the outspread canvas gladly wrings
> A drop to moisten Life's all-gasping springs;
> The savage foe escaped, to seek again
> More hospitable shelter from the main;
> The ghastly spectres which were doom'd at last
> To tell as true a tale of dangers past,
> As ever the dark annals of the deep
> Disclosed for man to dread or woman weep.

It is impossible not fully to accord with Bligh when he says, 'Thus happily ended, through the assistance of Divine Providence, without accident, a voyage of the most extraordinary nature that ever happened in the world,[11] let it be taken either in its extent, duration, or the want of every necessary of life.' We may go further and say, it is impossible to read this extraordinary and unparalleled voyage, without bestowing the meed of unqualified praise on the able and judicious conduct of its commander, who is in every respect, as far as this extraordinary enterprise is concerned, fully entitled to rank with Parry, Franklin, and Richardson. Few men, indeed, were ever placed for so long a period in a more trying, distressing, and perilous situation than he was; and it may safely be pronounced, that, to his discreet management of the men and their scanty resources, and to his ability as a thorough seaman, eighteen souls were saved from imminent and otherwise inevitable destruction, it was not alone the dangers of the sea, in an open boat, crowded with people, that he had to combat, though they required the most consummate nautical skill, to be enabled to contend successfully against them; but the unfortunate situation, to which the party were exposed, rendered him subject to the almost daily murmuring and caprice of people less conscious than himself of their real danger. From the experience they had acquired at Tofoa of the savage disposition of the people against the defenceless boat's crew, a lesson was learned how little was to be trusted, even to the mildest of uncivilized people, when a conscious superiority was in their hands. A striking proof of this was experienced in the unprovoked attack made by those amiable people, the Otaheitans, on Captain Wallis's ship, of whose power they had formed no just conception; but having once experienced the full force of it, on no future occasion was any attempt made to repeat the attack. Lieutenant Bligh, fully aware of his own weakness, deemed it expedient, therefore, to resist all desires and temptations to land at any of those islands, among which they passed in the course of the voyage, well knowing how little could be trusted to the forbearance of savages, unarmed and wholly defenceless as his party were.

But the circumstance of being tantalized with the appearance of land, clothed with perennial verdure, whose approach was forbidden to men chilled with wet and cold, and nearly perishing with hunger, was by no means the most difficult against which the commander had to struggle. 'It was not the least of my distresses,' he observes, 'to be constantly assailed with the melancholy demands of my people for an increase of allowance, which it grieved me to refuse.' He well knew that to reason with men reduced to the last stage of famine, yet denied the use of provisions within their reach, and with the power to seize upon them in their own hands, would be to no purpose. Something more must be done to ensure even the possibility of saving them from the effect of their own imprudence. The first thing he set about, therefore, was to ascertain the exact state of their provisions, which were found to amount to the ordinary consumption of five days, but which were to be spun out so as to last fifty days. This was at once distinctly stated to the men, and an agreement entered into, and a solemn promise made by all, that the settled allowance should never be deviated from, as they were made clearly to understand that on the strict observance of this agreement rested the only hope of their safety; and this was explained and made so evident to every man, at the time it was concluded, that they unanimously agreed to it; and by reminding them of this compact, whenever they became clamorous for more, and showing a firm determination not to swerve from it, Lieutenant Bligh succeeded in resisting all their solicitations.

This rigid adherence to the compact, in doling out their miserable pittance,--the constant exposure to wet,--the imminent peril of being swallowed up by the ocean,--their cramped and confined position,--and the unceasing reflection on their miserable and melancholy situation;--all these difficulties and sufferings made it not less than miraculous, that this voyage, itself a miracle, should have been completed, not only without the loss of a man from sickness, but with so little loss of health. 'With respect to the preservation of our health,' says the commander, 'during the course of sixteen days of heavy and almost continual rain, I would recommend to every one in a similar situation, the method we practised of dipping their clothes in salt-water, and to wring them out, as often as they become soaked with rain; it was the only resource we had, and I believe was of the greatest service to us, for it felt more like a change of dry clothes than could well be imagined. We had occasion to do this so often, that at length all our clothes were wrung to pieces.'

But the great art of all was to divert their attention from the almost hopeless situation in which they were placed, and to prevent despondency from taking possession of their minds; and in order to assist in effecting this, some employment was devised for them; among other things, a logline, an object of interest to all, was measured and marked; and the men were practised in counting seconds correctly, that the distance run on each day might be ascertained with a nearer approach to accuracy than by mere guessing. These little operations afforded them a temporary amusement; and the log being daily and hourly hove gave them also some employment, and diverted their thoughts for the moment from their melancholy situation. Then, every noon, when the sun was out, or at other times before and after noon, and also at night when the stars appeared, Lieutenant Bligh never neglected to take observations for the latitude, and to work the day's work for ascertaining the ship's place. The anxiety of the people to hear how they had proceeded, what progress had been made, and whereabouts they were on the wide ocean, also contributed for the time to drive away gloomy thoughts that but too frequently would intrude themselves. These observations were rigidly attended to, and sometimes made under the most difficult circumstances, the sea breaking over the observer, and the boat pitching and rolling so much, that he was obliged to be 'propped up,' while taking them. In this way, with now and then a little interrupted sleep, about a thousand long and anxious hours were consumed in pain and peril, and a space of sea passed over equal to four thousand five hundred miles, being at the rate of four and one-fifth miles an hour, or one hundred miles a day.

Lieutenant Bligh has expressed his conviction, that the six days spent among the coral islands, off the coast of New Holland, were the salvation of the whole party, by the refreshing sleep they here procured, by the exercise of walking about, and, above all, by the nutriment derived from the oysters and clams, the beans and berries, they procured while there; for that such, he says, was the exhausted condition of all on their arrival at the 'barrier reef,' that a few days more at sea must have terminated the existence of many of them. This stoppage, however, had likewise been nearly productive of fatal consequences to the whole party. In fact, another mutiny was within an ace of breaking out, which, if not checked at the moment, could only, in their desperate situation, have ended in irretrievable and total destruction. Bligh mentions, in his printed narrative, the mutinous conduct of a person to whom he gave a cutlass to defend himself. This affair, as stated in his original manuscript journal, wears a far more serious aspect.

'The carpenter (Purcell) began to be insolent to a high degree, and at last told me, with a mutinous aspect, he was as good a man as I was. I did not just now see where this was to end; I therefore determined to strike a final blow at it, and either to preserve my command or die in the attempt; and taking hold of a cutlass, I ordered the rascal to take hold of another and defend himself, when he called out that I was going to kill him, and began to make concessions. I was now only assisted by Mr. Nelson; and the master (Fryer) very deliberately called out to the boatswain, to put me under an arrest, and was stirring up a greater disturbance, when I declared, if he interfered, when I was in the execution of my duty to preserve order and regularity, and that in consequence any tumult arose, I would certainly put him to death the first person. This had a proper effect on this man, and he now assured me that, on the contrary, I might rely on him to support my orders and directions for the future. This is the outline of a tumult that lasted about a quarter of hour'; and he adds, 'I was told that the master and carpenter, at the last place, were endeavouring to produce altercations, and were the principal cause of their murmuring there.' This carpenter he brought to a court-martial on their arrival in England, on various charges, of which he was found guilty in part, and reprimanded. Purcell is said to be at this time in a mad-house.

On another occasion, when a stew of oysters was distributed among the people, Lieutenant Bligh observes (in the MS. Journal), 'In the distribution of it, the voraciousness of some and the moderation of others were very discernible. The ***master*** began to be dissatisfied the first, because it was not made into a larger quantity by the addition of water, and showed a turbulent disposition, until I laid my commands on him to be silent.' Again, on his refusing bread to the men, because they were collecting oysters, he says, 'this occasioned some murmuring with the master and carpenter, the former of whom endeavoured to prove the propriety of such an expenditure, and was troublesomely ignorant, tending to create disorder among those, if any were weak enough to listen to him.'

If what Bligh states with regard to the conduct of the master and the carpenter be true, it was such, on several occasions, as to provoke a man much less irritable than himself. He thus speaks of the latter, when in the ship and in the midst of the mutiny. 'The boatswain and carpenter were fully at liberty; the former was employed, on pain of death, to hoist the boats out, but the latter I saw acting the part of an idler, with an impudent and ill-looking countenance, which led me to believe he was one of the mutineers, until he was among the rest ordered to leave the ship, for it appeared to me to be a doubt with Christian, at first, whether he should keep the carpenter or his mate (Norman), but knowing the former to be a troublesome fellow, he determined on the latter.'

The following paragraph also appears in his original journal, on the day of the mutiny, but is not alluded to in his printed narrative. 'The master's cabin was opposite to mine; he saw them (the mutineers) in my cabin, for our eyes met each other through his door-window. He had a pair of ship's pistols loaded, and ammunition in his cabin--a firm resolution might have made a good use of them. After he had sent twice or thrice to Christian to be allowed to come on deck, he was at last permitted, and his question then was, "Will you let me remain in the ship?"--"No." "Have *you* any objection, Captain Bligh?" I whispered to him to knock him down--Martin is good (this is the man who gave the shaddock), for this was just before Martin was removed from me. Christian, however, pulled me back, and sent away the master, with orders to go again to his cabin, and I saw no more of him, until he was put into the boat. He afterwards told me that he could find nobody to act with him; that by staying in the ship he hoped to have retaken her, and that, as to the pistols, he was so flurried and surprised, that he did not recollect he had them.' This master tells a very different story respecting the pistols, in his evidence before the court-martial.

Whatever, therefore, on the whole, may have been the conduct of Bligh towards his officers, that of some of the latter appears to have been on several occasions provoking enough, and well calculated to stir up the irascible temper of a man, active and zealous in the extreme, as Bligh always was, in the execution of his duty. Some excuse may be found for hasty expressions uttered in a moment of irritation, when passion gets the better of reason; but no excuse can be found for one, who deeply and unfeelingly, without provocation, and in cold blood, inflicts a wound on the heart of a widowed mother, already torn with anguish and tortured with suspense for a beloved son, whose life was in imminent jeopardy: such a man was William Bligh. This charge is not loosely asserted; it is founded on documentary evidence under his own hand. Since the death of the late Captain Heywood, some papers have been brought to light, that throw a still more unfavourable stigma on the character of the two commanders, Bligh and Edwards, than any censure that has hitherto appeared in print, though the conduct of neither of them has been spared, whenever an occasion has presented itself for bringing their names before the public.

Bligh, it may be recollected, mentions young Heywood only as one of those left in the ship; he does not charge him with taking any active part in the mutiny; there is every reason, indeed, to believe that Bligh did not, and indeed could not, see him on the deck on that occasion: in point of fact, he never was within thirty feet of Captain Bligh, and the booms were between them. About the end of March, 1790, two months subsequent to the death of a most beloved and lamented husband, Mrs.

Heywood received the afflicting information, but by report only, of a mutiny having taken place on board the ***Bounty***. In that ship Mrs. Heywood's son had been serving as midshipman, who, when he left his home, in August, 1787, was under fifteen years of age, a boy deservedly admired and beloved by all who knew him, and, to his own family, almost an object of adoration, for his superior understanding and the amiable qualities of his disposition. In a state of mind little short of distraction, on hearing this fatal intelligence, which was at the same time aggravated by every circumstance of guilt that calumny or malice could invent with respect to this unfortunate youth, who was said to be one of the ringleaders, and to have gone armed into the captain's cabin, his mother addressed a letter to Captain Bligh, dictated by a mother's tenderness, and strongly expressive of the misery she must necessarily feel on such an occasion. The following is Bligh's reply:--

> '***London, April 2nd***, 1790.
>
> 'MADAM,--I received your letter this day, and feel for you very much, being perfectly sensible of the extreme distress you must suffer from the conduct of your son Peter. His baseness is beyond all description, but I hope you will endeavour to prevent the loss of him, heavy as the misfortune is, from afflicting you too severely. I imagine he is, with the rest of the mutineers, returned to Otaheite.--- I am, Madam,
>
> (Signed) 'WM. BLIGH.'

Colonel Holwell, the uncle of young Heywood, had previously addressed Bligh on the same melancholy subject, to whom he returned the following answer:--

> '***26th March***, 1790.
>
> 'SIR,--I have just this instant received your letter. With much concern I inform you that your nephew, Peter Hey wood, is

among the mutineers. His ingratitude to me is of the blackest dye, for I was a father to him in every respect, and he never once had an angry word from me through the whole course of the voyage, as his conduct always gave me much pleasure and satisfaction. I very much regret that so much baseness formed the character of a young man I had a real regard for, and it will give me much pleasure to hear that his friends can bear the loss of him without much concern.--I am, Sir, etc.

(Signed) 'WM. BLIGH.'

The only way of accounting for this ferocity of sentiment towards a youth, who had in point of fact no concern in the mutiny, is by a reference to certain points of evidence given by Hayward, Hallet, and Purcell on the court-martial, each point wholly unsupported. Those in the boat would no doubt, during their long passage, often discuss the conduct of their messmates left in the *Bounty*, and the unsupported evidence given by these three was well calculated to create in Bligh's mind a prejudice against young Heywood; yet, if so, it affords but a poor excuse for harrowing up the feelings of near and dear relatives.

As a contrast to these ungracious letters, it is a great relief to peruse the correspondence that took place, on this melancholy occasion, between this unfortunate young officer and his amiable but dreadfully afflicted family. The letters of his sister, Nessy Heywood (of which a few will be inserted in the course of this narrative), exhibit so lively and ardent an affection for her beloved brother, are couched in so high a tone of feeling for his honour, and confidence in his innocence, and are so nobly answered by the suffering youth, that no apology seems to be required for their introduction, more especially as their contents are strictly connected with the story of the ill-fated crew of the *Bounty*. After a state of long suspense, this amiable and accomplished young lady thus addresses her brother:--

'*Isle of Man, 2nd June*, 1792.

'In a situation of mind only rendered supportable by the long and painful state of misery and suspense we have suffered on his account, how shall I address my dear, my fondly beloved brother!--how describe the anguish we have felt at the idea of this long and painful separation, rendered still more distressing by the terrible circumstances attending it! Oh! my ever dearest boy, when I look back to that dreadful moment which brought us the fatal intelligence that you had remained in the ***Bounty*** after Mr. Bligh had quitted her, and were looked upon by him as a ***mutineer***!--when I contrast that day of horror with my present hopes of again beholding you, such as my most sanguine wishes could expect, I know not which is the most predominant sensation,--pity, compassion, and terror for your sufferings, or joy and satisfaction at the prospect of their being near a termination, and of once more embracing the dearest object of our affections.

'I will not ask you, my beloved brother, whether you are innocent of the dreadful crime of mutiny; if the transactions of that day were as Mr. Bligh has represented them, such is my conviction of your worth and honour, that I will, without hesitation, stake my life on your innocence. If, on the contrary, you were concerned in such a conspiracy against your commander, I shall be as firmly persuaded ***his*** conduct was the occasion of it; but, alas! could any occasion justify so atrocious an attempt to destroy a number of our fellow-creatures? No, my ever dearest brother, nothing but conviction from your own mouth can possibly persuade me, that you would commit an action in the smallest degree inconsistent with honour and duty; and the circumstance of your having swam off to the ***Pandora*** on her arrival at Otaheite (which filled us with joy to which no words can do justice), is sufficient to convince all who know you, that you certainly staid behind either by force or from views of preservation.

'How strange does it seem to me that I am now engaged in the delightful task of writing to you. Alas! my beloved brother, two years ago I never expected again to enjoy such a felicity, and even yet I am in the most painful uncertainty whether you are alive. Gracious God, grant that we may be at length blessed by your return I but, alas! the *Pandora's* people have been long expected, and are not even yet arrived. Should any accident have happened, after all the miseries you have already suffered, the poor gleam of hope with which we have been lately indulged, will render our situation ten thousand times more insupportable than if time had inured us to your loss. I send this to the care of Mr. Hayward, of Hackney, father to the young gentleman you so often mention in your letters while you were on board the *Bounty*, and who went out as third lieutenant of the *Pandora* -- a circumstance which gave us infinite satisfaction, as you would, on entering the *Pandora*, meet your old friend. On discovering old Mr. Hayward's residence, I wrote to him, as I hoped he could give me some information respecting the time of your arrival, and in return he sent me a most friendly letter, and has promised this shall be given to you when you reach England, as I well know how great must be your anxiety to hear of us, and how much satisfaction it will give you to have a letter immediately on your return. Let me conjure you, my dearest Peter, to write to us the very first moment--do not lose a post--'tis of no consequence how short your letter may be, if it only informs us you are well. I need not tell you that you are the first and dearest object of our affections. Think, then, my adored boy, of the anxiety we must feel on your account; for my own part, I can know no real joy or happiness independent of you, and if any misfortune should now deprive us of you, my hopes of felicity are fled for ever.

'We are at present making all possible interest with every friend and connexion we have, to ensure you a sufficient support and protection at your approaching trial; for a trial you must unavoidably undergo, in order to convince the world of that innocence, which those who know you will not for a moment doubt; but, alas! while circumstances are against you, the generality of mankind will judge severely. Bligh's representations to the Admiralty are, I am told, very unfavourable, and hitherto the tide of public opinion has been greatly in his favour. My mamma is at present well, considering the distress she has suffered since you left us; for, my dearest brother, we have experienced a complicated scene of misery from a variety of causes, which, however, when compared with the sorrow we felt on your account, was trifling and insignificant; *that* misfortune made all others light, and to see you once more returned, and safely restored to us, will be the summit of all earthly happiness.

'Farewell, my most beloved brother! God grant this may soon be put into your hands I Perhaps at this moment you are arrived in England, and I may soon have the dear delight of again beholding you. My mamma, brothers, and sisters, join with me in every sentiment of love and tenderness. Write to us immediately, my ever-loved Peter, and may the Almighty preserve you until you bless with your presence your fondly affectionate family, and particularly your unalterably faithful friend and sister,

(Signed) 'NESSY HEYWOOD.'[12]

The gleam of joy which this unhappy family derived from the circumstance, which had been related to them, of young Heywood's swimming off to the ***Pandora***, was dissipated by a letter from himself to his mother, soon after his arrival in England, in which he says:--'The question, my dear mother, in one of your letters, concerning my swimming off to the ***Pandora***, is one falsity among the too many, in which I have often thought of undeceiving you, and as frequently forgot. The story was this:--On the morning she arrived, accompanied by two of my friends (natives), I was going up the mountains, and having got about a hundred yards from my own house, another of my friends (for I was an universal favourite among those Indians, and perfectly conversant in their language) came running after me, and informed me there was a ship coming. I immediately ascended a rising ground, and saw, with indescribable joy, a ship laying-to off Hapiano; it was just after daylight, and thinking Coleman might not be awake, and therefore ignorant of this pleasing news, I sent one of my servants to inform him of it, upon which he immediately went off in a single canoe. There was a fresh breeze, and the ship working into the bay; he no sooner got alongside than the rippling capsized the canoe, and he being obliged to let go the tow-rope to get her righted, went astern, and was picked up the next tack and taken on board the ***Pandora***, he being the first person. I, along with my messmate Stewart, was then standing upon the beach with a double canoe, manned with twelve paddles ready for launching; and just as she made her last tack into her berth (for we did not think it requisite to go off sooner), we put off and got alongside just as they streamed the buoy; and being dressed in the country manner, tanned as brown as themselves, and I ***tattooed*** like them in the most curious manner, I do not in the least wonder at their taking us for natives. I was tattooed, not to gratify my own desire, but theirs; for it was my constant endeavour to acquiesce in any little custom which I thought would be agreeable to them, though painful in the process, provided I gained by it their friendship and esteem, which you may suppose is no inconsiderable object in an island where the natives are so numerous. The more a man or woman there is tattooed, the more they are respected; and a person having none of these marks is looked upon as bearing an unworthy badge of disgrace, and considered as a mere outcast of society.'

Among the many anxious friends and family connexions of the Heywoods, was Commodore Pasley, to whom this affectionate young lady addressed herself on the melancholy occasion; and the following is the reply she received from this officer.

'*Sheerness, June 8th*, 1792.

'Would to God, my dearest Nessy, that I could rejoice with you on the early prospect of your brother's arrival in England. One division of the ***Pandora's*** people has arrived, and now on board the ***Vengeance*** (my ship). Captain Edwards with the remainder, and all the prisoners late of the ***Bounty***, in number ten (four having been drowned on the loss of that ship), are daily expected. They have been most rigorously and closely confined since taken, and will continue so, no doubt, till Bligh's arrival. You have no chance of seeing him, for no bail can be offered. Your intelligence of his swimming off on the ***Pandoras*** arrival is not founded; a man of the name of Coleman swam off ere she anchored--your brother and Mr. Stewart the next day; this last youth, when the ***Pandora*** was lost, refused to allow his irons to be taken off to save his life.

'I cannot conceal it from you, my dearest Nessy, neither is it proper I should--your brother appears, by all accounts, to be the greatest culprit of all, Christian alone excepted. Every exertion, you may rest assured, I shall use to save his life, but on trial I have no hope of his not being condemned. Three of the ten who are expected are mentioned, in Bligh's narrative, as men detained against their inclination. Would to God your brother had been one of that number! I will not distress you more by enlarging on this subject; as intelligence arises on their arrival, you shall be made acquainted. Adieu! my dearest Nessy--present my affectionate remembrances to your mother and sisters, and believe me always, with the warmest affection,--Your uncle,
    THOS. PASLEY.'

How unlike is this from the letter of Bligh! while it frankly apprises this amiable lady of the real truth of the case, without disguise, as it was then understood to be from Mr. Bligh's representations, it assures her of his best exertions to save her brother's life. Every reader of sensibility will sympathise in the feeling displayed in her reply.

'*Isle of Man, 22nd June*, 1792.

'Harassed by the most torturing suspense, and miserably wretched as I have been, my dearest uncle, since the receipt of your last, conceive, if it is possible, the heartfelt joy and satisfaction we experienced yesterday morning, when, on the arrival of the packet, the dear delightful letter from our beloved Peter (a copy of which I send you enclosed) was brought to us. Surely, my excellent friend, you will agree with me in thinking there could not be a stronger proof of his innocence and worth, and that it must prejudice every person who reads it most powerfully in his favour. Such a letter in less distressful circumstances than those in which he writes, would, I am persuaded, reflect honour on the pen of a person much older than my poor brother. But when we consider his extreme youth (only sixteen at the time of the mutiny, and now but nineteen), his fortitude, patience, and manly resignation under the pressure of sufferings and misfortunes almost unheard of, and scarcely to be supported at any age, without the assistance of that which seems to be my dear brother's greatest comfort--- a quiet conscience, and a thorough conviction of his own innocence--when I add, at the same time, with real pleasure and satisfaction, that his relation corresponds in many particulars with the accounts we have hitherto heard of the fatal mutiny, and when I also add, with inconceivable pride and delight, that my beloved Peter never was known to breathe a syllable inconsistent with truth and honour;--when these circumstances, my dear uncle, are all united, what man on earth can doubt of the innocence which could dictate such a letter? In short, let it speak for him: the perusal of his artless and pathetic story will, I am persuaded, be a stronger recommendation in his favour than any thing I can urge.[13]

'I need not tire your patience, my ever loved uncle, by dwelling longer on this subject (the dearest and most interesting on earth to my heart); let me conjure you only, my kind friend, to read it, and consider the innocence and defenceless situation of its unfortunate author, which calls for, and I am sure deserves, all the pity and assistance his friends can afford him, and which, I am sure also, the goodness and benevolence of your heart will prompt you to exert in his behalf. It is perfectly unnecessary for me to add, after the anxiety I feel, and cannot but express, that no benefit conferred upon myself will be acknowledged with half the gratitude I must ever feel for the smallest instance of kindness shown to my beloved Peter. Farewell, my dearest uncle. With the firmest reliance on your kind and generous promises, I am, ever with the truest gratitude and sincerity,--Your most affectionate niece,

NESSY HEYWOOD.'

CHAPTER V
THE 'PANDORA'

>   --O! I have suffer'd
> With those that I saw suffer! a brave vessel,
> Who had, no doubt, some noble creatures in her,
> Dash'd all to pieces. O, the cry did knock
> Against my very heart! Poor souls! they perish'd
> Had I been any god of power, I would
> Have sunk the sea within the earth, or e'er
> It should the good ship so have swallow'd, and
> The freighting souls within her.

The tide of public applause set as strongly in favour of Bligh, on account of his sufferings and the successful issue of his daring enterprise, as its indignation was launched against Christian and his associates, for the audacious and criminal deed they had committed. Bligh was promoted by the Admiralty to the rank of Commander, and speedily sent out a second time to transport the bread-fruit to the West Indies, which he without the least obstruction successfully accomplished; and his Majesty's government were no sooner made acquainted with the atrocious act of piracy and mutiny, than it determined to adopt every possible means to apprehend and bring to condign punishment the perpetrators of so foul a deed. For this purpose, the ***Pandora*** frigate, of twenty-four guns and one hundred and sixty men, was despatched under the command of Captain Edward Edwards, with orders to proceed, in the first instance, to Otaheite, and not finding the mutineers there, to visit the different groups of the Society and Friendly Islands, and others in the neighbouring parts of the Pacific, using his best endeavours to seize and bring home in confinement the whole or such part of the delinquents as he might be able to discover.

This voyage was in the sequel almost as disastrous as that of the *Bounty*, but from a different cause. The waste of human life was much greater, occasioned by the wreck of the ship, and the distress experienced by the crew not much less, owing to the famine and thirst they had to suffer in a navigation of eleven hundred miles in open boats; but the Captain succeeded in fulfilling a part of his instructions, by taking fourteen of the mutineers, of whom ten were brought safe to England, the other four being drowned when the ship was wrecked.

The only published account of this voyage is contained in a small volume by Mr. George Hamilton, the surgeon, who appears to have been a coarse, vulgar, and illiterate man, more disposed to relate licentious scenes and adventures, in which he and his companions were engaged, than to give any information of proceedings and occurrences connected with the main object of the voyage. From this book, therefore, much information is not to be looked for. In a more modern publication, many abusive epithets have been bestowed on Captain Edwards, and observations made on the conduct of this officer highly injurious to his reputation, in regard to his inhuman treatment of, and disgraceful acts of cruelty towards, his prisoners, which it is to be feared have but too much foundation in fact.

The account of his proceedings, rendered by himself to the Admiralty, is vague and unsatisfactory; and had it not been for the journal of Morrison, and a circumstantial letter of young Heywood to his mother, no record would have remained of the unfeeling conduct of this officer towards his unfortunate prisoners, who were treated with a rigour which could not be justified on any ground of necessity or prudence.

The *Pandora* anchored in Matavai Bay on the 23rd March 1791. Captain Edwards, in his narrative, states that Joseph Coleman, the armourer of the *Bounty*, attempted to come on board before the *Pandora* had anchored; that on reaching the ship, he began to make inquiries of him after the *Bounty* and her people, and that he seemed to be ready to give him any information that was required; that the next who came on board, just after the ship had anchored, were Mr. Peter Heywood and Mr. Stewart, before any boat had been sent on shore; that they were brought down to his cabin, when, after some conversation, Heywood asked if Mr. Hayward (midshipman of the *Bounty*, but now lieutenant of the *Pandora*) was on board, as he had heard that he was; that Lieutenant Hayward, whom he sent for, treated Heywood. with a sort of contemptuous look, and began to enter into conversation with him respecting the *Bounty*; but Edwards ordered him to desist, and called in the sentinel to take the prisoners into safe custody, and to put them in irons; that four other mutineers soon made their appearance; and that, from them and some of the natives, he learned that the rest of the *Bounty's* people had built a schooner, with which they had sailed the day before from Matavai Bay to the north-west part of the island.

He goes on to say that, on this intelligence, he despatched the two lieutenants, Corner and Hayward, with the pinnace and launch, to endeavour to intercept her. They soon got sight of her and chased her out to sea, but the schooner gained so much upon them, and night coming on, they were compelled to give up the pursuit and return to the ship. It was soon made known, however, that she had returned to Paparre, on which they were again despatched in search of her. Lieutenant Corner had taken three of the mutineers, and Hayward, on arriving at Paparre, found the schooner there, but the mutineers had abandoned her and fled to the mountains. He carried off the schooner, and returned next day, when he learned they were not far off; and the following morning, on hearing they were coming down, he drew up his party in order to receive them, and when within hearing, called to them to lay down their arms and to go on one side, which they did, when they were confined and brought as prisoners to the ship.

The following were the persons received on Board the *Pandora*:

PETER HEYWOOD	Midshipman.
GEORGE STEWART	Ditto.
JAMES MORRISON	Boatswain's mate.
CHARLES NORMAN	Carpenter's mate.
THOMAS M'INTOSH	Carpenter's crew.
JOSEPH COLEMAN	Armourer.
RICHARD SKINNER }	
THOMAS ELLISON }	
HENRY HILLBRANT }	

THOMAS BURKITT }	Seamen.
JOHN MILLWARD }	
JOHN SUMNER }	
WILLIAM MUSPRATT }	
MICHAEL BYRNE }	

In all fourteen. The other two, which made up the sixteen that had been left on the island, were murdered, as will appear presently.

Captain Edwards will himself explain how he disposed of his prisoners. 'I put the pirates,' he says, 'into a round-house which I built on the after part of the quarter-deck, for their more effectual security in this airy and healthy situation, and to separate them from, and to prevent their having communication with, or to crowd and incommode, the ship's company.' Dr. Hamilton calls it the most desirable place in the ship, and adds, that 'orders were given that the prisoners should be victualled, in every respect, the same as the ship's company, both in meat, liquor, and all the extra indulgences with which they were so liberally supplied, notwithstanding the established laws of the service, which restrict prisoners to two-thirds allowance; but Captain Edwards very humanely commiserated their unhappy and inevitable length of confinement.' Mr. Morrison, one of the prisoners, gives a very different account of their treatment from that of Edwards or Hamilton. He says that Captain Edwards put both legs of the two midshipmen in irons, and that he branded them with the opprobrious epithet of 'piratical villains': that they, with the rest, being strongly handcuffed, were put into a kind of round-house only eleven feet long, built as a prison, and aptly named '*Pandora's* Box,' which was entered by a scuttle in the roof, about eighteen inches square. This was done in order that they might be kept separate from the crew, and also the more effectually to prevent them from having any communication with the natives; that such of those friendly creatures as ventured to look pitifully towards them were instantly turned out of the ship, and never again allowed to come on board. But two sentinels were kept constantly upon the roof of the prison, with orders to shoot the first of its inmates who should attempt to address another in the Otaheitan dialect.

That Captain Edwards took every precaution to keep his prisoners in safe custody, and place them in confinement, as by his instructions he was directed to do, may be well imagined,[14] but Mr. Morrison will probably be thought to go somewhat beyond credibility in stating that orders were given 'to **shoot** any of the prisoners,' when confined in irons. Captain Edwards must have known that such an act would have cost him his commission or something more. The fact is, that information was given to Edwards, at least he so asserts, by the brother of the King of Otaheite, an intelligent chief, that a conspiracy was formed among the natives to cut the ship's cables the first strong wind that should blow on the shore, which was considered to be the more probable, as many of the prisoners were said to be married to the most respectable chiefs' daughters in the district opposite to the anchorage; that the midshipman Stewart, in particular, had married the daughter of a man of great landed property near Matavai Bay. This intelligence, no doubt, weighed with the Captain in giving his orders for the close confinement of the prisoners; and particularly in restricting the visits of the natives; but so far is it from being true that all communication between the mutineers and the natives was cut off, that we are distinctly told by Mr. Hamilton, that 'the prisoners' wives visited the ship daily, and brought their children, who were permitted to be carried to their unhappy fathers. To see the poor captives in irons,' he says, 'weeping over their tender offspring, was too moving a scene for any feeling heart, Their wives brought them ample supplies of every delicacy that the country afforded, while we lay there, and behaved with the greatest fidelity and affection to them.'[15]

Of the fidelity and attachment of these simple-minded creatures an instance is afforded in the affecting story which is told, in the first **Missionary Voyage of the Duff**, of the unfortunate wife of the reputed mutineer Mr. Stewart. It would seem also to exonerate Edwards from some part of the charges which have been brought against him.

'The history of Peggy Stewart marks a tenderness of heart that never will be heard without emotion: she was the daughter of a chief, and taken for his wife by Mr. Stewart, one of the unhappy mutineers. They had lived with the old chief in the most tender state of endearment; a beautiful little girl had been the fruit of their union, and was at the breast when the **Pandora** arrived, seized the criminals, and secured them in irons on board the ship. Frantic with grief, the unhappy Peggy (for so he had named her) flew with her infant in a canoe to the arms of her husband. The interview was so affecting and afflicting, that the officers on board were overwhelmed with anguish, and Stewart himself, unable to bear the heartrending scene, begged she might not be admitted again on board. She was separated from him by violence, and conveyed on shore in a state of despair and grief too big for utterance. Withheld from him, and forbidden to come any more on board, she sunk into the deepest dejection; it preyed on her vitals; she lost all relish for food and life, rejoiced no more, pined under a rapid decay of two months, and fell a victim to her feelings, dying literally of a broken heart. Her child is yet alive, and the tender object of our care, having been brought up by a sister, who nursed it as her own, and has discharged all the duties of an affectionate mother to the orphan infant.'[16]

It does not appear that young Heywood formed any matrimonial engagement during his abode in Otaheite. He was not, however, insensible to the amiable and good qualities of these people. In some laudatory verses which he wrote while on the island, their numerous good qualities are spoken of in terms of the highest commendation.

All the mutineers that were left on the island being received on board the ***Pandora***, that ship proceeded in search of those who had gone away in the ***Bounty***. It may be mentioned, however, that two of the most active in the mutiny, Churchill and Thompson, had perished on the island before her arrival, by violent deaths. These two men had accompanied a chief, who was the ***tayo***, or sworn friend, of Churchill, and having died without children, this mutineer succeeded to his property and dignity, according to the custom of the country. Thompson, for some real or fancied insult, took an opportunity of shooting his companion. The natives assembled, and came to a resolution to avenge the murder, and literally stoned Thompson to death, and his skull was brought on board the ***Pandora***. This horrible wretch had some time before slain a man and a child through mere wantonness, but escaped punishment by a mistake that had nearly proved fatal to young Heywood. It seems that the description of a person in Otaheite is usually given by some distinguishing figure of the ***tattoo***, and Heywood, having the same marks as Thompson, was taken for him; and just as the club was raised to dash out his brains, the interposition of an old chief, with whom he was travelling round the island, was just in time to avert the blow.

Captain Edwards had no clue to guide him as to the route taken by the ***Bounty***, but he learnt from different people and from journals kept on board that ship, which were found in the chests of the mutineers at Otaheite, the proceedings of Christian and his associates after Lieutenant Bligh and his companions had been turned adrift in the launch. From these it appears that the pirates proceeded in the first instance to the island of Toobouai, in lat. 20 deg. 13' S., long. 149 deg. 35' W., where they anchored on the 25th May, 1789. They had thrown overboard the greater part of the bread-fruit plants, and divided among themselves the property of the officers and men who had been so inhumanly turned adrift. At this island they intended to form a settlement, but the opposition of the natives, the want of many necessary materials, and quarrels among themselves, determined them to go to Otaheite to procure what might be required to effect their purpose, provided they should agree to prosecute their original intention. They accordingly sailed from Toobouai about the latter end of the month, and arrived at Otaheite on the 6th June. The Otoo, or reigning sovereign, and other principal natives, were very inquisitive and anxious to know what had become of Lieutenant Bligh and the rest of the crew, and also what had been done with the bread-fruit plants? They were told they had most unexpectedly fallen in with Captain Cook at an island he had just discovered, called Whytootakee, where he intended to form a settlement, and where the plants had been landed; and that Lieutenant Bligh and the others were stopping there to assist Captain Cook in the business he had in hand, and that he had appointed Mr. Christian commander of the ***Bounty***; and that he was now come by his orders for an additional supply of hogs, goats, fowls, bread-fruit, and various other articles which Otaheite could supply.

This artful story was quite sufficient to impose on the credulity of these humane and simple-minded islanders; and so overcome with joy were they to hear that their old friend Captain Cook was alive, and about to settle so near them, that every possible means were forthwith made use of to procure the things that were wanted; so that in the course of a very few days the ***Bounty*** received on board three hundred and twelve hogs, thirty-eight goats, eight dozen of fowls, a bull and a cow, and a large quantity of bread-fruit, plantains, bananas, and other fruits. They also took with them eight men, nine women, and seven boys. With these supplies they left Otaheite on the 19th June, and arrived a second time at Toobouai on the 26th. They warped the ship up the harbour, landed the live stock, and set about building a fort of fifty yards square.

While this work was carrying on, quarrels and disagreements were daily happening among them, and continual disputes and skirmishes were taking place with the natives, generally brought on by the violent conduct of the invaders, and by depredations committed on their property. Retaliations were attempted by the natives without success, numbers of whom being pursued with fire-arms were put to death. Still the situation of the mutineers became so disagreeable and unsafe, the work went on so slowly and reluctantly, that the building of the fort was agreed to be discontinued. Christian, in fact, had very soon perceived that his authority was on the wane, and that no peaceful establishment was likely to be accomplished at Toobouai; he therefore held a consultation as to what would be the most advisable step to take. After much angry discussion, it was at length determined that Toobouai should be abandoned; that the ship should once more be taken to Otaheite; and that those who might choose to go on shore there might do so, and those who preferred to remain in the ship might proceed in her to whatever place they should agree upon among themselves.

In consequence of this determination they sailed from Toobouai on the 15th, and arrived at Matavai Bay on the 20th September, 1789. Here sixteen of the mutineers were put on shore, at their own request, fourteen of whom were received on board the ***Pandora***, and two of them, as before mentioned, were murdered on the island. The remaining nine agreed to continue in the ***Bounty***. The small arms, powder, canvas, and the small stores belonging to the ship, were equally divided among the whole crew. The ***Bounty*** sailed finally from Otaheite on the night of the 21st September, and was last seen the following morning to the north-west of Point Venus. They took with them seven Otaheitan men and twelve women. It was not even conjectured whither they meant to go; but Christian had frequently been heard to say, that his object was to discover some unknown or uninhabited island, in which there was no harbour for shipping; that he would run the ***Bounty*** on shore, and make use of her materials to form a settlement; but this was the only account, vague as it was, that could be procured to direct Captain Edwards in his intended search.

It appears that when the schooner, of which we have spoken, had been finished, six of the fourteen mutineers that were left on Otaheite embarked in her, with the intention of proceeding to the East Indies, and actually put to sea; but meeting with bad weather, and suspecting the nautical abilities of Morrison, whom they had elected as commanding officer, to conduct her in safety, they resolved on returning to Otaheite. Morrison, it seems, first undertook the construction of this schooner, being himself a tolerable mechanic, in which he was assisted by the two carpenters, the cooper, and some others. To this little band of architects, we are told, Morrison acted both as director and chaplain, distinguishing the Sabbath day by reading to them the Church Liturgy, and hoisting the British colours on a flagstaff erected near the scene of their operations. Conscious of his innocence, his object is stated to have been that of reaching Batavia in time to secure a passage home in the next fleet bound to Holland; but that their return was occasioned, not by any distrust of Morrison's talents, but by a refusal, on the part of the natives, to give them a sufficient quantity of matting and other necessaries for so long a voyage, being, in fact, desirous of retaining them on the island. Stewart and young Heywood took no part in this transaction, having made up their minds to remain at Otaheite, and there to await the arrival of a king's ship, it being morally certain that ere long one would be sent out thither to search for them, whatever might have been the fate of Bligh and his companions; and that this was really their intention is evident by the alacrity they displayed in getting on board the ***Pandora***, the moment of her arrival.

On the 8th of May, this frigate left Otaheite, accompanied by the little schooner which the mutineers had built, and the history of which is somewhat remarkable. In point of size she was not a great deal larger than Lieutenant Bligh's launch, her dimensions being thirty feet length of keel; thirty-five feet length on deck; nine feet and a half extreme breadth; five feet depth of the hold. She parted from the ***Pandora*** near the Palmerston Islands, when searching for the ***Bounty***, and was not heard of till the arrival of the ***Pandora's*** crew at Samarang, in Java, where they found her lying at anchor, the crew having suffered so dreadfully from famine and the want of water, that one of the young gentlemen belonging to her became delirious. She was a remarkably swift sailer, and, being afterwards employed in the sea-otter trade, is stated to have made one of the quickest passages ever known from China to the Sandwich Islands. This memorable little vessel was purchased at Canton by the late Captain Broughton, to assist him in surveying the coast of Tartary, and became the means of preserving the crew of his Majesty's ship ***Providence***, amounting to one hundred and twelve men, when wrecked to the eastward of Formosa, in the year 1797.

The ***Pandora*** called at numerous islands without success, but on Lieutenant Corner having landed on one of the Palmerston's group, he found a yard and some spars with the broad arrow upon them, and marked ***Bounty***. This induced the captain to cause a very minute search to be made in all these islands, in the course of which the ***Pandora***, being driven out to sea by blowing weather, and very thick and hazy, lost sight of the little tender and a jolly boat, the latter of which was never more heard of. This gives occasion to a little splenetic effusion from a writer in a periodical journal,[17] which was hardly called for, 'When this boat,' says the writer, 'with a midshipman and several men (four), had been inhumanly ordered from alongside, it was known that there was nothing in her but one piece of salt-beef, compassionately thrown in by a seaman; and horrid as must have been their fate, the flippant surgeon, after detailing the disgraceful fact, adds--"that this is the way the world was peopled"--or words to that effect, for we quote only from memory.' The following is quoted from the book:--

'It may be difficult to surmise,' says the surgeon, 'what has been the fate of those unfortunate men. They had a piece of salt-beef thrown into the boat to them on leaving the ship; and it rained a good deal that night and the following day, which might satiate their thirst. It is by these accidents the Divine Ruler of the universe has peopled the southern hemisphere.' This is no more than asserting an acknowledged fact that can hardly admit of a dispute, and there appears nothing in the paragraph which at all affects the character of Captain Edwards, against whom it is levelled.

After a fruitless search of three months, the ***Pandora*** arrived, on the 29th August, on the coast of New Holland, and close to that extraordinary reef of coral rocks called the 'Barrier Reef,' which runs along the greater part of the eastern coast, but at a considerable distance from it. The boat had been sent out to look for an opening, which was soon discovered, but in the course of the night the ship had drifted past it. 'On getting soundings,' says Captain Edwards, in his narrative laid before the court-martial, 'the topsails were filled; but before the tacks were hauled on board and other sail made and trimmed, the ship struck upon a reef; we had a quarter less two fathoms on the larboard side, and three fathoms on the starboard side; the sails were braced about different ways to endeavour to get her off, but to no purpose; they were then clewed up and afterwards furled, the top-gallant yards got down and the top-gallant masts struck. Boats were hoisted out with a view to carry out an anchor, but before that could be effected the ship struck so violently on the reef, that the carpenter reported she made eighteen inches of water in five minutes; and in five minutes after this, that there were four feet of water in the hold. Finding the leak increasing so fast, it was thought necessary to turn the hands to the pumps, and to bail at the different hatchways; but she still continued to gain upon us so fast, that in little more than an hour and a half after she struck, there were eight feet and a half of water in the hold. About ten we perceived that the ship had beaten over the reef, and was in ten fathoms water; we therefore let go the small bower anchor, cleared away a cable, and let go the best bower anchor in fifteen and a half fathoms water under foot, to steady the ship. Some of her guns were thrown overboard, and the water gained upon us only in a small degree, and we flattered ourselves that by the assistance of a thrummed topsail, which we were preparing to haul under the ship's bottom, we might be able to lessen the leak, and to free her of water: but these flattering hopes did not continue long; for, as she settled in the water, the leak increased again, and in so great a degree, that there was reason to apprehend she would sink before daylight. During the night two of the pumps were unfortunately for some time rendered useless; one of them, however, was repaired, and we continued baling and pumping the remainder of the night; and every effort that was thought of was made to keep afloat and preserve the ship. Daylight fortunately appeared, and gave us the opportunity of seeing our situation and the surrounding danger, and it was evident the ship had been carried to the northward by a tide or current.

'The officers, whom I had consulted on the subject of our situation, gave it as their opinion that nothing more could be done for the preservation of the ship; it then became necessary to endeavour to provide and to find means for the preservation of the people. Our four boats, which consisted of one launch, one eight-oared pinnace, and two six-oared yawls, with careful hands in them, were kept astern of the ship; a small quantity of bread, water, and other necessary articles, were put into them; two canoes, which we had on board, were lashed together and put into the water; rafts were made, and all floating things upon deck were unlashed.

'About half-past six in the morning of the 29th the hold was full, and the water was between decks, and it also washed in at the upper deck ports, and there were strong indications that the ship was on the very point of sinking, and we began to leap overboard and take to the boats, and before everybody could get out of her she actually sunk. The boats continued astern of the ship in the direction of the drift of the tide from her, and took up the people that had hold of rafts and other floating things that had been cast loose, for the purpose of supporting them on the water. The double canoe, that was able to support a considerable number of men, broke adrift with only one man, and was bulged upon a reef, and afforded us no assistance when she was so much wanted on this trying and melancholy occasion. Two of the boats were laden with men and sent to a small sandy island (or key) about four miles from the wreck; and I remained near the ship for some time with the other two boats, and picked up all the people that could be seen, and then followed the two first boats to the key; and having landed the men and cleared the boats, they were immediately despatched again to look about the wreck and the adjoining reef for any that might be missing, but they returned without having found a single person. On mustering the people that were saved, it appeared that eighty-nine of the ship's company, and ten of the mutineers that had been prisoners on board, answered to their names; but thirty-one of the ship's company, and four mutineers, were lost with the ship.'

It is remarkable enough that so little notice is taken of the mutineers in this narrative of the captain; and as the following statement is supposed to come from the late Lieutenant Corner, who was second lieutenant of the *Pandora*, it is entitled to be considered as authentic, and if so, Captain Edwards must have deserved the character, ascribed to him, of being altogether destitute of the common feelings of humanity.

'Three of the *Bounty's* people, Coleman, Norman, and M'Intosh, were now let out of irons, and sent to work at the pumps. The others offered their assistance, and begged to be allowed a chance of saving their lives; instead of which, two additional sentinels were placed over them, with orders to shoot any who should attempt to get rid of their fetters. Seeing no prospect of escape, they betook themselves to prayer, and prepared to meet their fate, every one expecting that the ship would soon go to pieces, her rudder and part of the stern-post being already beat away.'

When the ship was actually sinking, and every effort making for the preservation of the crew, it is asserted that 'no notice was taken of the prisoners, as is falsely stated by the author of the ***Pandora's Voyage***, although Captain Edwards was entreated by Mr. Heywood to have mercy upon them, when he passed over their prison, to make his own escape, the ship then lying on her broadside, with the larboard bow completely under water. Fortunately the master-at-arms, either by accident or design, when slipping from the roof of "***Pandora's*** Box" into the sea, let the keys of the irons fall through the scuttle or entrance, which he had just before opened, and thus enabled them to commence their own liberation, in which they were generously assisted, at the imminent risk of his own life, by William Moulter, a boatswain's mate, who clung to the coamings, and pulled the long bars through the shackles, saying he would set them free, or go to the bottom with them.

'Scarcely was this effected when the ship went down, leaving nothing visible but the top-mast cross-trees. The master-at-arms and all the sentinels sunk to rise no more. The cries of them and the other drowning men were awful in the extreme; and more than half an hour had elapsed before the survivors could be taken up by the boats. Among the former were Mr. Stewart, John Sumner, Richard Skinner, and Henry Hillbrant, the whole of whom perished with their hands still in manacles.

'On this melancholy occasion Mr. Heywood was the last person but three who escaped from the prison, into which the water had already found its way through the bulk-head scuttles. Jumping overboard, he seized a plank, and was swimming towards a small sandy quay (key) about three miles distant, when a boat picked him up, and conveyed him thither in a state of nudity. It is worthy of remark, that James Morrison endeavoured to follow his young companion's example, and, although handcuffed, managed to keep afloat until a boat came to his assistance.'

This account would appear almost incredible. It is true men are sometimes found to act the part of inhuman monsters, but then they are generally actuated by some motive or extraordinary excitement; here, however, there was neither; but on the contrary, the condition of the poor prisoners appealed most forcibly to the mercy and humanity of their jailor. The surgeon of the ship states, in his account of her loss, that as soon as the spars, booms, hen-coops, and other buoyant articles were cut loose, 'the prisoners were ordered to be let out of irons.' One would imagine, indeed, that the officers on this dreadful emergency would not be witness to such inhumanity, without remonstrating effectually against keeping these unfortunate men confined a moment beyond the period when it became evident that the ship must sink. It will be seen, however, presently, from Mr. Heywood's own statement, that they were so kept, and that the brutal and unfeeling conduct which has been imputed to Captain Edwards is but too true.

It is an awful moment when a ship takes her last heel, just before going down. When the *Pandora* sunk, the surgeon says, 'the crew had just time to leap overboard, accompanying it with a most dreadful yell. The cries of the men drowning in the water was at first awful in the extreme; but as they sunk and became faint, they died away by degrees.' How accurately has Byron described the whole progress of a shipwreck to the final catastrophe! He might have been a spectator of the *Pandora*, at the moment of her foundering, when

> She gave a heel, and then a lurch to port,
> And, going down head foremost--sunk....
>
> Then rose from sea to sky the wild farewell--
>   Then shriek'd the timid and stood still the brave--
> Then some leap'd overboard with dreadful yell,
>   As eager to anticipate their grave;
> And the sea yawn'd around her like a hell,
>   And down she suck'd with her the whirling wave,
> Like one who grapples with his enemy,
> And strives to strangle him before he die.
>
> And first one universal shriek there rush'd,
>   Louder than the loud ocean, like a crash
> Of echoing thunder; and then all was hush'd,
>   Save the wild wind and the remorseless dash
> Of billows; but at intervals there gush'd,
>   Accompanied with a convulsive splash,
> A solitary shriek, the bubbling cry
> Of some strong swimmer in his agony.

On the sandy key which fortunately presented itself, the shipwrecked seamen hauled up the boats, to repair those that were damaged, and to stretch canvas round the gunwales, the better to keep out the sea from breaking into them. The heat of the sun and the reflection from the sand are described as excruciating, and the thirst of the men was rendered intolerable, from their stomachs being filled with salt water in the length of time they had to swim before being picked up. Mr. Hamilton says they were greatly disturbed in the night, by the irregular behaviour of one of the seamen, named Connell, which made them suspect he had got drunk with some wine that had been saved; but it turned out that the excruciating torture he suffered from thirst had induced him to drink salt water; 'by which means he went mad, and died in the sequel of the voyage.' It seems, a small keg of water, and some biscuits, had been thrown into one of the boats, which they found, by calculation, would be sufficient to last sixteen days, on an allowance of two wine-glasses of water per day to each man, and a very small quantity of bread, the weight of which was accurately ascertained by a musket-ball, and a pair of wooden scales made for each boat.

The crew and the prisoners were now distributed among the four boats. At Bligh's 'Mountainous Island,' they entered a bay where swarms of natives came down and made signs for their landing; but this they declined to do; on which an arrow was discharged and struck one of the boats; and as the savages were seen to be collecting their bows and arrows, a volley of muskets, a few of which happened to be in the boats, was discharged, which put them to flight. While sailing among the islands and near the shore, they now and then stopped to pick up a few oysters, and procure a little fresh water. On the 2nd September, they passed the north-west point of New Holland, and launched into the great Indian Ocean, having a voyage of about a thousand miles still to perform.

It will be recollected that Captain Bligh's people received warmth and comfort by wringing out their clothes in salt-water. The same practice was adopted by the crews of the *Pandora's* boats; but the doctor observes, that 'this wetting their bodies with salt water is not advisable, if protracted beyond three or four days, as, after that time, the great absorption from the skin that takes place, taints the fluids with the bitter part of salt water, so that the saliva becomes intolerable in the mouth.' Their mouths, indeed, he says, became so parched, that few attempted to eat the slender allowance of bread. He also remarks, that as the sufferings of the people continued, their temper became cross and savage. In the captain's boat, it is stated, one of the mutineers took to praying; but that 'the captain, suspecting the purity of his doctrines, and unwilling that he should have a monopoly of the business, gave prayers himself.'

On the 13th, they saw the island of Timor, and the next morning landed and got some water, and a few small fish from the natives; and on the night of the 15th, anchored opposite the fort of Coupang. Nothing could exceed the kindness and hospitality of the governor and other Dutch officers of this settlement, in affording every possible assistance and relief in their distressed condition. Having remained here three weeks, they embarked on the 6th October, on board the ***Rembang*** Dutch Indiaman, and on the 30th, anchored at Samarang, where they were agreeably surprised to find their little Tender, which they had so long given up for lost. On the 7th November they arrived at Batavia, where Captain Edwards agreed with the Dutch East India Company, to divide the whole of the ship's company and prisoners among four of their ships proceeding to Europe. The latter the captain took with him in the ***Vreedenburgh***; but finding his Majesty's ship ***Gorgon*** at the Cape, he transhipped himself and prisoners, and proceeded in her to Spithead, where he arrived on the 19th June, 1792.

Captain Edwards, in his meagre narrative, takes no more notice of his prisoners with regard to the mode in which they were disposed of at Coupang and Batavia, than he does when the ***Pandora*** went down. In fact, he suppresses all information respecting them, from the day in which they were consigned to '***Pandora's*** Box.' From this total indifference towards these unfortunate men, and their almost unparalleled sufferings, Captain Edwards must be set down as a man, whose only feeling was to stick to the letter of his instructions, and rigidly to adhere to what he considered the strict line of his duty; that he was a man of a cold phlegmatic disposition, whom no distress could move, and whose feelings were not easily disturbed by the sufferings of his fellow-creatures. He appears to have been one of those mortals, who might say, with Manfred--

My spirit walk'd not with the souls of men;

* * * * *

> My joys, my griefs, my passions, and my powers,
> Made me a stranger; though I wore the form,
> I had no sympathy with breathing flesh!

There seems to have been a general feeling at and before the court-martial, that Captain Edwards had exercised a harsh, unnecessary, and undue degree of severity on his prisoners. It is the custom, sanctioned no doubt by long usage, to place in irons all such as may have been guilty of mutiny in a ship of war, and the necessity of so doing is obvious enough--to prevent, in the most effectual manner, communication with the rest of the ship's company, who might be contaminated by their intercourse with such mischievous and designing men; men whose crime is of that dye, that, if found guilty, they have little hope to escape the punishment of death, to which a mutineer must, by the naval articles of war, be sentenced; no alternative being left to a court-martial, in such a case, but to pronounce a sentence of acquittal or of death.

In the present case, however, most of the prisoners had surrendered themselves; many of them had taken no active part in the mutiny; and others had been forcibly compelled to remain in the ship. It was not likely, therefore, that any danger could arise from indulging them occasionally, and in turns, with a few hours of fresh air on deck. As little danger was there of their escaping; where indeed could they escape to--especially when the ship was going down, at a great distance from any shore, and the nearest one known to be inhabited by savages? All or most of them were desirous of getting home, and throwing themselves on God and their country. The captain, however, had no 'compunctious visitings of nature' to shake his purpose, which seems to have been, to keep them strictly in irons during the whole passage, and to deliver them over in that state on his arrival in England.

Perhaps the circumstance of the crime of piracy, being superadded to that of mutiny, may have operated on his stern nature, and induced him to inflict a greater severity of punishment than he might otherwise have done, and which he certainly did far beyond the letter and spirit of his instructions. He might have considered that, in all ages and among all nations, with the exception of some of the Greek states,[18] piracy has been held in the utmost abhorrence, and those guilty of it treated with singular and barbarous severity; and that the most sanguinary laws were established for the protection of person and property in maritime adventure. The laws of Oleron, which were composed under the immediate direction of our Richard I., and became the common usage among maritime states, whose vessels passed through British seas, are conceived in a spirit of the most barbarous cruelty. [19] Thus, if a poor pilot, through ignorance, lost the vessel, he was either required to make full satisfaction to the merchant for damages sustained, or to lose his head. In the case of wrecks, where the lord of the coast (something like our present vice-admiral) should be found to be in league with the pilots, and run the ships on rocks, in order to get salvage, the said lord, the salvers, and all concerned, are declared to be accursed and excommunicated, and punished as thieves and robbers; and the pilot condemned to be hanged upon a high gibbet, which is to abide and remain to succeeding ages, on the place where erected, as a visible caution to other ships sailing thereby. Nor was the fate of the lord of the coast less severe,--his property was to be confiscated, and himself fastened to a post in the midst of his own mansion, which being fired at the four corners, were all to be burned together; the walls thereof demolished; and the spot on which it stood be converted into a market-place, for the sale only of hogs and swine, to all posterity.

These and many other barbarous usages were transferred into the institutions of Wisbuy, which formed the ***jus mercatorum*** for a long period, and in which great care was taken for the security of ships against their crews. Among other articles are the following.--Whoever draws a sword upon the master of a vessel, or wilfully falsifies the compass, shall have his right hand nailed to the mast.--Whoever behaves riotously shall be punished by being keel-hauled.--Whoever is guilty of rebellion (or mutiny) shall be thrown overboard.

For the suppression of piracy, the Portuguese, in their early intercourse with India, had a summary punishment, and accompanied it with a terrible example to deter others from the commission of the crime. Whenever they took a pirate ship, they instantly hanged every man, carried away the sails, rudder, and everything that was valuable in the ship, and left her to be buffeted about by the winds and the waves, with the carcasses of the criminals dangling from the yards, a horrid object of terror to all who might chance to fall in with her. Even to this day, a spice of the laws of Oleron still remains in the maritime code of European nations, as far as regards mutiny and piracy; and a feeling of this kind may have operated on the mind of Captain Edwards, especially as a tendency even to mutiny, or mutinous expressions, are considered, by the usage of the service, as justifying the commander of a ship of war to put the offenders in irons. Besides, the treatment of Bligh, whose admirable conduct under the unparalleled sufferings of himself and all who accompanied him in the open boat, had roused the people of England to the highest pitch of indignation against Christian and his associates, in which Edwards no doubt participated.

The following letter of Mr. Peter Heywood to his mother removes all doubt as to the character and conduct of this officer. It is an artless and pathetic tale, and, as his amiable sister says, 'breathes not a syllable inconsistent with truth and honour.'

'*Batavia, November 20th*, 1791.

'MY EVER-HONOURED AND DEAREST MOTHER,
 --At length the time has arrived when you are once more to hear from your ill-fated son, whose conduct at the capture of that ship, in which it was my fortune to embark, has, I fear, from what has since happened to me, been grossly misrepresented to you by Lieutenant Bligh, who, by not knowing the real cause of my remaining on board, naturally suspected me, unhappily for me, to be a coadjutor in the mutiny; but I never, to my knowledge, whilst under his command, behaved myself in a manner unbecoming the station I occupied, nor so much as even entertained a thought derogatory to his honour, so as to give him the least grounds for entertaining an opinion of me so ungenerous and undeserved; for I flatter myself he cannot give a character of my conduct, whilst I was under his tuition,

that could merit the slightest scrutiny. Oh! my dearest mother, I hope you have not so easily credited such an account of me; do but let me vindicate my conduct, and declare to you the true cause of my remaining in the ship, and you will then see how little I deserve censure, and how I have been injured by so gross an aspersion. I shall then give you a short and cursory account of what has happened to me since; but I am afraid to say a hundredth part of what I have got in store, for I am not allowed the use of writing materials, if known, so that this is done by stealth; but if it should ever come to your hands, it will, I hope, have the desired effect of removing your uneasiness on my account, when I assure you, before the face of God, of my innocence of what is laid to my charge. How I came to remain on board was thus:--

'The morning the ship was taken, it being my watch below, happening to awake just after daylight, and looking out of my hammock, I saw a man sitting upon the arm-chest in the main hatchway, with a drawn cutlass in his hand, the reason of which I could not divine; so I got out of bed and inquired of him what was the cause of it. He told me that Mr. Christian, assisted by some of the ship's company had seized the captain and put him in confinement; had taken the command of the ship and meant to carry Bligh home a prisoner, in order to try him by court-martial, for his long tyrannical and oppressive conduct to his people. I was quite thunderstruck; and hurrying into my berth again, told one of my messmates, whom I awakened out of his sleep, what had happened. Then dressing myself, I went up the fore-hatchway, and saw what he had told me was but too true; and again, I asked some of the people, who were under arms, what was going to be done with the captain, who was then on the larboard side of the quarter-deck, with his hands tied behind his back, and Mr. Christian alongside him with a pistol and drawn bayonet. I now heard a very different story, and that the captain was to be sent ashore to Tofoa in the launch, and that those who would not join Mr. Christian might either accompany the captain, or would be taken in irons to Otaheite and left there. The relation of two stories so different, left me unable to judge which could be the true one; but seeing them hoisting the boats out, it seemed to prove the latter.

'In this trying situation, young and inexperienced as I was, and without an adviser (every person being as it were infatuated, and not knowing what to do), I remained for awhile a silent spectator of what was going on; and after revolving the matter in my mind, I determined to choose what I thought the lesser of two evils and stay by the ship; for I had no doubt that those who went on shore, in the launch, would be put to death by the savage natives, whereas the Otaheitans being a humane and generous race, one might have a hope of being kindly received, and remain there until the arrival of some ship, which seemed, to silly me, the most consistent with reason and rectitude.

'While this resolution possessed my mind, at the same time lending my assistance to hoist out the boats, the hurry and confusion affairs were in, and thinking my intention just, I never thought of going to Mr. Bligh for advice; besides, what confirmed me in it was, my seeing two experienced officers, when ordered into the boat by Mr. Christian, desire his permission to remain in the ship (one of whom, my own messmate, Mr. Hayward), and I being assisting to clear the launch of yams, he asked me what I intended to do? I told him, to remain in the ship. Now this answer, I imagine, he has told Mr, Bligh I made to him; from which, together with my not speaking to him that morning, his suspicions of me have arisen, construing my conduct into what is foreign to my nature.

'Thus, my dearest mother, it was all owing to my youth and unadvised inexperience, but has been interpreted into villany and disregard of my country's laws, the ill effects of which I at present, and still am to, labour under for some months longer. And now, after what I have asserted, I may still once more retrieve my injured reputation, be again reinstated in the affection and favour of the most tender of mothers, and be still considered as her ever dutiful son.

'I was not undeceived in my erroneous decision till too late, which was after the captain was in the launch; for while I was talking to the master-at-arms, one of the ringleaders in the affair, my other messmate whom I had left in his hammock in the berth (Mr. Stewart), came up to me, and asked me, if I was not going in the launch? I replied, No--upon which he told me not to think of such a thing as remaining behind, but take his advice and go down below with him to get a few necessary things, and make haste to go with him into the launch; adding that, by remaining in the ship, I should incur an equal share of guilt with the mutineers themselves. I reluctantly followed his advice--I say ***reluctantly***, because I knew no better, and was foolish; and the boat swimming very deep in the water--the land being far distant--the thoughts of being sacrificed by the natives--and the self-consciousness of my first intention being just--all these considerations almost staggered my resolution; however, I preferred my companion's judgement to my own, and we both jumped down the main-hatchway to prepare ourselves for the boat--but, no sooner were we in the berth, than the master-at-arms ordered the sentry to keep us both in the berth till he should receive orders to release us. We desired the master-at-arms to acquaint Mr. Bligh of our intention, which we had reason to think he never did, nor were we permitted to come on deck until the launch was a long way astern. I now, when too late, saw my error.

'At the latter end of May, we got to an island to the southward of Taheite, called Tooboui, where they intended to make a settlement, but finding no stock there of any kind, they agreed to go to Taheite, and, after procuring hogs and fowls, to return to Tooboui and remain. So, on the 6th June, we arrived at Taheite, where I was in hopes I might find an opportunity of running away, and remaining on shore, but I could not effect it, as there was always too good a look-out kept to prevent any such steps being taken. And besides, they had all sworn that should any one make his escape, they would force the natives to restore him, and would then shoot him as an example to the rest; well knowing, that any one by remaining there might be the means (should a ship arrive) of discovering their intended place of abode. Finding it therefore impracticable, I saw no other alternative but to rest as content as possible and return to Tooboui, and there wait till the masts of the *Bounty* should be taken out, and then take the boat which might carry me to Taheite, and disable those remaining from pursuit.[20] But Providence so ordered it, that we had no occasion to try our fortune at such a hazard, for, upon returning there and remaining till the latter end of August, in which time a fort was almost built, but nothing could be effected; and as the natives could not be brought to friendly terms, and with whom we had many skirmishes, and narrow escapes from being cut off by them, and, what was still worse, internal broils and discontent,--these things determined part of the people to leave the island and go to Taheite, which was carried by a majority of votes.

'This being carried into execution on the 22nd September, and having anchored in Matavai bay, the next morning my messmate (Mr. Stewart) and I went on shore, to the house of an old landed proprietor, our former friend; and being now set free from a lawless crew, determined to remain as much apart from them as possible, and wait patiently for the arrival of a ship. Fourteen more of the ***Bounty's*** people came likewise on shore, and Mr. Christian and eight men went away with the ship, but God knows whither. Whilst we remained here, we were treated by our kind and friendly natives with a generosity and humanity almost unparalleled, and such as we could hardly have expected from the most civilized people.

'To be brief--having remained here till the latter end of March, 1791, on the 26th of that month, his Majesty's ship ***Pandora*** arrived, and had scarcely anchored, when my messmate and I went on board and made ourselves known; and having learnt from one of the natives who had been off in a canoe, that our former messmate Mr. Hayward, now promoted to the rank of lieutenant, was on board, we asked for him, supposing he might prove the assertions of our innocence. But he (like all worldlings when raised a little in life) received us very coolly, and pretended ignorance of our affairs; yet formerly, he and I were bound in brotherly love and friendship. Appearances being so much against us, we were ordered to be put in irons, and looked upon--oh, infernal words!--as ***piratical villains***. A rebuff so severe as this was, to a person unused to troubles, would perhaps have been insupportable, but to me, who had now been long inured to the frowns of fortune, and feeling myself supported by an inward consciousness of not deserving it, it was received with the greatest composure, and a full determination to bear it with patience.

'My sufferings, however, I have not power to describe; but though they are great, yet I thank God for enabling me to bear them without repining. I endeavour to qualify my affliction with these three considerations, first, my innocence not deserving them; secondly, that they cannot last long; and thirdly, that the change may be for the better. The first improves my hopes; the second, my patience; and the third, my courage. I am young in years, but old in what the world calls adversity; and it has had such an effect, as to make me consider it the most beneficial incident that could have occurred at my age. It has made me acquainted with three things which are little known, and as little believed by any but those who have felt their effects: first, the villany and censoriousness of mankind; secondly, the futility of all human hopes; and thirdly, the happiness of being content in whatever station it may please Providence to place me. In short, it has made me more of a philosopher, than many years of a life spent in ease and pleasure would have done.

'As they will no doubt proceed to the greatest lengths against me, I being the only surviving officer, and they most inclined to believe a prior story, all that can be said to confute it will probably be looked upon as mere falsity and invention. Should that be my unhappy case, and they resolved upon my destruction as an example to futurity, may God enable me to bear my fate with the fortitude of a man, conscious that misfortune, not any misconduct, is the cause, and that the Almighty can attest my innocence. Yet why should I despond? I have, I hope, still a friend in that Providence which hath preserved me amidst many greater dangers, and upon whom alone I now depend for safety. God will always protect those who deserve it. These are the sole considerations which have enabled me to make myself easy and content under my past misfortunes.

'Twelve more of the people who were at Otaheite having delivered themselves up, there was a sort of prison built on the after-part of the quarter-deck, into which we were all put in close confinement with both legs and both hands in irons, and were treated with great rigour, not being allowed ever to get out of this den; and, being obliged to eat, drink, sleep, and obey the calls of nature here, you may form some idea of the disagreeable situation I must have been in, unable as I was to help myself (being deprived of the use of both my legs and hands), but by no means adequate to the reality.

'On the 9th May we left Otaheite, and proceeded to the Friendly Islands, and about the beginning of August, got in among the reefs of New Holland, to endeavour to discover a passage through them; but it was not effected, for the *Pandora*, ever unlucky, and as if devoted by heaven to destruction, was driven by a current upon the patch of a reef, and on which, there being a heavy surf, she was soon almost bulged to pieces; but having thrown all the guns on one side overboard, and the tide flowing at the same time, she beat over the reef into a basin and brought up in fourteen or fifteen fathoms; but she was so much damaged while on the reef, that imagining she would go to pieces every moment, we had contrived to wrench ourselves out of our irons, and applied to the captain to have mercy on us, and suffer us to take our chance for the preservation of our lives; but it was all in vain--he was even so inhuman as to order us all to be put in irons again, though the ship was expected to go down every moment, being scarcely able to keep her under with all the pumps at work.

'In this miserable situation, with an expected death before our eyes, without the least hope of relief, and in the most trying state of suspense, we spent the night, the ship being by the hand of Providence kept up till the morning. The boats by this time had all been prepared; and as the captain and officers were coming upon the poop or roof of our prison, to abandon the ship, the water being then up to the coamings of the hatchways, we again implored his mercy; upon which he sent the corporal and an armourer down to let some of us out of irons, but three only were suffered to go up, and the scuttle being then clapped on, and the master-at-arms upon it, the armourer had only time to let two persons out of irons, the rest, except three, letting themselves out; two of these three went down with them on their hands, and the third was picked up. She now began to heel over to port so very much, that the master-at-arms, sliding overboard, and leaving the scuttle vacant, we all tried to get up, and I was the last out but three. The water was then pouring in at the bulk-head scuttles, yet I succeeded in getting out, and was scarcely in the sea when I could see nothing above it but the cross-trees, and nothing around me but a scene of the greatest distress. I took a plank (being stark-naked) and swam towards an island about three miles off, but was picked up on my passage by one of the boats. When we got ashore to the small sandy key, we found there were thirty-four men drowned, four of whom were prisoners, and among these was my unfortunate messmate (Mr. Stewart); ten of us, and eighty-nine of the *Pandora's* crew, were saved.

'When a survey was made of what provisions had been saved, they were found to consist of two or three bags of bread, two or three breakers of water, and a little wine; so we subsisted three days upon two wine-glasses of water, and two ounces of bread per day. On the 1st September we left the island, and on the 16th, arrived at Coupang in the island of Timor, having been on short allowance eighteen days. We were put in confinement in the castle, where we remained till October, and on the 5th of that month were sent on board a Dutch ship bound for Batavia.

'Though I have been eight months in close confinement in a hot climate, I have kept my health in a most surprising manner, without the least indisposition, and am still perfectly well in every respect, in mind as well as body; but without a friend, and only a shirt and pair of trousers to put on, and carry me home. Yet with all this I have a contented mind, entirely resigned to the will of Providence, which conduct alone enables me to soar above the reach of unhappiness.'

In a subsequent letter to his sister he says,
'I send you two little sketches of the manner in which his Majesty's ship *Pandora* went down on the 29th August, and of the appearance which we who survived made on the small sandy key within the reef, about ninety yards long and sixty broad, in all ninety-nine souls; here we remained three days, subsisting on a single wine-glass of wine or water, and two ounces of bread a day, with no shelter from the meridian and then vertical sun. Captain Edwards had tents erected for himself and his people, and we prisoners petitioned him for an old sail which was lying useless, part of the wreck, but he refused it; and the only shelter we had was to bury ourselves up to the neck in the burning sand, which scorched the skin entirely off our bodies, for we were quite naked, and we appeared as if dipped

in large tubs of boiling water. We were nineteen days in the same miserable situation before we landed at Coupang. I was in the ship, in irons, hands and feet, much longer than till the position you now see her in, the poop alone being above water (and that knee deep), when a kind Providence assisted me to get out of irons and escape from her.'

The treatment of these unhappy men was almost as bad at Batavia as in the *Pandora*, being closely confined in irons in the castle, and fed on very bad provisions; and the hardships they endured on their passage to England, in Dutch ships, were very severe, having, as he says, slept on nothing but hard boards on wet canvas, without any bed, for seventeen months, always subsisting on short allowance of execrable provisions, and without any clothes for some time, except such as the charity of two young men in the ship supplied him with. He had during his confinement at Batavia learned to make straw hats, and finished several with both his hands in fetters, which he sold for half-a-crown a-piece; and with the produce of these he procured a suit of coarse clothes, in which, with a cheerful and light heart, notwithstanding all his sufferings, he arrived at Portsmouth. How he preserved his health under the dreadful sufferings he endured, and in eight months' close confinement in a hot climate, is quite wonderful.

On the second day after the arrival of the *Gorgon* at Spithead the prisoners were transferred to the *Hector*, commanded by Captain (the late Admiral Sir George) Montague, where they were treated with the greatest humanity, and every indulgence allowed that could with propriety be extended to men in their unhappy situation, until the period when they were to be arraigned before the competent authority, and put on their trials for mutiny and piracy, which did not take place until the month of September.

In this period of anxious and awful suspense, a most interesting correspondence was carried on between this unfortunate youth and his numerous friends, which exhibits the character of himself and the whole family in the most amiable and affectionate colours, and in a more particular manner, of that adorable creature, his sister Nessy, who, in one of her letters, accounts for the peculiar warmth of her attachment and expressions by their being nearly of the same age, and engaged in the same pursuits, whether of study or amusement in their juvenile years. The poor mother, on hearing of his arrival, thus addresses her unfortunate son:--

'*Isle of Man, June 29th,* 1792.

'Oh! my ever dearly-beloved and long-lost son, with what anxiety have I waited for this period! I have counted the days, hours, and even minutes, since I first heard of the horrid and unfortunate mutiny which has so long deprived me of my dearest boy: but now the happy time is come when, though I cannot have the unspeakable pleasure of seeing and embracing you, yet I hope we may be allowed to correspond; surely there can be nothing improper in a liberty of this sort between an affectionate mother and her dutiful and beloved son, who, I am perfectly convinced, was never guilty of the crime he has been suspected of by those who did not know his worth and truth. I have not the least doubt but that the all-gracious God, who of his good providence has protected you so long, and brought you safe through so many dangers and difficulties, will still protect you, and at your trial make your innocence appear as clear as the light. All your letters have come safe to me, and to my very dear good Nessy. Ah! Peter, with what real joy did we all receive them, and how happy are we that you are now safe in England! I will endeavour, my dearest lad, to make your present situation as comfortable as possible, for so affectionate and good a son deserves my utmost attention. Nessy has written to our faithful and kind friend, Mr. Heywood, of Plymouth, for his advice, whether it would be proper for her to come up to you; if he consents to her so doing, not a moment shall be lost, and how happy shall I be when she is with you! Such a sister as she is! Oh! Peter, she is a most valuable girl,' etc.

On the same day this 'most valuable girl' thus writes:--[21]

'MY DEAREST AND MOST BELOVED BROTHER
--Thanks to that Almighty Providence which has so miraculously preserved you, your fond, anxious, and, till now, miserable Nessy, is at last permitted to address the object of her tenderest affection in England! Oh! my admirable, my heroic boy, what have we felt on your account! yet how small, how infinitely trifling was the misery of our situation when compared with the horror of yours! Let me now, however, with confidence hope that the God of all mercies has not so long protected you in vain, but will at length crown your fortitude and pious resignation to His will with that peace and happiness you so richly merit. How blest did your delightful and yet dreadful letter from Batavia make us all! Surely, my beloved boy, you could not for a moment imagine we ever supposed you guilty of the crime of mutiny. No, no; believe me, no earthly power could have persuaded us that it was possible for you to do anything inconsistent with strict honour and duty. So well did we know your amiable, steady principles, that we were assured your reasons for staying behind would turn out such as you represent them; and I firmly trust that Providence will at length restore you to those dear and affectionate friends, who can know no happiness until they are blest with your loved society. Take care of your precious health, my angelic boy. I shall soon be with you; I have written to Mr. Heywood (your and our excellent friend and protector) for his permission to go to you immediately, which my uncle Heywood, without first obtaining it, would not allow, fearing lest any precipitate step might injure you at present; and I only wait the arrival of his next letter to fly into your arms. Oh! my best beloved Peter, how I anticipate the rapture of that moment!--for alas! I have no

joy, no happiness, but in your beloved society, and no hopes, no fears, no wishes, but for you.'

Mr. Heywood's sisters all address their unfortunate brother in the same affectionate, but less impassioned strain; and a little trait of good feeling is mentioned, on the part of an old female servant, that shows what a happy and attached family the Heywoods were, previous to the melancholy affair in which their boy became entangled. Mrs. Heywood says, 'my good honest Birket is very well, and says your safe return has made her more happy than she has been for these two and forty years she has been in our family.' And Miss Nessy tells him, 'Poor Birket, the most faithful and worthiest of servants, desires me to tell you that she almost dies with joy at the thought of your safe arrival in England. What agony, my dear boy, has she felt on your account! her affection for you knows no bounds, and her misery has indeed been extreme; but she still lives to bless your virtues.'

The poor prisoner thus replies, from his Majesty's ship *Hector*, to his 'beloved sisters all':--

'This day I had the supreme happiness of your long-expected letters, and I am not able to express the pleasure and joy they afforded me; at the sight of them my spirits, low and dejected, were at once exhilarated; my heart had long and greatly suffered from my impatience to hear of those most dear to me, and was tossed and tormented by the storms of fearful conjecture--but they are now subsided, and my bosom has at length attained that long-lost serenity and calmness it once enjoyed: for you may believe me when I say it never yet has suffered any disquiet from my own misfortunes, but from a truly anxious solicitude for, and desire to hear of, your welfare. God be thanked, you still entertain such an opinion of me as I will flatter myself I have deserved; but why do I say so? can I make myself too worthy the affectionate praises of such amiable sisters? Oh! my Nessy, it grieves me to think I must be under the necessity, however heart-breaking to myself, of desiring you will relinquish your most affectionate design of coming to see me; it is too long and tedious a journey, and even on your arrival, you would not be allowed the wished-for happiness, both to you and myself, of seeing, much less conversing with, your unfortunate brother: the rules of the service are so strict, that prisoners are not permitted to have any communication with female relations; thus even the sight of, and conversation with, so truly affectionate a sister is for the present denied me! The happiness of such an interview let us defer till a time (which, please God, will arrive) when it can be enjoyed with more freedom, and unobserved by the gazing eyes of an inquisitive world, which in my present place of confinement would of course not be the case.

'I am very happy to hear that poor old Birket is still alive; remember me to her, and tell her not to *heave aback*, until God grants me the pleasure of seeing her.

'And now, my dear Nessy, cease to anticipate the happiness of personal communication with your poor, but resigned brother, until wished-for freedom removes the indignant shackles I now bear, from the feet of your fond and most affectionate brother, P.H.'

In a subsequent letter to his sister, he says, 'Let us at present be resigned to our fate, contented with this sort of communication, and be thankful to God for having even allowed us that happiness--for be assured the present confinement is *liberty*, compared with what it has been for the fifteen months last past.' On the 15th July, Commodore Pasley addresses the following business-like letter to Miss Heywood.

> 'I received your letter, my dearest Nessy, with the enclosure [her brother's narrative], but did not choose to answer it until I had made a thorough investigation; that is, seen personally all the principal evidences, which has ever since occupied my whole thoughts and time. I have also had some letters from himself; and notwithstanding he must still continue in confinement, every attention and indulgence possible is granted him by Captain Montague of the *Hector*, who is my particular friend. I have no doubt of the truth of your brother's narrative; the master, boatswain, gunner, and carpenter, late of the *Bounty*, I have seen, and have the pleasure to assure you that they are all favourable, and corroborate what he says. That *fellow*, Captain Edwards, whose inhuman rigour of confinement I shall never forget, I have likewise seen; he cannot deny that Peter avowed himself late of the *Bounty* when he came voluntarily aboard; this is a favourable circumstance. I have been at the Admiralty, and read over all the depositions taken and sent home by Bligh and his officers from Batavia, likewise the court-martial on himself; in none of which appears anything against Peter. As soon as Lieutenant Hayward arrives with the remainder of the *Pandora's* crew, the court-martial is to take place. I shall certainly attend, and we must have an able counsellor to assist, for I will not deceive you, my dear Nessy, however favourable circumstances may appear, our martial law is severe; by the tenor of it, the man who stands neuter is equally guilty with him who lifts his arm against his captain in such cases. His extreme youth and his delivering himself up, are the strong points of his defence. Adieu! my dearest

Nessy; present my love to your mother and sisters, and rest assured of my utmost exertions to extricate your brother.--Your affectionate uncle, T. PASLEY.'

This excellent man did not stop here: knowing that sea-officers have a great aversion from counsel, he writes to say, 'A friend of mine, Mr. Graham, who has been secretary to the different Admirals on the Newfoundland station for these twelve years, and consequently has acted as judge-advocate at courts-martial all that time, has offered me to attend you; he has a thorough knowledge of the service, uncommon abilities, and is a very good lawyer. He has already had most of the evidences with him. Adieu! my young friend; keep up your spirits, and rest assured I shall be watchful for your good. My heart will be more at ease, if I can get my friend Graham to go down, than if you were attended by the first counsel in England.'[22] Mr. Graham accordingly attended, and was of the greatest service at the trial.

Nessy Heywood[23] having in one of her letters inquired of her brother how tall he was, and having received information on this point, expressed some surprise that he was not taller. 'And so,' he replies, 'you are surprised I am not taller!--Ah, Nessy! let me ask you this--suppose the two last years of *your* growth had been retarded by close confinement--nearly deprived of all kinds of necessary aliment--shut up from the all-cheering light of the sun for the space of five months, and never suffered to breathe the fresh air (an enjoyment which Providence denies to none of His creatures) during all that time--and without any kind of exercise to stretch and supple your limbs--besides many other inconveniences which I will not pain you by mentioning--how tall should you have been, my dear sister?--answer, four feet nothing: but enough of nonsense.'

Nessy Heywood had expressed a strong desire to see her brother, but was told the rules of the service would not allow it; also, that it would agitate him, when he ought to be cool and collected, to meet his approaching trial. This was quite enough:--'But as for myself,' she says, 'no danger, no fatigue, no difficulties, would deter me--I have youth, and health, and excellent natural spirits--these and the strength of my affection would support me through it all; if I were not allowed to see you, yet being in the same place which contains you, would be joy inexpressible! I will not, however, any longer desire it, but will learn to imitate your fortitude and patience.'

Mr. Heywood of Maristow, and his daughter, Mrs. Bertie, had intimated the same thing. These excellent people, from the moment of young Heywood's arrival, had shown him every kindness, supplied him with money, and what was better, with friends, who could give him the best advice. To this worthy lady, Miss Nessy Heywood thus addresses herself.

> 'Overwhelmed with sensations of gratitude and pleasure, which she is too much agitated to express, permit me, dearest Madam, at my mamma's request, to offer you hers and our most sincere acknowledgements for your invaluable letter, which, from the detention of the packet, she did not receive till yesterday. By a letter from my beloved brother, of the same date, we are informed that Mr. Larkham (whom I suppose to be the gentleman you mention having sent to see him) has been on board the *Hector*, and has kindly offered him the most salutary advice relative to his present situation, for which allow me to request you will present him our best thanks. He also speaks with every expression a grateful heart can dictate of your excellent father's goodness in providing for all his wants, even before he could have received any letters from us to that purpose.
>
> 'Ah! my dear Madam, how truly characteristic is this of the kind friendship with which he has ever honoured our family! But my beloved Peter does not know that Mr. Heywood has a daughter, whose generosity is equal to his own, and whose amiable compassion for his sufferings it will be as impossible for us to forget, as it is to express the admiration and gratitude it has inspired. It would, I am convinced, be unnecessary, as well as a very bad compliment to you, Madam, were I to presume to point out anything particular to be done for our poor boy, as I have not the least doubt your goodness

and kind intention have long ago rendered every care of that sort on our part unnecessary. I shall only add, that my mamma begs every wish he forms may be granted, and sure I am, he will not desire a single gratification that can be deemed in the smallest degree improper.

'In one of my brother's letters, dated the 23rd, he hints that he shall not be permitted to see any of his relations till his trial is over, and that he therefore does not expect us. I have, however, written to Mr. Heywood (without whose approbation I would by no means take any step) for permission to go to him. If it is absolutely impossible for me to see him (though in the presence of witnesses), yet even that prohibition, cruel as it is, I could bear with patience, provided I might be near him, to see the ship in which he at present exists--to behold those objects, which, perhaps, at the same moment, attract his notice--to breathe the same air which he breathes.--Ah! my dearest Madam, these are inestimable gratifications, and would convey sensations of rapture and delight to the fond bosom of a sister, which it is far, very far beyond my power to describe. Besides, the anxiety and impatience produced by the immense distance which now separates us from him, and the uncertainty attending the packet, render it difficult and sometimes impossible to hear of him so often as we would wish--and, may I not add (though Heaven in its mercy forbid it--for alas! the bare idea is too dreadful, yet it is in the scale of possibility), that some accident might happen to deprive us of my dearest brother: how insupportably bitter would then be our reflections, for having omitted the opportunity, when it was in our power, of administering comfort and consolation to him in person. For these reasons, I earnestly hope Mr. Heywood will not judge it improper to comply with my request, and shall wait with eager impatience the arrival of his next letter. Think not, my dear Madam, that it is want of confidence in your care and attention which makes me solicitous to be with my beloved brother. Be assured we are all as perfectly easy in that respect as if we were on the spot; but I am convinced you will pardon the dictates of an affection which an absence of five years, rendered still more painful by his sufferings, has heightened almost to a degree of adoration. I shall, with your permission, take the liberty of enclosing a letter to my brother, which I leave open for perusal, and at the same time request your pardon for mentioning you to him in such terms as I am apprehensive will wound the delicacy which ever accompanies generosity like yours; but indeed, my dearest Madam, I cannot, must not, suffer my beloved boy to remain in ignorance of that worth and excellence which has prompted you to become his kind protectress.

'I have the honour to be, with every sentiment of gratitude, &c., &c, &c,

'NESSY HEYWOOD.'

Among the numerous friends that interested themselves in the fate of this unhappy youth, was his uncle, Colonel Holwell. The testimony he bears to his excellent character is corroborated by all who knew him while a boy at home. About a fortnight before the trial he writes to him thus:--

'*21st August*, 1792.

'MY VERY DEAR PETER,--I have this day received yours of the 18th, and am happy to find by its contents that, notwithstanding your long and cruel confinement, you still preserve your health, and write in good spirits. Preserve it,

my dear boy, awful as the approaching period must be, even to
the most innocent, but from which all who know you have not a
doubt of your rising as immaculate as a new-born infant. I
have known you from your cradle, and have often marked with
pleasure and surprise the many assiduous instances (far beyond
your years) you have given of filial duty and paternal
affection to the best of parents, and to brothers and sisters
who doated on you. Your education has been the best; and from
these considerations alone, without the very clear evidence of
your own testimony, I would as soon believe the Archbishop of
Canterbury would set fire to the city of London as suppose you
could, directly or indirectly, join in such a d----d absurd
piece of business. Truly sorry am I that my state of health
will not permit me to go down to Portsmouth to give this
testimony publicly before that respectable tribunal where your
country's laws have justly ordained you must appear; but
consider this as the *touchstone*, my dear boy, by which your
worth must be known. Six years in the navy myself, and
twenty-eight years a soldier, I flatter myself my judgement
will not prove erroneous. That Power, my dear Peter, of whose
grace and mercy you seem to have so just a sense, will not now
forsake you. Your dear aunt is as must be expected in such a
trying situation, but more from your present sufferings than
any apprehension of what is to follow,' &c.

With similar testimonies and most favourable auguries from
Commodore Pasley, the Rev. Dr. Scott, of the Isle of Man, and
others, young Heywood went to his long and anxiously expected
trial, which took place on the 12th September, and continued
to the 18th of that month. Mrs. Heywood had been anxious that
Erskine and Mingay should be employed as counsel, but Mr.
Graham, whom Commodore Pasley had so highly recommended, gave
his best assistance; as did also Mr. Const, who had been

retained, for which the Commodore expresses his sorrow, as sea officers, he says, have a great aversion to lawyers. Mr. Peter Heywood assigns a better reason; in a letter to his sister Mary he says, that 'Counsel to a naval prisoner is of no effect, and as they are not allowed to speak, their eloquence is not of the least efficacy; I request, therefore, you will desire my dear mother to revoke the letter she has been so good to write to retain Mr. Erskine and Mr. Mingay, and to forbear putting herself to so great and needless an expense, from which no good can accrue. No, no! Mary--it is not the same as a trial on shore; it would then be highly requisite; but, in this case, *I* alone must fight my own battle; and I think my telling the truth undisguised, in a plain, short, and concise manner, is as likely to be deserving the victory, as the most elaborate eloquence of a Cicero upon the same subject.'

At this anxious moment many painfully interesting letters passed to and from the family in the Isle of Man: the last letter from his beloved Nessy previous to the awful event thus concludes:--May that Almighty Providence whose tender care has hitherto preserved you be still your powerful protector! may He instil into the hearts of your judges every sentiment of justice, generosity, and compassion! may hope, innocence, and integrity be your firm support! and liberty, glory, and honour your just reward! may all good angels guard you from even the appearance of danger! and may you at length be restored to us, the delight, the pride of your adoring friends, and the sole happiness and felicity of that fond heart which animates the bosom of my dear Peter's most faithful and truly affectionate sister,

N.H.'

CHAPTER VI
THE COURT-MARTIAL

If any person in or belonging to the fleet shall make, or endeavour to make, any mutinous assembly, upon any pretence whatsoever, every person offending herein, and being convicted thereof, by the sentence of the Court-martial, shall suffer DEATH.
Naval Articles of War, **Art.** 19.

The Court assembled to try the prisoners on board his Majesty's ship *Duke*, on the 12th September, 1792, and continued by adjournment from day to day (Sunday excepted) until the 18th of the same month.[24]

PRESENT

Vice-Admiral Lord Hood, **President**.
Capt. Sir Andrew Snape Hamond, Bart.,
  " John Colpoys,
  " Sir George Montagu,
  " Sir Roger Curtis,
  " John Bazeley,
  " Sir Andrew Snape Douglas,
  " John Thomas Duckworth,
  " John Nicholson Inglefield,

"   John Knight,
"   Albemarle Bertie,
"   Richard Goodwin Keats.

The charges set forth that Fletcher Christian, who was mate of the ***Bounty***, assisted by others of the inferior officers and men, armed with muskets and bayonets, had violently and forcibly taken that ship from her commander, Lieutenant Bligh; and that he, together with the master, boatswain, gunner, and carpenter, and other persons (being nineteen in number), were forced into the launch and cast adrift;--that Captain Edwards, in the ***Pandora***, was directed to proceed to Otaheite, and other islands in the South Seas, and to use his best endeavours to recover the said vessel, and to bring in confinement to England the said Fletcher Christian and his associates, or as many of them as he might be able to apprehend, in order that they might be brought to condign punishment, &c. That Peter Heywood, James Morrison, Charles Norman, Joseph Coleman, Thomas Ellison, Thomas M'Intosh, Thomas Burkitt, John Millward, William Muspratt, and Michael Byrne, had been brought to England, &c., and were now put on their trial.

Mr. Fryer, the master of the ***Bounty***, being first sworn, deposed--

That he had the first watch; that between ten and eleven o'clock Mr. Bligh came on deck, according to custom, and after a short conversation, and having given his orders for the night, left the deck; that at twelve he was relieved by the gunner, and retired, leaving all quiet; that at dawn of day he was greatly alarmed by an unusual noise; and that, on attempting to jump up, John Sumner and Matthew Quintal laid their hands upon his breast and desired him to lie still, saying he was their prisoner; that on expostulating with them, he was told, 'Hold your tongue, or you are a dead man, but if you remain quiet there is none on board will hurt a hair of your head'; he further deposes, that on raising himself on the locker, he saw on the ladder, going upon deck, Mr. Bligh in his shirt, with his hands tied behind him, and Christian holding him by the cord; that the master-at-arms, Churchill, then came to his cabin and took a brace of pistols and a hanger, saying, 'I will take care of these, Mr. Fryer'; that he asked, on seeing Mr. Bligh bound, what they were going to do with the captain; that Sumner replied, 'D---- n his eyes, put him into the boat, and let the see if he can live upon three-fourths of a pound of yams a day';

that he remonstrated with such conduct, but in vain. They said he must go in the small cutter. 'The small cutter!' Mr. Fryer exclaimed; 'why her bottom is almost out, and very much eaten by the worms!' to which Sumner and Quintal both said, 'D---- n his eyes, the boat is too good for him'; that after much entreaty he prevailed on them to ask Christian if he might be allowed to go on deck, which, after some hesitation, was granted. When I came on deck, says Mr. Fryer, Mr. Bligh was standing by the mizen-mast, with his hands tied behind him, and Christian holding the cord with one hand, and a bayonet in the other. I said, 'Christian, consider what you are about.' 'Hold your tongue, Sir,' he said; 'I have been in hell for weeks past; Captain Bligh has brought all this on himself.' I told him that Mr. Bligh and he not agreeing was no reason for taking the ship. 'Hold your tongue, Sir,' he said. I said,--Mr. Christian, you and I have been on friendly terms during the voyage, therefore give me leave to speak,--let Mr. Bligh go down to his cabin, and I make no doubt we shall all be friends again;--he then repeated, 'Hold your tongue, Sir; it is too late'; and threatening me if I said anything more. Mr. Fryer then asked him to give a better boat than the cutter; he said, 'No, that boat is good enough.' Bligh now said to the master, that the man behind the hen-coops (Isaac Martin) was his friend, and desired him (the master) to knock Christian down, which Christian must have heard, but took no notice; that Fryer then attempted to get past Christian to speak to Martin, but he put his bayonet to his breast, saying, 'Sir, if you advance an inch farther, I will run you through,' and ordered two armed men to take him down to his cabin. Shortly afterwards he was desired to go on deck, when Christian ordered him into the boat: he said, 'I will stay with you, if you will give me leave.' 'No, Sir,' he replied, 'go directly into the boat.' Bligh, then on the gangway, said, 'Mr. Fryer, stay in the ship.' 'No, by G---- d, Sir,' Christian said, 'go into the boat, or I will run you through.' Mr. Fryer states, that during this time very bad language was used by the people towards Mr. Bligh; that with great difficulty they prevailed on Christian to suffer a few articles to be put into the boat; that after the persons were ordered into the boat to the number of nineteen, such opprobrious language continued to be used, several of the men calling out 'Shoot the----,' that Cole, the boatswain, advised they should cast off and take their chance, as the mutineers would certainly do them a mischief if they stayed much longer. Mr. Fryer then states the names of those who were under arms; and that Joseph Coleman, Thomas M'Intosh, Charles

Norman, and Michael Byrne (prisoners), wished to come into the boat, declaring they had nothing to do in the business; that he did not perceive Mr. Peter Heywood on deck at the seizure of the ship.

On being asked what he supposed Christian meant when he said he had been in hell for a fortnight? he said, from the frequent quarrels that they had, and the abuse he had received from Mr. Bligh, and that the day before the mutiny Mr. Bligh had challenged all the young gentlemen and people with stealing his cocoa-nuts.

Mr. Cole, the boatswain, deposes,--that he had the middle watch; was awakened out of his sleep in the morning, and heard a man calling out to the carpenter, that they had mutinied and taken the ship; that Christian had the command, and that the captain was a prisoner on the quarter-deck; that he went up the hatchway, having seen Mr. Heywood and Mr. Young in the opposite berth; that coming on deck he saw the captain with his hands tied behind him, and four sentinels standing over him, two of which were Ellison and Burkitt, the prisoners; that he asked Mr. Christian what he meant to do, and was answered by his ordering him to hoist the boat out, and shook the bayonet, threatening him and damning him if he did not take care; that when he found the captain was to be sent out of the ship, he again went aft with the carpenter to ask for the long-boat; that they asked three or four times before he granted it; that he saw Mr. Peter Heywood, one of the prisoners, lending a hand to get the fore-stayfall along, and when the boat was hooked on, spoke something to him, but what it was does not know, as Christian was threatening him at the time; that Heywood then went below, and does not remember seeing him afterwards; that after the few things were got into the boat, and most of the people in her, they were trying for the carpenter's tool-chest, when Quintal said, 'D---- n them, if we let them have these things they will build a vessel in a month'; but when all were in the boat she was veered astern, when Coleman, Norman, and M'Intosh, prisoners, were crying at the gangway, wishing to go in the boat; and Byrne in the cutter alongside was also crying; that he advised Mr. Bligh to cast off, as he feared they would fire into the boat.

The Court asked if he had any reason to believe that any other of the prisoners than those named were detained contrary to their inclinations? Answer--'I believe Mr. Heywood was; I thought all along he was intending to come away; he had no arms, and he assisted to get the boat out, and then went below; I heard Churchill call out, 'Keep them below.' *The Court*--'Do you think he meant Heywood?' 'I have no reason to think any other.'

Mr. Peckover the gunner's evidence is similar to that of Mr. Cole's, and need not be detailed.

Mr. Purcell, the carpenter, corroborated, generally, the testimony of the three who had been examined. *The Court* asked, 'Did you see Mr. Heywood standing upon the booms?' 'Yes; he was leaning the flat part of his hand on a cutlass, when I exclaimed, In the name of God, Peter, what do you with that? when he instantly dropped it, and assisted in hoisting the launch out, and handing the things into the boat, and then went down below, when I heard Churchill call to Thompson to keep them below, but could not tell whom he meant; I did not see Mr. Heywood after that.' *The Court*--'In what light did you look upon Mr. Heywood, at the time you say he dropped the cutlass on your speaking to him?' *Witness*--'I looked upon him as a person confused, and that he did not know he had the weapon in his hand, or his hand being on it, for it was not in his hand; I considered him to be confused, by his instantly dropping it, and assisting in hoisting the boat out, which convinced me in my own mind that he had no hand in the conspiracy; that after this he went below, as I think, on his own account, in order to collect some of his things to put into the boat.' *The Court*--'Do you, upon the solemn oath you have taken, believe that Mr. Heywood, by being armed with a cutlass at the time you have mentioned, by anything that you could collect from his gestures or speeches, had any intention of opposing, or joining others that might oppose, to stop the progress of the mutiny?' *Witness*--'No.' *The Court*--'In the time that Mr. Heywood was assisting you to get the things into the boat, did he, in any degree whatever, manifest a disposition to assist in the mutiny?' *Witness*--'No.' *The Court*--'Was he, during that time, deliberate or frightened, and in what manner did he behave himself?' *Witness*--'I had not an opportunity of observing his every action, being myself at that time engaged in getting several things into the boat, so that I cannot tell.' *The Court*--'Putting every circumstance together, declare to this court, upon the oath you have taken, how you considered his behaviour, whether as a person joined in the mutiny, or as a person wishing well to Captain Bligh?' *Witness*--'I by no means considered him as a person concerned in the mutiny or conspiracy.'

Lieutenant Thomas Hayward, late third lieutenant of the ***Pandora***, and formerly midshipman of the ***Bounty***, deposes,--that he had the morning watch; that at four o'clock Fletcher Christian relieved the watch as usual; that at five he ordered him, as master's mate of his watch, to look out, while he went down to lash his hammock up; that while looking at a shark astern of the ship, to his unutterable surprise, he saw Fletcher Christian, Charles Churchill, Thomas Burkitt (the prisoner), John Sumner, Matthew Quintal, William M'Koy, Isaac Martin, Henry Hillbrant, and Alexander Smith, coming aft, armed with muskets and bayonets; that on going forward, he asked Christian the cause of such an act, who told him to hold his tongue instantly; and leaving Isaac Martin as a sentinel on deck, he proceeded with the rest of his party below to Lieutenant Bligh's cabin; that the people on deck were Mr. John Hallet, myself, Robert Lamb, Butcher, Thomas Ellison (prisoner) at the helm, and John Mills at the conn; that he asked Mills if he knew any thing of the matter, who pleaded total ignorance, and Thomas Ellison quitted the helm and armed himself with a bayonet; that the decks now became thronged with armed men; that Peter Heywood, James Morrison (two of the prisoners), and George Stewart, were unarmed on the booms; that Fletcher Christian and his gang had not been down long before he heard the cry of murder from Lieutenant Bligh, and Churchill calling out for a rope, on which Mills, contrary to all orders and entreaties, cut the deep-sea line and carried a piece of it to their assistance; that soon after Lieutenant Bligh was brought upon the quarter-deck with his hands bound behind him, and was surrounded by most of those who came last on deck.

This witness then states, that on the arrival of the ***Pandora*** at Matavai Bay, Joseph Coleman was the first that came on board; that he was upset in a canoe and assisted by the natives; that as soon as the ship was at anchor, George Stewart and Peter Heywood came on board; that they made themselves known to Captain Edwards, and expressed their happiness that he was arrived; that he asked them how they came to go away with his Majesty's ship the ***Bounty***, when George Stewart said, when called upon hereafter, he would answer all particulars; that he was prevented by Captain Edwards from answering further questions, and they were sent out of the cabin to be confined. He then describes the manner in which the rest of the mutineers were taken on the island. Having stated that when he went below to get some things he saw Peter Heywood in his berth, and told him to go into the boat, he was asked by *the Court* if Heywood was prevented by any force from going upon deck, he answered, 'No.' *The Court*--'Did you, from his behaviour, consider him as a person attached to his duty, or to the party of the mutineers?' *Witness*--'I should rather suppose, after my having told him to go into the boat, and he not joining us, to be on the side of the mutineers; but that must be understood only as an opinion, as he was not in the least employed during the active part of it.' *The Court*--'Did you observe any marks of joy or sorrow on his countenance or behaviour?' *Witness*--'Sorrow.'

Lieutenant Hallet, late midshipman of the *Bounty*, states,--that he had the morning-watch; that he heard Lieutenant Bligh call out murder, and presently after saw him brought upon deck naked, excepting his shirt, with his hands tied behind him, and Christian holding the end of the cord which tied them in one hand, and either a bayonet or a cutlass in the other; that the cutter was hoisted out, and Mr. Samuel, Mr. Hayward, and myself ordered to go into her; but the boatswain and carpenter going aft, and telling Christian they wished to go with the captain rather than stay in the ship, and asking to have the launch, it was granted. On being asked if he saw Peter Heywood on that day, he replied, once, on the platform, standing still and looking attentively towards Captain Bligh; never saw him under arms nor spoke to him; does not know if he offered to go in the boat, nor did he hear any one propose to him to go in the boat; that when standing on the platform, Captain Bligh said something to him, but what he did not hear, upon which Heywood laughed, turned round, and walked away.

Captain Edwards being then called and sworn, was desired by the Court to state the conversation that passed between him and Coleman, Peter Heywood, and George Stewart, when they came on board the *Pandora*.

Edwards--'Joseph Coleman attempted to come on board before the ship came to an anchor at Otaheite; he was soon afterwards taken up by canoes and came on board before the ship came to an anchor; I began to make inquiries of him after the *Bounty* and her people. The next who came on board were Stewart and Peter Heywood; they came after the ship was at anchor, but before any boat was on shore. I did not see them come alongside. I desired Lieutenant Larkin to bring them down to the cabin. I asked them what news; Peter Heywood, I think, said he supposed

I had heard of the affair of the *Bounty*. I don't recollect all the conversation that passed between us; he sometimes interrupted me by asking for Mr. Hayward, the lieutenant of the *Pandora*, whether he was on board or not--he had heard that he was; at last I acknowledged that he was, and I desired him to come out of my state-room, where I had desired him to go into, as he happened to be with me at the time. Lieutenant Hayward treated him with a sort of contemptuous look, and began to enter into conversation with him respecting the *Bounty*, but I called the sentinel in to take them into custody, and ordered Lieutenant Hayward to desist, and I ordered them to be put into irons; some words passed, and Peter Heywood said he should be able to vindicate his conduct.

Lieutenant Corner, of the *Pandora*, merely states his being sent to bring the rest of the mutineers on board, who were at some distance from Matavai Bay.

The prisoners being called on for their defence, the witnesses were again separately called and examined on the part of the prisoners.

Mr. Fryer, the master, called in and examined by Mr. Heywood.--'If you had been permitted, would you have stayed in the ship in preference to going into the boat?' *Witness*--'Yes.' *Prisoner*--'Had you stayed in the ship in expectation of retaking her, was my conduct such, from the first moment you knew me to this, as would have induced you to intrust me with your design; and do you believe I would have favoured it, and given you all the assistance in my power?' *Witness*--'I believe he would: I should not have hesitated a moment in asking of him when I had had an opportunity of opening my mind to him.'

The same question being put to *Mr. Cole*, the boatswain, *Mr. Peckover*, the gunner, and *Mr. Purcell*, the carpenter, they all answered in the affirmative.

Mr. Heywood asked, 'What was my general conduct, temper, and disposition on board the ship?' *Witness*--'Beloved by everybody, to the best of my recollection.' To the same question, *Mr. Cole* answers, 'Always a very good character.' *Mr. Peckover*--'The most amiable, and deserving of every one's esteem.' *Mr. Purcell*--'In every respect becoming the character of a gentleman, and such as merited the esteem of everybody.'

Mr. Cole being examined, gave his testimony,--that he never saw Mr. Heywood armed; that he did not consider him of the mutineers' party; that he saw nothing of levity or apparent merriment in his conduct; that when he was below with Stewart, he heard Churchill call out, 'Keep them below,' and that he believes Heywood was one of the persons meant--has no doubt of it at all; that Bligh could not have spoken to him, when on the booms, loud enough to be heard; that Hayward was alarmed, and Hallet alarmed; that he by no means considers Heywood or Morrison as mutineers.

Mr. Purcell being examined, states,--that, respecting the cutlass on which he saw Mr. Heywood's hand resting, he does not consider him as being an armed man; that he never thought him as of the mutineers' party; that he never heard Captain Bligh speak to him; that he thinks, from his situation, he could not have heard him; that he was by no means guilty of levity or apparent merriment; that he heard the master-at-arms call out to keep them below; that Mr. Hallet appeared to him to be very much confused; and that Mr. Hayward likewise appeared to be very much confused.

The Court asked,--'As you say you did not look upon the prisoner as a person armed, to what did you allude when you exclaimed, "Good God, Peter, what do you do with that?"' *Witness*--'I look upon it as an accidental thing.'

Captain Edwards, being asked by Heywood--'Did I surrender myself to you upon the arrival of the *Pandora* at Otaheite?' *Witness*--'Not to me, to the Lieutenant. I apprehend he put himself in my power. I always understood he came voluntarily; our boats were not in the water.' *Prisoner*--'Did I give you such information respecting myself and the *Bounty* as afterwards proved true?' *Witness*--'He gave me some information respecting the people on the island, that corroborated with Coleman's. I do not recollect the particular conversation, but in general it agreed with the account given by Coleman.' *Prisoner*--'When I told you that I went away the first time from Otaheite with the pirates, did I not at the same time inform you that it was not possible for me to separate myself from Christian, who would not permit any man of the party to leave him at that time, lest, by giving intelligence, they might have been discovered whenever a ship should arrive?' *Witness*--'Yes, but I do not recollect the latter part of it, respecting giving intelligence.'

Mr. Fryer again called in and examined by Mr. Morrison.--Mr. Fryer states, he saw him assist in hoisting out the boats; that he said to him (Fryer), 'Go down below.' ***The Court*** asked, 'Whether it might not have been from a laudable motive, as supposing your assistance at that time might have prevented a more advantageous effort?' ***Witness***--'Probably it might: had I stayed in the ship, he would have been one of the first that I should have opened my mind to, from his good behaviour in the former part of the voyage': states his belief, that he addressed him as advice; and that, in hoisting out the boat, he was assisting Captain Bligh.

Mr. Cole, the boatswain, states, that he ordered Morrison to go and help them with the cutter; that he told him the boat was overloaded; that Captain Bligh had begged that no more people should go in her, and said he would take his chance in the ship; that he shook Morrison by the hand, and said he would do him justice in England; that he had no reason to suppose him concerned in the mutiny.

Lieutenant Thomas Hayward states, that Morrison appeared joyful, and supposed him to be one of the mutineers; on being asked by Morrison if he could declare before God and the Court that what he stated was not the result of a private pique? ***Witness***--'Not the result of any private pique, but an opinion formed after quitting the ship, from his not coming with us, there being more boats than one; cannot say they might have had the cutter.' This witness was pleased to remember nothing that was in favour of the prisoner.

Lieutenant Hallet states, he saw Morrison under arms; being asked in what part of the ship, he says, 'I did not see him under arms till the boat was veered astern, and he was then looking over the taffrail, and called out, in a jeering manner, "If my friends inquire after me, tell them I am somewhere in the South Seas."'

Captain Edwards bore testimony that Morrison voluntarily surrendered himself.

Mr. Fryer did not see Morrison armed; he was in his watch, and he considered him a steady, sober, attentive, good man; and acknowledged, that if he had remained in the ship, with the view of retaking her, Morrison would have been one of the first he should have called to his assistance.

Mr. Cole gave testimony to his being a man of good character, attentive to his duty, and he never knew any harm of him.

Mr. Purcell bore witness to his good character, being always diligent and attentive; did not see him under arms on the taffrail; never heard him use any jeering speeches. Respecting the prisoner **Muspratt, Mr. Cole's** evidence proves that he had a musket in his hands, but not till the latter part of the business; it is also proved that he assisted in getting things into the launch. **Mr. Peckover** saw him standing on the forecastle doing nothing--he was not armed.

Lieutenant Hayward saw Muspratt among the armed men: was asked, when Captain Bligh used the words, 'Don't let the boat be overloaded, my lads'--'I'll do you justice'; do you understand the latter words, 'My lads, I'll do you justice,' to apply to clothes or to men, whom he apprehended might go into the boat? **Witness**--If Captain Bligh made use of the words "my lads," it was to the people already in the boat, and not to those in the ship.' **The Court**--'To whom do you imagine Captain Bligh alluded: was it, in your opinion, to the men in the boat with him, or to any persons then remaining in the ship?' **Witness**--'To persons remaining in the ship.'

Against the prisoners Ellison, Burkitt, and Millward, the evidence given by all the witnesses so clearly and distinctly proved they were under arms the whole time, and actively employed against Bligh, that it is unnecessary to go into any detail as far as they are concerned.

The Court having called on the prisoners, each separately, for his defence, Mr. Heywood delivered his as follows:--

'My lords and gentlemen of this honourable Court,--Your attention has already been sufficiently exercised in the painful narrative of this trial; it is therefore my duty to trespass further on it as little as possible.

'The crime of mutiny, for which I am now arraigned, is so seriously pregnant with every danger and mischief, that it makes the person so accused, in the eyes, not only of military men of every description, but of every nation, appear at once the object of unpardonable guilt and exemplary vengeance.

'In such a character it is my misfortune to appear before this tribunal, and no doubt I must have been gazed at with all that horror and indignation which the conspirators of such a mutiny as that in Captain Bligh's ship so immediately provoke; hard, then, indeed is my fate, that circumstances should so occur to point me out as one of them.

'Appearances, probably, are against me, but they are appearances only; for unless I may be deemed guilty for feeling a repugnance at embracing death unnecessarily, I declare before this Court and the tribunal of Almighty God, I am innocent of the charge.

'I chose rather to defer asking any questions of the witnesses until I heard the whole of the evidence; as the charge itself, although I knew it generally, was not in its full extent, nor in particular points, made known to me before I heard it read by the Judge Advocate at the beginning of the trial: and I feel myself relieved by having adopted such a mode, as it enables me to set right a few particulars of a narrative which I had the honour to transmit to the Earl of Chatham, containing an account of all that passed on the fatal morning of the 28th of April, 1789, but which, from the confusion the ship was in during the mutiny, I might have mistaken, or from the errors of an imperfect recollection I might have mis-stated; the difference, however, will now be open to correction; and I have great satisfaction in observing, that the mistakes but very slightly respect my part of the transaction, and I shall consequently escape the imputation of endeavouring to save myself by imposing on my judges.

'When first this sad event took place I was sleeping in my hammock; nor, till the very moment of being awakened from it, had I the least intimation of what was going on. The spectacle was as sudden to my eyes, as it was unknown to my heart; and both were convulsed at the scene.

'Matthew Thompson was the first that claimed my attention upon waking: he was sitting as a sentinel over the arm-chest and my berth, and informed me that the captain was a prisoner, and Christian had taken the command of the ship. I entreated for permission to go upon deck; and soon after the boatswain and carpenter had seen me in my berth, as they were going up the fore-hatchway, I followed them, as is stated in their evidence. It is not in my power to describe my feelings upon seeing the captain as I did, who, with his hands tied behind him, was standing on the quarter-deck, a little abaft the mizen-mast, and Christian by his side. My faculties were benumbed, and I did not recover the power of recollection until called to by somebody to take hold of the tackle-fall, and assist to get out the launch, which I found was to be given to the captain instead of the large cutter, already in the water alongside the ship. It were in vain to say what things I put into the boat, but many were handed in by me; and in doing this it was that my hand touched the cutlass (for I will not attempt to deny what the carpenter has deposed), though, on my conscience, I am persuaded it was of momentary duration, and innocent as to intention. The former is evident, from its being unobserved by every witness who saw me upon deck, some of whom must have noticed it had it continued a single minute; and the latter is proved by the only person who took notice of the circumstance, and has also deposed that, at the moment he beheld me, I was apparently in a state of absolute stupor. The poison, therefore, carries with it its antidote; and it seems needless to make any further comment on the subject, for no man can be weak enough to suppose, that if I had been armed for the purpose of assisting in the mutiny, I should have resumed a weapon in the moment of triumph, and when the ship was so completely in the possession of the party, that (as more than one witness has emphatically expressed it) all attempts at recovering her would have been impracticable.

'The boat and ship, it is true, presented themselves to me without its once occurring that I was at liberty to choose, much less that the choice I should make would be afterwards deemed criminal; and I bitterly deplore that my extreme youth and inexperience concurred in torturing me with apprehensions, and prevented me from preferring the former; for as things have turned out, it would have saved me from the disgrace of appearing before you as I do at this day--it would have spared the sharp conflicts of my own mind ever since, and the agonizing tears of a tender mother and my much-beloved sisters.

'Add to my youth and inexperience, that I was influenced in my conduct by the example of my messmates, Mr. Hallet and Mr. Hayward, the former of whom was very much agitated, and the latter, though he had been many years at sea, yet, when Christian ordered him into the boat, he was evidently alarmed at the perilous situation, and so much overcome by the harsh command, that he actually shed tears.

'My own apprehensions were far from being lessened at such a circumstance as this, and I fearfully beheld the preparations for the captain's departure as the preliminaries of inevitable destruction, which, although I did not think could be more certain, yet I feared would be more speedy, by the least addition to their number.

'To show that I have no disposition to impose upon this Court, by endeavouring to paint the situation of the boat to be worse than it really was, I need only refer to the captain's own narrative, wherein he says that she would have sunk with them on the evening of the 3rd May, had it not been for his timely caution of throwing out some of the stores, and all the clothes belonging to the people, excepting two suits for each.

'Now what clothes or stores could they have spared which in weight would have been equal to that of two men? (for if I had been in her, and the poor fellow, Norton, had not been murdered at Tofoa, she would have been encumbered with our additional weight), and if it be true that she was saved by those means, which the captain says she was, it must follow that if Norton and myself had been in her (to say nothing of Coleman, M'Intosh, Norman, and Byrne, who, 'tis confessed, were desirous of leaving the ship), she must either have gone down with us, or, to prevent it, we must have lightened her of the provisions and other necessary articles, and thereby have perished for want--dreadful alternative!

'A choice of deaths to those who are certain of dying may be a matter of indifference; but where, on one hand, death appears inevitable, and the means of salvation present themselves on the other, however imprudent it might be to resort to those means in any other less trying situation, I think (and hope even at my present time of life) that I shall not be suspected of a want of courage for saying, few men would hesitate to embrace the latter.

'Such, then, was exactly my situation on board the *Bounty*; to be starved to death, or drowned, appeared to be inevitable if I went in the boat; and surely it is not to be wondered at, if, at the age of sixteen years, with no one to advise with, and so ignorant of the discipline of the service (having never been at sea before) as not to know or even suppose it was possible that what I should determine upon might afterwards be alleged against me as a crime--I say, under such circumstances, in so trying a situation, can it be wondered at, if I suffered the preservation of my life to be the first, and to supersede every other, consideration.

'Besides, through the medium of the master, the captain had directed the rest of the officers to remain on board, in hopes of retaking the ship. Such is the master's assertion, and such the report on board, and as it accorded with my own wishes for the preservation of my life, I felt myself doubly justified in staying on board, not only as it appeared to be safer than going in the boat, but from a consideration also of being in the way to be useful in assisting to accomplish so desirable a wish of the captain.

'Let it not--for God's sake--let it not be argued that my fears were groundless, and that the arrival of the boat at Timor is a proof that my conduct was wrong. This would be judging from the event, and I think I have plainly shown that, but for the death of Norton at Tofoa, and the prudent order of the captain not to overload the boat, neither himself nor any of the people who were saved with him, would at this moment have been alive to have preferred any charge against me, or given evidence at this trial.

'If deliberate guilt be necessarily affixed to all who continued on board the ship, and that in consequence they must be numbered with Christian's party--in such a strict view of matters it must irrevocably impeach the armourer and two carpenter's mates, as well as Martin and Byrne, who certainly wished to quit the ship. And if Christian's first intention of sending away the captain, with a few persons only, in the small cutter, had not been given up, or if even the large cutter had not been exchanged for the launch, more than half of those who did go with him would have been obliged to stay with me. Forgetful for a moment of my own misfortunes, I cannot help being agitated at the bare thought of their narrow escape.

'Every body must, and I am sure that this Court will, allow that my case is a peculiarly hard one, inasmuch as the running away with the ship is a proof of the mutiny having been committed. The innocent and the guilty are upon exactly the same footing--had the former been confined by sickness, without a leg to stand on, or an arm to assist them in opposing the mutineers, they must have been put upon their trial, and instead of the captain being obliged to prove their guilt, it would have been incumbent upon them to have proved themselves innocent. How can this be done but negatively? If all who wished it could not accompany the captain, they were necessarily compelled to stay with Christian; and being with him, were dependent on him, subject to his orders, however disinclined to obey them, for force in such a state is paramount to every thing. But when, on the contrary, instead of being in arms, or obeying any orders of the mutineers, I did every thing in my power to assist the captain, and those who went with him, and by all my actions (except in neglecting to do what, if I had done, must have endangered the lives of those who were so fortunate as to quit the ship) I showed myself faithful to the last moment of the captain's stay, what is there to leave a doubt in the minds of impartial and dispassionate men of my being perfectly innocent? Happy indeed should I have been if the master had stayed on board, which he probably would have done, if his reasons for wishing to do so had not been overheard by the man who was in the bread-room.

'Captain Bligh in his narrative acknowledges that he had left some friends on board the ***Bounty***, and no part of my conduct could have induced him to believe that I ought not to be reckoned of the number. Indeed from his attention to and very kind treatment of me personally, I should have been a monster of depravity to have betrayed him. The idea alone is sufficient to disturb a mind where humanity and gratitude have, I hope, ever been noticed as its characteristic features; and yet Mr. Hallet has said that he saw me laugh at a time when, Heaven knows, the conflict in my own mind, independent of the captain's situation, rendered such a want of decency impossible. The charge in its nature is dreadful, but I boldly declare, notwithstanding an internal conviction of my innocence has enabled me to endure my sufferings for the last sixteen months, could I have laid to my heart so heavy an accusation, I should not have lived to defend myself from it. And this brings to my recollection another part of Captain Bligh's narrative, in which he says, "I was kept apart from every one, and all I could do was by speaking to them in general, but my endeavours were of no avail, for I was kept securely bound, and no one but the guard was suffered to come near me."

'If the captain, whose narrative we may suppose to have been a detail of every thing which happened, could only recollect that he had spoken generally to the people, I trust it will hardly be believed that Mr. Hallet, without notes, at so distant a period as this, should be capable of recollecting that he heard him speak to any one in particular; and here it may not be improper to observe that, at the time to which I allude, Mr. Hallet (if I am rightly informed) could not have been more than fifteen years of age. I mean not to impeach his courage, but I think if circumstances be considered, and an adequate idea of the confused state of the ship can be formed by this Court, it will not appear probable that this young gentleman should have been so perfectly unembarrassed as to have been able to particularize the muscles of a man's countenance, even at a considerable distance from him; and what is still more extraordinary is, that he heard the captain call to me from abaft the mizen to the platform where I was standing, which required an exertion of voice, and must have been heard and noticed by all who were present, as the captain and Christian were at that awful moment the objects of every one's peculiar attention; yet he who was standing between us, and noticing the transactions of us both, could not hear what was said.

'To me it has ever occurred that diffidence is very becoming, and of all human attainments a knowledge of ourselves is the most difficult; and if, in the ordinary course of life, it is not an easy matter precisely to account for our own actions, how much more difficult and hazardous must it be, in new and momentous scenes, when the mind is hurried and distressed by conflicting passions, to judge of another's conduct; and yet here are two young men, who, after a lapse of near four years (in which period one of them, like myself, has grown from a boy to be a man), without hesitation, in a matter on which my life is depending, undertake to account for some of my actions, at a time, too, when some of the most experienced officers in the ship are not ashamed to acknowledge they were overcome by the confusion which the mutiny occasioned, and are incapable of recollecting a number of their own transactions on that day.

'I can only oppose to such open boldness the calm suggestions of reason, and would willingly be persuaded that the impression under which this evidence has been given is not in any degree open to suspicion. I would be understood, at the same time, not to mean anything injurious to the character of Mr. Hallet, and for Mr. Hayward, I ever loved him, and must do him the justice to declare, that whatever cause I may have to deplore the effect of his evidence, or rather his opinion, for he has deposed no fact against me, yet I am convinced it was given conscientiously, and with a tenderness and feeling becoming a man of honour.

'But may they not both be mistaken? Let it be remembered that their long intimacy with Captain Bligh, in whose distresses they were partakers, and whose sufferings were severely felt by them, naturally begot an abhorrence towards those whom they thought the authors of their misery,--might they not forget that the story had been told to them, and by first of all believing, then constantly thinking of it, be persuaded at last it was a fact within the compass of their own knowledge.

'It is the more natural to believe it is so, from Mr. Hallet's forgetting what the captain said upon the occasion, which, had he been so collected as he pretends to have been, he certainly must have heard. Mr. Hayward, also, it is evident, has made a mistake in point of time as to the seeing me with Morrison and Millward upon the booms; for the boatswain and carpenter in their evidence have said, and the concurring testimony of every one supports the fact, that the mutiny had taken place, and the captain was on deck, before they came up, and it was not till after that time that the boatswain called Morrison and Millward out of their hammocks; therefore to have seen me at all upon the booms with those two men, it must have been long after the time that Mr. Hayward has said it was. Again, Mr. Hayward has said that he could not recollect the day nor even the month when the *Pandora* arrived at Otaheite. Neither did Captain Edwards recollect when, on his return, he wrote to the Admiralty, that Michael Byrne had surrendered himself as one of the *Bounty's* people, but in that letter he reported him as having been apprehended, which plainly shows that the memory is fallible to a very great degree; and it is a fair conclusion to draw that, if when the mind is at rest, which must have been the case with Mr. Hayward in the *Pandora*, and things of a few months' date are difficult to be remembered, it is next to impossible, in the state which every body was on board the *Bounty*, to remember their particular actions at the distance of three years and a half after they were observed.

'As to the advice he says he gave me, to go into the boat, I can only say, I have a faint recollection of a short conversation with somebody--I thought it was Mr. Stewart--but be that as it may, I think I may take upon me to say it was on deck and not below, for on hearing it suggested that I should be deemed guilty if I stayed in the ship, I went down directly, and in passing Mr. Cole, told him, in a low tone of voice, that I would fetch a few necessaries in a bag and follow him into the boat, which at that time I meant to do, but was afterwards prevented.

'Surely I shall not be deemed criminal that I hesitated at getting into a boat whose gunnel, when she left the ship, was not quite eight inches above the surface of the water. And if, in the moment of unexpected trial, fear and confusion assailed my untaught judgement, and that by remaining in the ship I appeared to deny my commander, it was in appearance only--it was the sin of my head--for I solemnly assure you before God, that it was not the vileness of my heart.

'I was surprised into my error by a mixture of ignorance, apprehension, and the prevalence of example; and, alarmed as I was from my sleep, there was little opportunity and less time for better recollection. The captain, I am persuaded, did not see me during the mutiny, for I retired, as it were, in sorrowful suspense, alternately agitated between hope and fear, not knowing what to do. The dread of being asked by him, or of being ordered by Christian to go into the boat,--or, which appeared to me worse than either, of being desired by the latter to join his party, induced me to keep out of the sight of both, until I was a second time confined in my berth by Thompson, when the determination I had made was too late to be useful.

'One instance of my conduct I had nearly forgot, which, with much anxiety and great astonishment, I have heard observed upon and considered as a fault, though I had imagined it blameless, if not laudable--I mean the assistance I gave in hoisting out the launch, which, by a mode of expression of the boatswain's, who says I did it voluntarily (meaning that I did not refuse my assistance when he asked me to give it), the Court, I am afraid, has considered it as giving assistance to the mutineers, and not done with a view to help the captain; of which, however, I have no doubt of being able to give a satisfactory explanation in evidence.

'Observations on matters of opinion I will endeavour to forbear where they appear to have been formed from the impulse of the moment; but I shall be pardoned for remembering Mr. Hayward's (given I will allow with great deliberation, and after long weighing the question which called for it), which cannot be reckoned of that description, for although he says he rather considered me as a friend to Christian's party, he states that his last words to me were, "Peter, go into the boat," which words could not have been addressed to one who was of the party of the mutineers. And I am sure, if the countenance is at all an index to the heart, mine must have betrayed the sorrow and distress he has so accurately described.

'It were trespassing unnecessarily upon the patience of the Court, to be giving a tedious history of what happened in consequence of the mutiny, and how, through one very imprudent step, I was unavoidably led into others.

'But, amidst all this pilgrimage of distress, I had a conscience, thank heaven, which lulled away the pain of personal difficulties, dangers, and distress. It was this conscious principle which determined me not to hide myself as if guilty. No--I welcomed the arrival of the *Pandora* at Otaheite, and embraced the earliest opportunity of freely surrendering myself to the captain of that ship.

'By his order I was chained and punished with incredible severity, though the ship was threatened with instant destruction: when fear and trembling came on every man on board, in vain, for a long time, were my earnest repeated cries, that the galling irons might not, in that moment of affrighting consternation, prevent my hands from being lifted up to heaven for mercy.

'But though it cannot fail deeply to interest the humanity of this Court, and kindle in the breast of every member of it compassion for my sufferings, yet as it is not relative to the point, and as I cannot for a moment believe that it proceeded from any improper motive on the part of Captain Edwards, whose character in the navy stands high in estimation both as an officer and a man of humanity, but rather that he was actuated in his conduct towards me by the imperious dictates of the laws of the service, I shall, therefore, waive it, and say no more upon the subject.

'Believe me, again I entreat you will believe me, when, in the name of the tremendous judge of heaven and earth (before whose vindictive Majesty I may be destined soon to appear), I now assert my innocence of plotting, abetting, or assisting, either by word or deed, the mutiny for which I am tried--for, young as I am, I am still younger in the school of art and such matured infamy.

'My parents (but I have only one left, a solitary and mournful mother, who is at home weeping and trembling for the event of this day), thanks to their fostering care, taught me betimes to reverence God, to honour the king, and be obedient to his laws; and at no one time have I resolutely or designedly been an apostate to either.

'To this honourable Court, then, I now commit myself.

'My character and my life are at your disposal; and as the former is as sacred to me as the latter is precious, the consolation or settled misery of a dear mother and two sisters, who mingle their tears together, and are all but frantic for my situation--pause for your verdict.

'If I am found worthy of life, it shall be improved by past experience, and especially taught from the serious lesson of what has lately happened; but if nothing but death itself can atone for my pitiable indiscretion, I bow with submission and all due respect to your impartial decision.

'Not with sullen indifference shall I then meditate on my doom as not deserving it--no, such behaviour would be an insult to God and an affront to man, and the attentive and candid deportment of my judges in this place requires more becoming manners in me.

'Yet, if I am found guilty this day, they will not construe it, I trust, as the least disrespect offered to their discernment and opinion, if I solemnly declare that my heart will rely with confidence in its own innocence, until that awful period when my spirit shall be about to be separated from my body to take its everlasting flight, and be ushered into the presence of that unerring Judge, before whom all hearts are open and from whom no secrets are hid.

'P. HEYWOOD.'

Mr. Morrison's Defence

Sets out by stating that he was waked at daylight by Mr. Cole the boatswain, who told him that the ship was taken by Christian; that he assisted in clearing out the boat at Mr. Cole's desire, and says, 'While I was thus employed Mr. Fryer came to me and asked if I had any hand in the mutiny; I told him No. He then desired me to see who I could find to assist me, and try to rescue the ship; I told him I feared it was then too late, but would do my endeavour; when John Millward, who stood by me, and heard what Mr. Fryer said, swore he would stand by me if an opportunity offered. Mr. Fryer was about to speak again, but was prevented by Matthew Quintal, who, with a pistol in one hand, collared him with the other, saying, "Come, Mr. Fryer, you must go down into your cabin"; and hauled him away. Churchill then came, and shaking his cutlass at me, demanded what Mr. Fryer said. I told him that he only asked me if they were going to have the long-boat, upon which Alexander Smith (Adams), who stood on the opposite side of the boat, said, "It's a d--d lie, Charley, for I saw him and Millward shake hands when the master spoke to them." Churchill then said to me, "I would have you mind how you come on, for I have an eye upon you." Smith at the same time called out, "Stand to your arms, for they intend to make a rush." This, as it was intended, put the mutineers on their guard, and I found it necessary to be very cautious how I acted; and I heard Captain Bligh say to Smith, "I did not expect you would be against me, Smith"; but I could not hear what answer he made.'

He says that, while clearing the boat, he heard Christian order Churchill to see that no arms were put into her; to keep Norman, M'Intosh, and Coleman in the ship, and get the officers into the boat as fast as possible; that Mr. Fryer begged permission to stay, but to no purpose. On seeing Mr. Fryer and most of the officers going into the boat, without the least appearance of an effort to rescue the ship, I began to reflect on my own situation; and seeing the situation of the boat, and considering that she was at least a thousand leagues from any friendly settlement, and judging, from what I had seen of the Friendly Islanders but a few days before, that nothing could be expected from them but to be plundered or killed, and seeing no choice but of one evil, I chose, as I thought the least, to stay in the ship, especially as I considered it as obeying Captain Bligh's orders, and depending on his promise to do justice to those who remained. I informed Mr. Cole of my intention, who made me the like promise, taking me by the hand and saying, "God bless you, my boy; I will do you justice if ever I reach England."

'I also informed Mr. Hayward of my intention; and on his dropping a hint to me that he intended to knock Churchill down, I told him I would second him, pointing to some of the Friendly Island clubs which were sticking in the booms, and saying, "There were tools enough": but (he adds) 'I was suddenly damped to find that he went into the boat without making the attempt he had proposed.'

He then appeals to the members of the Court, as to the alternative they would themselves have taken:--'A boat alongside, already crowded; those who were in her crying out she would sink; and Captain Bligh desiring no more might go in--with a slender stock of provisions,--what hope could there be to reach any friendly shore, or withstand the hostile attacks of the boisterous elements? The perils those underwent who reached the island of Timor, and whom nothing but the apparent interference of Divine Providence could have saved, fully justify my fears, and prove beyond a doubt that they rested on a solid foundation; for by staying in the ship, an opportunity might offer of escaping, but by going in the boat nothing but death appeared, either from the lingering torments of hunger and thirst, or from the murderous weapons of cruel savages, or being swallowed up by the deep.

'I have endeavoured,' he says, 'to recall to Mr. Hayward's remembrance a proposal he at one time made, by words, of attacking the mutineers, and of my encouraging him to the attempt, promising to back him. He says he has but a faint recollection of the business--so faint indeed that he cannot recall to his memory the particulars, but owns there was something passed to that effect. Faint, however, as his remembrance is (which for me is the more unfortunate), ought it not to do away all doubt with respect to the motives by which I was then influenced?' And, in conclusion, he says, 'I beg leave most humbly to remind the members of this honourable Court, that I did freely, and of my own accord, deliver myself up to Lieutenant Robert Corner, of H.M.S. *Pandora*, on the first certain notice of her arrival.'

William Muspratt's Defence

Declares his innocence of any participation in the mutiny; admits he assisted in hoisting out the boat, and in putting several articles into her; after which he sat down on the booms, when Millward came and mentioned to him Mr. Fryer's intention to rescue the ship, when he said he would stand by Mr. Fryer as far as he could; and with that intention, and for that purpose only, he took up a musket which one of the people had laid down, and which he quitted the moment he saw Bligh's people get into the boat. Solemnly denies the charge of Mr. Purcell against him, of handing liquor to the ship's company. Mr. Hayward's evidence, he trusts, must stand so impeached before the Court, as not to receive the least attention, when the lives of so many men are to be affected by it--for, he observes, he swears that Morrison was a mutineer, because he assisted in hoisting out the boats; and that M'Intosh was not a mutineer, notwithstanding he was precisely employed on the same business--that he criminated Morrison from the appearance of his countenance--that he had only a faint remembrance of that material and striking circumstance of Morrison offering to join him to retake the ship--that, in answer to his (Muspratt's) question respecting Captain Bligh's words, 'My lads, I'll do you justice' he considered them applied to the people in the boat, and not to those in the ship--to the same question put by the Court, he said they applied to persons remaining in the ship. And he notices some other instances which he thinks most materially affect Mr. Hayward's credit; and says, that if he had been under arms when Hayward swore he was, he humbly submits Mr. Hallet must have seen him. And he concludes with asserting (what indeed was a very general opinion), 'that the great misfortune attending this unhappy business is, that no one ever attempted to rescue the ship; that it might have been done, Thompson being the only sentinel over the arm-chest.'

Michael Byrne's Defence

was very short. He says, 'It has pleased the Almighty, among the events of His unsearchable providence, nearly to deprive me of sight, which often puts it out of my power to carry the intentions of my mind into execution.

'I make no doubt but it appears to this honourable Court, that on the 28th of April, 1789, my intention was to quit his Majesty's ship ***Bounty*** with the officers and men who went away, and that the sorrow I expressed at being detained was real and unfeigned.

'I do not know whether I may be able to repeat the exact words that were spoken on the occasion, but some said, "We must not part with our fiddler"; and Charles Churchill threatened to send me to the shades if I attempted to quit the cutter, into which I had gone for the purpose of attending Lieutenant Bligh': and, without further trespassing on the time of the Court, he submits his case to its judgement and mercy.

It is not necessary to notice any parts of the defence made by Coleman, Norman, and M'Intosh, as it is clear, from the whole evidence and from Bligh's certificates, that those men were anxious to go in the boat, but were kept in the ship by force.

It is equally clear, that Ellison, Millward, and Burkitt, were concerned in every stage of the mutiny, and had little to offer in their defence in exculpation of the crime of which they were accused.

On the sixth day, namely, on the 18th of September, 1792, the Court met,--the prisoners were brought in, audience admitted, when the president, having asked the prisoners if they or any of them had anything more to offer in their defence, the Court was cleared, and agreed,--

'That the charges had been proved against the said Peter Heywood, James Morrison, Thomas Ellison, Thomas Burkitt, John Millward, and William Muspratt; and did adjudge them, and each of them, to suffer death, by being hanged by the neck, on board such of his Majesty's ship or ships of war, and at such time or times, and at such place or places, as the commissioners for executing the office of Lord High Admiral of Great Britain and Ireland, etc., or any three of them, for the time being, should, in writing, under their hands, direct; but the Court, in consideration of various circumstances, did humbly and most earnestly recommend the said Peter Heywood and James Morrison to his Majesty's mercy; and the Court further agreed, that the charges had not been proved against the said Charles Norman, Joseph Coleman, Thomas M'Intosh, and Michael Byrne, and did adjudge them, and each of them, to be acquitted.'

The Court was then opened and audience admitted, and sentence passed accordingly.

CHAPTER VII
THE KING'S WARRANT

>Well, believe this--
>No ceremony that to great ones 'longs,
>Not the king's crown, nor the deputed sword,
>The marshal's truncheon, nor the judge's robe,
>Become them with one half so good a grace,
>As mercy does.

It was a very common feeling that Heywood and Morrison, the former in particular, had been hardly dealt with by the Court in passing upon them a sentence of death, tempered as it was with the recommendation to the king's mercy. It should, however, have been recollected, that the Court had no discretional power to pass any other sentence but that, or a full acquittal. But earnestly, no doubt, as the Court was disposed towards the latter alternative, it could not, consistently with the rules and feelings of the service, be adopted. It is not enough in cases of mutiny (and this case was aggravated by the piratical seizure of a king's ship) that the officers and men in his Majesty's naval service should take no active part;--to be neutral or passive is considered as tantamount to aiding and abetting. Besides, in the present case, the remaining in the ship along with the mutineers, without having recourse to such means as offered of leaving her, presumes a voluntary adhesion to the criminal party. The only fault of Heywood, and a pardonable one on account of his youth and inexperience, was his not asking Christian to be allowed to go with his captain,--his not *trying* to go in time. M'Intosh, Norman, Byrne, and Coleman were acquitted because they expressed a strong desire to go, but were forced to remain. This was not only clearly proved, but they were in possession of written testimonies from Bligh to that effect; and so would Heywood have had, but for some prejudice Bligh had taken against him, in the course of the boat-voyage home, for it will be shown that he knew he was confined to his berth below.

In favour of three of the four men condemned without a recommendation, there were unhappily no palliating circumstances. Millward, Burkitt, and Ellison were under arms from first to last; and Ellison not only left the helm to take up arms, but, rushing aft towards Bligh, called out, 'D--n him, I'll be sentry over him.' The fourth man, Muspratt, was condemned on the evidence of Lieutenant Hayward, which, however, appears to have been duly appreciated by the Lords Commissioners of the Admiralty, and in consequence of which the poor man escaped an ignominious death.

The family of young Heywood in the Isle of Man had been buoyed up, from various quarters, with the almost certainty of his full acquittal. From the 12th September, when the court-martial first sat, till the 24th of that month, they were prevented, by the strong and contrary winds which cut off all communication with England, from receiving any tidings whatever. But while Mrs. Heywood and her daughters were fondly flattering themselves with everything being most happily concluded, one evening, as they were indulging these pleasing hopes, a little boy, the son of one of their particular friends, ran into the room and told them, in the most abrupt manner, that the trial was over and all the prisoners condemned, but that Peter Heywood was recommended to mercy; he added that a man whose name he mentioned had told him this. The man was sent for, questioned, and replied he had seen it in a newspaper at Liverpool, from which place he was just arrived in a small fishing-boat, but had forgotten to bring the paper with him. In this state of doubtful uncertainty this wretched family remained another whole week, harassed by the most cruel agony of mind, which no language can express.[26]

The affectionate Nessy determined at once to proceed to Liverpool, and so on to London. She urges her brother James at Liverpool to hasten to Portsmouth: 'Don't wait for me, I can go alone; fear and even despair will support me through the journey; think only of our poor unfortunate and adored boy, bestow not one thought on me.' And she adds, 'yet, if I could listen to reason (which is indeed difficult), it is not likely that anything serious has taken place, or will do so, as we should then certainly have had an express.' She had a tempestuous passage of forty-nine hours, and to save two hours got into an open fishing-boat at the mouth of the Mersey, the sea running high and washing over her every moment; but, she observes, 'let me but be blessed with the cheering influence of *hope*, and I have spirit to undertake anything.' From Liverpool she set off the same night in the mail for London; and arrived at Mr. Graham's on the 5th October, who received her with the greatest kindness, and desired her to make his house her home.

The suspense into which the afflicted family in the Isle of Man had been thrown, by the delay of the packet, was painfully relieved on its arrival in the night of the 29th September, by the following letter from Mr. Graham to the Rev. Dr. Scott, which the latter carried to Mrs. Heywood's family the following morning.

' *Portsmouth, Tuesday, 18th September*.
'

'SIR,--Although a stranger, I make no apology in writing to you. I have attended and given my assistance at Mr. Heywood's trial, which was finished and the sentence passed about half an hour ago. Before I tell you what that sentence is, I must inform you that his life is safe, notwithstanding it is at present at the mercy of the king, to which he is in the strongest terms recommended by the Court. That any unnecessary fears may not be productive of misery to the family, I must add, that the king's attorney-general (who with Judge Ashurst attended the trial) desired me to make myself perfectly easy, for that my friend was as safe as if he had not been condemned. I would have avoided making use of this dreadful word, but it must have come to your knowledge, and perhaps unaccompanied by many others of a pleasing kind. To prevent its being improperly communicated to Mrs. or the Misses Heywood, whose distresses first engaged me in the business, and could not fail to call forth my best exertions upon the occasion, I send you this by express. The mode of communication I must leave to your discretion; and shall only add that, although from a combination of circumstances, ill-nature, and mistaken friendship, the sentence is in itself terrible, yet it is incumbent on me to assure you that, from the same combination of circumstances, everybody who attended the trial is perfectly satisfied in his own mind that he was hardly guilty in appearance, in intention he was perfectly innocent. I shall of course write to Commodore Pasley, whose mind, from my letter to him of yesterday, must be dreadfully agitated, and take his advice about what is to be done when Mr. Heywood is released. I shall stay here till then, and my intention is afterwards to take him to my house in town, where I think he had better stay till one of the family calls for him: for he will require a great deal of tender management after all his sufferings; and it would perhaps be a necessary preparation for seeing his mother, that one or both his sisters should be previously prepared to support her on so trying an occasion.'

On the following day Mr. Graham again writes to Dr. Scott, and among other things observes, 'It will be a great satisfaction to his family to learn, that the declarations of some of the other prisoners, since the trial, put it past all doubt that the evidence upon which he was convicted must have been (to say nothing worse of it) an unfortunate belief, on the part of the witness, of circumstances which either never had existence, or were applicable to one of the other gentlemen who remained in the ship, and not to Mr. Heywood.'[27]

On the 20th September Mr. Heywood addresses the first letter he wrote, after his conviction, to Dr. Scott.

'HONOURED AND DEAR SIR,--On Wednesday the 12th instant the awful trial commenced, and on ***that*** day, ***when in Court***, I had the pleasure of receiving your most kind and parental letter,[28] in answer to which I now communicate to you the melancholy issue of it, which, as I desired my friend Mr. Graham to inform you of immediately, will be no dreadful news to you. The morning lowers, and all my hope of worldly joy is fled. On Tuesday morning the 18th the dreadful sentence of death was pronounced upon me, to which (being the just decree of that Divine Providence who first gave me breath) I bow my devoted head, with that fortitude, cheerfulness, and resignation, which is the duty of every member of the church of our blessed Saviour and Redeemer Christ Jesus. To Him alone I now look up for succour, in full hope that perhaps a few days more will open to the view of my astonished and fearful soul His kingdom of eternal and incomprehensible bliss, prepared only for the righteous of heart.

'I have not been found guilty of the slightest act connected with that detestable crime of mutiny, but am doomed to die for not being active in my endeavours to suppress it. Could the witnesses who appeared on the Court-martial be themselves tried, **they** would also suffer for the very same and only crime of which I have been found guilty. But I am to be the victim. Alas! my youthful inexperience, and not depravity of will, is the sole cause to which I can attribute my misfortunes. But so far from repining at my fate, I receive it with a dreadful kind of joy, composure, and serenity of mind; well assured that it has pleased God to point me out as a subject through which some greatly useful (though at present unsearchable) intention of the divine attributes may be carried into execution for the future benefit of my country. Then why should I repine at being made a sacrifice for the good, perhaps, of thousands of my fellow-creatures; forbid it, Heaven! Why should I be sorry to leave a world in which I have met with nothing but misfortunes and all their concomitant evils? I shall on the contrary endeavour to divest myself of all wishes for the futile and sublunary enjoyments of it, and prepare my soul for its reception into the bosom of its Redeemer. For though the very strong recommendation I have had to his Majesty's mercy by all the members of the Court may meet with his approbation, yet that is but the balance of a straw, a mere uncertainty, upon which no hope can be built; the other is a certainty that must one day happen to every mortal, and therefore the salvation of my soul requires my most prompt and powerful exertions during the short time I may have to remain on earth.

'As this is too tender a subject for me to inform my unhappy and distressed mother and sisters of, I trust, dear Sir, you will either show them this letter, or make known to them the truly dreadful intelligence in such a manner as (assisted by your wholesome and paternal advice) may enable them to bear it with Christian fortitude. The only worldly feelings I am now possessed of are for their happiness and welfare; but even these, in my present situation, I must endeavour, with God's assistance, to eradicate from my heart, how hard soever the task. I must strive against cherishing any temporal affections. But, my dear Sir, endeavour to mitigate my distressed mother's sorrow. Give my everlasting duty to her, and unabated love to my disconsolate brothers and sisters, and all my other relations. Encourage them, by my example, to bear up with fortitude and resignation to the Divine will, under their load of misfortunes, almost too great for female nature to support, and teach them to be fully persuaded that all hopes of happiness on earth are vain. On my own account I still enjoy the most easy serenity of mind; and am, dear Sir, for ever your greatly indebted and most dutiful, but ill-fated,

'PETER HEYWOOD.'

His next letter is to his dearly beloved Nessy.

'Had I not a strong idea that, ere this mournful epistle from your ill-fated brother can reach the trembling hand of my ever dear and much afflicted Nessy, she must have been informed of the final issue of my trial on Wednesday morning, by my honoured friend Dr. Scott, I would not now add trouble to the afflicted by a confirmation of it. Though I have indeed fallen an early victim to the rigid rules of the service, and though the jaws of death are once more opened upon me, yet do I not now nor ever will bow to the tyranny of base-born fear. Conscious of having done my duty to God and man, I feel not one moment's anxiety on my own account, but cherish a full and sanguine hope that perhaps a few days more will free me from the load of misfortune which has ever been my portion in this transient period of existence; and that I shall find an everlasting asylum in those blessed regions of eternal bliss, where the galling yoke of tyranny and oppression is felt no more.

'If earthly Majesty, to whose mercy I have been recommended by the Court, should refuse to put forth its lenient hand and rescue me from what is ***fancifully*** called an ignominious death, there is a heavenly King and Redeemer ready to receive the righteous penitent, on whose gracious mercy alone I, as we all should, depend, with that pious resignation which is the duty of every Christian; well convinced that, without His express permission, not even a hair of our head can fall to the ground.

'Oh! my sister, my heart yearns when I picture to myself the affliction, indescribable affliction, which this melancholy intelligence must have caused in the mind of my much honoured mother. But let it be your peculiar endeavour to watch over her grief and mitigate her pain. I hope, indeed, this little advice from me will be unnecessary; for I know the holy precepts of that inspired religion, which, thank heaven! have been implanted in the bosoms of us all, will point out to you, and all my dear relatives, that fortitude and resignation which are required of us in the conflicts of human nature, and prevent you from arraigning the wisdom of that omniscient Providence, of which we ought all to have the fullest sense.

'I have had all my dear Nessy's letters; the one of the 17th this morning, but alas! what do they now avail? Their contents only serve to prove the instability of all human hopes and expectations; but, my dear sister, I begin to feel the pangs which you must suffer from the perusal of this melancholy paper, and will therefore desist, for I know it is more than your nature can support. The contrast between last week's correspondence and this is great indeed; but why? we had only hope then; and have we not the same now? certainly. Endeavour then, my love, to cherish that hope, and with faith rely upon the mercy of that God who does as to Him seems best and most conducive to the general good of His miserable creatures.

'Bear it then with Christian patience, and instil into the mind of my dear and now sorrowful sisters, by your advice, the same disposition; and, for heaven's sake, let not despair touch the soul of my dear mother--for then all would be over. Let James also employ all his efforts to cheer her spirits under her weight of woe. I will write no more. Adieu, my dearest love! Write but little to me, and pray for your ever affectionate but ill-fated brother.

'P.S.--I am in perfect spirits, therefore let not your sympathizing feelings for my sufferings hurt your own precious health, which is dearer to me than life itself. Adieu!--'

In a letter to his mother he assures her of the perfect tranquillity of his mind; advises her not to entertain too sanguine hopes, but at the same time not to be uneasy; and he adds, 'A minister of the gospel, who now attends me, has advised me not to say too much to any of my dear relations, but now and then I cannot avoid it.' To his dearest Nessy, who encourages him to take hope, he says, 'Alas! it is but a broken stick which *I* have leaned on, and it has pierced my soul in such a manner that I will never more trust to it, but wait with a contented mind and patience for the final accomplishment of the Divine will.... Mrs. **Hope** is a faithless and ungrateful acquaintance, with whom I have now broken off all connexions, and in her stead have endeavoured to cultivate a more sure friendship with **Resignation**, in full trust of finding her more constant.' He desires her to write through her brother James who is with him; and says that the reason for his having desired her not to write much was, lest she might hurt herself by it; and he adds, 'from an idea that your exalted sentiments upon so tender a subject ought not to be known by an inquiring world; but,' he continues, 'do just as you like best: I am conscious that your good sense will prompt you to nothing inconsistent with our present circumstances.' To this she replies, in the true spirit of a character like her own. 'Yes! my ever dearest brother, I *will* write to you, and I know I need not add, that in *that* employment (while thus deprived of your loved society) consists my only happiness. But why not express my sentiments to yourself? I have nothing to say which I should blush to have known to all the world;--nothing to express in my letters to you but love and affection, and shall I blush for this? Or can I have a wish to conceal sentiments of such a nature for an object who I am so certain merits all my regard, and in whom the admiration of surrounding friends convinces me I am not mistaken. No, surely; 'tis my pride, my chiefest glory, to love you; and when you think me worthy of commendation, *that* praise, and *that* only, can make me vain.

I shall not therefore write to you, my dearest brother, in a private manner, for it is unnecessary, and I abhor all deceit; in which I know you agree with me.'

To her sister Mary in the Isle of Man she says, 'With respect to that little wretch Hallet, his intrepidity in court was astonishing; and after every evidence had spoken highly in Peter's favour, and given testimony of his innocence, so strong that not a doubt was entertained of his acquittal, *he* declared, unasked, that while Bligh was upon deck, he (Hallet) saw him look at and speak to Peter. What he said to him Hallet could not hear, (being at the distance of twenty feet from Bligh, and Peter was twenty feet farther off, consequently a distance of forty feet separated Mr. Bligh and my brother); but he added that Peter, on *hearing* what Mr. Bligh said to him, *laughed* and turned contemptuously away. No other witness saw Peter laugh but Hallet; on the contrary, all agreed he wore a countenance on that day remarkably sorrowful; yet the effect of this cruel evidence was wonderful upon the minds of the Court, and they concluded by pronouncing the dreadful sentence, though at the same time accompanied by the strongest recommendation to mercy. Assure yourselves (I have it from Mr. Graham's own mouth), that Peter's honour is and will be as secure as his own; that every professional man, as well as every man of sense, of whatever denomination, does and will esteem him highly; that my dear uncle Pasley (who was in town the night before my arrival) is delighted with his worth; and that, in short, we shall at length be happy.'

From this time a daily correspondence passed between Peter Heywood and his sister Nessy, the latter indulging hope, even to a certainty, that she will not be deceived,--the other preaching up patience and resignation, with a full reliance on his innocence and integrity. 'Cheer up then,' says he, 'my dear Nessy; cherish *your hope*, and I will exercise *my patience*.' Indeed so perfectly calm was this young man under his dreadful calamity, that in a very few days after condemnation his brother says, 'While I write this, Peter is sitting by me making an Otaheitan vocabulary, and so happy and intent upon it, that I have scarcely an opportunity of saying a word to him; he is in excellent spirits, and I am convinced they are better and better every day.'

This vocabulary is a very extraordinary performance; it consists of one hundred full-written folio pages, the words alphabetically arranged, and all the syllables accented. It appears, from a passage in the *Voyage of the Duff*, that a copy of this vocabulary was of great use to the missionaries who were first sent to Otaheite in this ship.

During the delay which took place in carrying the sentence into execution, Commodore Pasley, Mr. Graham, and others, were indefatigable in their inquiries and exertions to ascertain what progress had been made in bringing to a happy issue the recommendation to the fountain of mercy: not less so was Nessy Heywood: from Mr. Graham she learnt what this excellent man considered to be the principal parts of the evidence that led to the conviction of her unhappy brother, which, having understood to be the following, she transmitted to her brother:--

First. That he assisted in hoisting out the launch.

Second. That he was seen by the carpenter resting his hand upon a cutlass.

Third. That on being called to by Lieutenant Bligh, he laughed.

Fourth. That he remained in the *Bounty* instead of accompanying Bligh in the launch.

On these points of the evidence, Mr. Heywood made the following comments, which he sent from Portsmouth to his sister in town.

> 'Peter Heywood's Remarks upon material points of the evidence which was given at his trial, on board the *Duke*, in Portsmouth Harbour.
>
> '**First. *That I assisted in hoisting out the launch.*** --This boat was asked for by the captain and his officers, and whoever assisted in hoisting her out were their friends; for if the captain had been sent away in the cutter (which was Christian's first intention), he could not have taken with him more than nine or ten men, whereas the launch carried nineteen. The boatswain, the master, the gunner, and the carpenter say, in their evidence, that they considered me as helping the captain on this occasion.
>
> 'Second. That I was seen by the carpenter resting my hand on a cutlass.--I was seen in this position by no other person

than the carpenter--no other person therefore could be intimidated by my appearance. Was the carpenter intimidated by it?--No. So far from being afraid of me, he did not even look upon me in the light of a person armed, but pointed out to me the danger there was of my being thought so, and I immediately took away my hand from the cutlass, upon which I had very innocently put it when I was in a state of stupor. The Court was particularly pointed in its inquiries into this circumstance; and the carpenter was pressed to declare, on the oath he had taken, and after maturely considering the matter, whether he did, at the time he saw me so situated, or had since been inclined to believe, that, under all the circumstances of the case, I could be considered as an armed man, to which he unequivocally answered, No; and he gave some good reasons (which will be found in his evidence) for thinking that I had not a wish to be armed during the mutiny. The master, the boatswain, the gunner, Mr. Hayward, Mr. Hallet, and John Smith (who, with the carpenter, were all the witnesses belonging to the *Bounty*), say, in their evidence, that they did not, ***any of them,*** see me armed; and the boatswain and the carpenter further say, in the most pointed terms, that they considered me to be one of the captain's party, and ***by no means*** as belonging to the mutineers: and the master, the boatswain, the carpenter, the gunner, all declare that, from what they observed on my conduct during the mutiny, and from a recollection of my behaviour previous thereto, they were convinced I would have afforded them all the assistance in my power, if an opportunity had offered to retake the ship.

'Third. That, upon being called to by the captain, I laughed.--If this was believed by the Court, it must have had, I am afraid, a very great effect upon its judgement; for, if viewed in too serious a light, it would seem to bring together and combine a number of trifling circumstances, which by themselves could only be treated merely as matters of suspicion. It was no doubt, therefore, received with caution, and considered with the utmost candour. The countenance, I grant, on some other occasions, may warrant an opinion of good or evil existing in the mind; but on the momentous events of life and death, it is surely by much too indefinite and hazardous even to listen to for a moment. The different ways of expressing our various passions are, with many, as variable as the features they wear. Tears have often been, nay generally are, the relief of excessive joy, while misery and dejection have, many a time, disguised themselves in a smile; and convulsive laughs have betrayed the anguish of an almost broken heart. To judge, therefore, the principles of the heart, by the barometer of the face, is as erroneous as it would be absurd and unjust. This matter may likewise be considered in another point of view. Mr. Hallet says I laughed in consequence of being called to by the captain, who was abaft the mizen-mast, while I was upon the platform near the fore hatchway, a distance of more than thirty feet: if the captain intended I should hear him, and there can be no doubt that he wished it--if he really called to me, he must have exerted his voice, and very considerably too, upon such an occasion and in such a situation; and yet Mr. Hallet himself, who, by being on the quarter-deck, could not have been half the distance from the captain that I was, even he, I say, could not hear what was said to me: how then, in the name of God, was it possible that I should have heard the captain at all, situated, as I must have been, in the midst of noisy confusion? And if I did not hear him, which I most solemnly aver to be the truth, even granting that I laughed (which, however, in my present awful situation I declare I believe I did not), it could not have been at what the captain said. Upon this ground, then, I hope I shall stand acquitted of this charge, for if the crime derives its guilt from the knowledge I had of the captain's speaking to me, it follows, of course, that if I did not hear him speak, there could be no crime in my laughing. It may, however, very fairly be asked, why Mr. Hallet did not make known that the captain was calling to me? His duty to the captain, if not his friendship for me, should have prompted him to it; and the peculiarity of our situation required this act of kindness at his hands.[29] I shall only observe further upon this head, that the boatswain, the carpenter, and Mr. Hayward, who saw more of me than any other of the witnesses, did say in their evidence, that I had rather a sorrowful countenance on the day of the mutiny.

'Fourth. That I remained on board the ship, instead of going in the boat with the captain.--That I was at first alarmed and afraid of going into the boat I will not pretend to deny; but that afterwards I wished to accompany the captain, and should have done it, if I had not been prevented by Thompson, who confined me below by the order of Churchill, is clearly proved by the evidence of several of the witnesses. The boatswain says, that just before he left the ship I went below, and in passing him said something about a bag--(it was, that I would put a few things into a bag and follow him); the carpenter says he saw me go below at this time; and both those witnesses say that they heard the master-at-arms call to Thompson "*to keep them below*." The point, therefore, will be to prove to whom this order, "*keep them below*," would apply. The boatswain and carpenter say they have no doubt of its meaning me as one; and that it must have been so, I shall have very little difficulty in showing, by the following statement:--

'There remained on board the ship after the boat put off, twenty-five men. Messrs. Hayward and Hallet have proved that the following were under arms:--Christian, Hillbrant, Millward, Burkitt, Muspratt, Ellison, Sumner, Smith, Young, Skinner, Churchill, M'Koy, Quintal, Morrison, Williams, Thompson, Mills, and Brown, in all eighteen. The master (and upon this occasion I may be allowed to quote from the captain's printed narrative) mentions Martin as one, which makes the number of armed men nineteen, none of whom, we may reasonably suppose, were ordered to be kept below. Indeed, Mr. Hayward says, that there were at the least eighteen of them upon deck, when he went into the boat; and if Thompson, the sentinel over the arm-chest, be added to them, it exactly agrees with the number above-named; there remains then six, to whom Churchill's order, "*keep them below,*" might apply, namely, Heywood, Stewart, Coleman, Norman, M'Intosh, and Byrne.

'Could Byrne have been one of them? *No*, for he was in the cutter alongside. Could Coleman have been one of them? *No*, for he was at the gangway when the captain and officers went into the launch, and aft upon the taffrail when the boat was veered astern. Could Norman have been one of them? *No*, for he was speaking to the officers. Could M'Intosh have been one of them? *No*, for he was with Coleman and Norman, desiring the captain and officers to take notice that they were not concerned in the mutiny. It could then have applied to nobody but to Mr. Stewart and myself; and by this order of Churchill, therefore, was I prevented from going with the captain in the boat.

'The foregoing appear to me the most material points of

evidence on the part of the prosecution. My defence being very full, and the body of evidence in my favour too great to admit of observation in this concise manner, I shall refer for an opinion thereon to the minutes of the court-martial.

(Signed) 'P. HEYWOOD.'

There is a note in Marshall's *Naval Biography*,[30] furnished by Captain Heywood, which shows one motive for keeping him and Stewart in the ship. It is as follows:--'Mr. Stewart was no sooner released than he demanded of Christian the reason of his detention; upon which the latter denied having given any directions to that effect; and his assertion was corroborated by Churchill, who declared that he had kept both him and Mr. Heywood below, knowing it was their intention to go away with Bligh; "in which case," added he, "what would become of us, if any thing should happen to you; who is there but yourself and them to depend upon in navigating the ship?"' It may be suspected, however, that neither Christian nor Churchill told the exact truth, and that Mr. Heywood's case is, in point of fact, much stronger than he ever could have imagined; and that if Bligh had not acted the part of a prejudiced and unfair man towards him, he would have been acquitted by the Court on the same ground that Coleman, Norman, M'Intosh, and Byrne were,--namely, that they were detained in the ship against their will, as stated by Bligh in the narrative on which they were tried, and also in his printed report. It has before been observed, that many things are set down in Bligh's original manuscript journal, that have not appeared in any published document; and on this part of the subject there is, in the former, the following very important admission. 'As for the officers, whose cabins were in the cockpit, there was no relief for them; **they endeavoured to come to my assistance, but were not allowed to put their heads above the hatchway**.' To say, therefore, that in the suppression of this passage Bligh acted with prejudice and unfairness, is to make use of mild terms; it has more the appearance of a deliberate act of malice, by which two innocent men might have been condemned to suffer an ignominious death, one of whom was actually brought into this predicament;--the other only escaped it by a premature death. It may be asked, how did Bligh know that Stewart and Heywood endeavoured, but were not allowed, to come to his assistance? Confined as he was on the quarter-deck, how could he know what was going on below? The answer is, he must have known it from Christian himself; Churchill, no doubt, acted entirely by his leader's orders, and the latter could give no orders that were not heard by Bligh, whom he never left, but held the cord by which his hands were fettered, till he was forced into the boat. Churchill was quite right as to the motive of keeping these young officers; but Christian had no doubt another and a stronger motive: he knew how necessary it was to interpose a sort of barrier between himself and his mutinous gang; he was too good an adept not to know that seamen will always pay a more ready and cheerful obedience to officers who are **_gentlemen_**, than to those who may have risen to command from among themselves. It is indeed a common observation in the service, that officers who have risen from **_before the mast_** are generally the greatest tyrants.[31] It was Bligh's misfortune not to have been educated in the cockpit of a man of war, among young gentlemen, which is to the navy what a public school is to those who are to move in civil society. What painful sufferings to the individual, and how much misery to an affectionate family might have been spared, had Bligh, instead of suppressing, only suffered the passage to stand as originally written in his journal!

The **_remarks_** of young Heywood above recited, were received and transmitted by his sister Nessy in a letter to the Earl of Chatham, then first Lord of the Admiralty, of which the following is a copy.

'**_Great Russell Street, 11th Oct_**. 1792.

> 'MY LORD,--To a nobleman of your lordship's known humanity and
> excellence of heart, I dare hope that the unfortunate cannot
> plead in vain. Deeply impressed as I therefore am, with
> sentiments of the most profound respect for a character which
> I have been ever taught to revere, and alas I nearly
> interested as I must be in the subject of these lines, may I
> request your lordship will generously pardon a sorrowful and
> mourning sister, for presuming to offer the enclosed [remarks]
> for your candid perusal. It contains a few observations made

> by my most unfortunate and tenderly beloved brother, Peter Heywood, endeavouring to elucidate some parts of the evidence given at the court-martial lately held at Portsmouth upon himself and other prisoners of his Majesty's ship ***Bounty***. When I assure you, my lord, that he is dearer and more precious to me than any object on earth--nay, infinitely more valuable than life itself--that, deprived of him, the word misery would but ill express my complicated wretchedness--and that, on his fate, my own, and (shall I not add?) that of a tender, fond, and alas! widowed mother, depends, I am persuaded you will not wonder, nor be offended, that I am thus bold in conjuring your lordship will consider, with your usual candour and benevolence, the "Observations" I now offer you, as well as the painful situation of my dear and unhappy brother.--I have the honour, etc.
>
> NESSY HEYWOOD.'

Whether this letter and its enclosure produced any effect on the mind of Lord Chatham does not appear; but no immediate steps were taken, nor was any answer given; and this amiable young lady and her friends were suffered to remain in the most painful state of suspense for another fortnight. A day or two before the warrant was despatched, that excellent man, Mr. Graham, writes thus to Mrs. Heywood.

> 'MY DEAR MADAM,--If feeling for the distresses and rejoicing in the happiness of others denote a heart which entitles the owner of it to the confidence of the good and virtuous, I would fain be persuaded that mine has been so far interested in your misfortunes, and is now so pleased with the prospect of your being made happy, as cannot fail to procure me the friendship of your family, which, as it is my ambition, it cannot cease to be my desire to cultivate.

'Unused to the common rewards which are sought after in this world, I will profess to anticipate more real pleasure and satisfaction from the simple declaration of you and yours, that "we accept of your services, and we thank you for them," than it is in common minds to conceive; but, fearful lest a too grateful sense should be entertained of the friendly offices I have been engaged in (which, however, I ought to confess, I was prompted to, in the first place, by a remembrance of the many obligations I owed to Commodore Pasley), I must beg you will recollect that, by sending to me your charming Nessy (and if strong affection may plead such a privilege, I may be allowed to call her *my* daughter also), you would have over-paid me if my trouble had been ten times, and my uneasiness ten thousand times greater than they were, upon what I once thought the melancholy, but now deem the fortunate, occasion which has given me the happiness of her acquaintance. Thus far, my dear Madam, I have written to please myself. Now, for what must please you--and in which, too, I have my share of satisfaction.

'The business, though not publicly known, is most certainly finished, and what I had my doubts about yesterday, I am satisfied of to-day. Happy, happy, happy family! accept of my congratulations--not for what it is in the power of words to express--but for what I know you will feel, upon being told that your beloved Peter will soon be restored to your bosom, with every virtue that can adorn a man, and ensure to him an affectionate, a tender, and truly welcome reception.'

At the foot of this letter Nessy writes thus:--

'Now, my dearest mamma, did you ever in all your life read so charming a letter? Be assured it is exactly characteristic of the benevolent writer. What would I give to be transported (though only for a moment) to your elbow, that I might see you read it? What will you feel, when you know assuredly that you may with certainty believe its contents? Well may Mr. Graham call us happy! for never felicity could equal ours! Don't expect connected sentences from me at present, for this joy makes me almost delirious. Adieu! love to all--I need not say be happy and blessed as I am at this dear hour, my beloved mother.--Your most affectionate,

N. H.'

On the 24th October, the king's warrant was despatched from the Admiralty, granting a full and free pardon to Heywood and Morrison, a respite for Muspratt, which was followed by a pardon; and for carrying the sentence of Ellison, Burkitt, and Millward into execution, which was done on the 29th, on board his Majesty's ship ***Brunswick***, in Portsmouth harbour. On this melancholy occasion, Captain Hamond reports that 'the criminals behaved with great penitence and decorum, acknowledged the justice of their sentence for the crime of which they had been found guilty, and exhorted their fellow-sailors to take warning by their untimely fate, and whatever might be their hardships, never to forget their obedience to their officers, as a duty they owed to their king and country.' The captain adds, 'A party from each ship in the harbour, and at Spithead, attended the execution, and from the reports I have received, the example seems to have made a great impression upon the minds of all the ships' companies present.'

The same warrant that carried with it affliction to the friends of these unfortunate men, was the harbinger of joy to the family and friends of young Heywood. The happy intelligence was communicated to his affectionate Nessy on the 26th, who instantly despatched the joyful tidings to her anxious mother in the following characteristic note:--

Friday, 26th October, four o'clock.

>'Oh, blessed hour!--little did I think, my beloved friends, when I closed my letter this morning, that before night I should be out of my senses with joy!--this moment, this ecstatic moment, brought the enclosed.[32] I cannot speak my happiness; let it be sufficient to say, that in a very few hours our angel Peter will be FREE! Mr. Graham goes this night to Portsmouth, and to-morrow, or next day at farthest, I shall be--oh, heavens! what shall I be? I am already transported, even to pain; then how shall I bear to clasp him to the bosom of your happy, ah! how very happy, and affectionate
>
>NESSY HEYWOOD.'

>'I am too *mad* to write sense, but 'tis a pleasure I would not forgo to be the most reasonable being on earth. I asked Mr. Graham, who is at my elbow, if he would say anything to you, "Lord!" said he, "I can't say anything"; he is almost as mad as myself.'[33]

Mr. Graham writes, 'I have however my senses sufficiently about me not to suffer this to go without begging leave to congratulate you upon, and to assure you that I most sincerely sympathize and participate in the happiness which I am sure the enclosed will convey to the mother and sisters of my charming and beloved Nessy.'

This 'charming' girl next writes to Mr. Const, who attended as counsel for her brother, to acquaint him with the joyful intelligence, and thus concludes. 'I flatter myself you will partake in the joy which, notwithstanding it is so excessive at this moment, as almost to deprive me of my faculties, leaves me however sufficiently collected to assure you of the eternal gratitude and esteem with which I am,' etc.

To which Mr. Const, after congratulations and thanks for her polite attention, observes, 'Give me leave, my dear Miss Heywood, to assure you that the intelligence has given me a degree of pleasure which I have not terms to express, and it is even increased by knowing what you must experience on the event. Nor is it an immaterial reflection, that although your brother was unfortunately involved in the general calamity which gave birth to the charge, he is uncontaminated by the crime, for there was not a credible testimony of the slightest fact against him that can make the strictest friend deplore anything that has passed, except his sufferings; and his uniform conduct under them only proved how little he deserved them.'

Mr. Graham's impatience and generous anxiety to give the finishing stroke to this joyful event would not permit him to delay one moment in setting out for Portsmouth, and bringing up to his house in town the innocent sufferer, where they arrived on the morning of the 29th October. Miss Heywood can best speak of her own feelings.

> '*Great Russell Street, Monday Morning, 29th October,*
> *half-past ten o'clock--the brightest moment of my existence*!
>
>> 'MY DEAREST MAMMA,--I have seen him, clasped him to my bosom, and my felicity is beyond expression! In person he is almost even now as I could wish; in mind you know him an angel. I can write no more, but to tell you, that the three happiest beings at this moment on earth, are your most dutiful and affectionate children,
>>
>> 'NESSY HEYWOOD. 'PETER HEYWOOD. 'JAMES HEYWOOD.
>>
>> 'Love to and from all ten thousand times.'

The worthy Mr. Graham adds,

> 'If, my dearest Madam, it were ever given for mortals to be supremely blest on earth, mine to be sure must be the happy family. Heavens! with what unbounded extravagance have we been forming our wishes! and yet how far beyond our most unbounded

> wishes we are blest! Nessy, Maria,[34] Peter, and James, I see, have all been endeavouring to express their feelings. I will not fail in any such attempt, for I will not attempt anything beyond an assurance that the scene I have been witness of, and in which I am happily so great a sharer, beggars all description. Permit me however to offer my most sincere congratulations upon the joyful occasion.'

This amiable young lady, some of whose letters have been introduced into this narrative, did not long survive her brother's liberty. This impassioned and most affectionate of sisters, with an excess of sensibility, which acted too powerfully on her bodily frame, sunk, as is often the case with such susceptible minds, on the first attack of consumption. She died within the year of her brother's liberation. On this occasion the following note from her afflicted mother appears among the papers from which the letters and poetry are taken.

> 'My dearest Nessy was seized, while on a visit at Major Yorke's, at Bishop's Grove near Tonbridge Wells, with a violent cold, and not taking proper care of herself, it soon turned to inflammation on her lungs, which carried her off at Hastings, to which place she was taken on the 5th September, to try if the change of air, and being near the sea, would recover her; but alas! it was too late for her to receive the wished for benefit, and she died there on the 25th of the same month 1793, and has left her only surviving parent a disconsolate mother, to lament, while ever she lives, with the most sincere and deep affliction, the irreparable loss of her most valuable, affectionate, and darling daughter.'[35]

But to return to Mr. Heywood. When the king's full and free pardon had been read to this young officer by Captain Montagu, with a suitable admonition and congratulation, he addressed that officer in the following terms,--so suitably characteristic of his noble and manly conduct throughout the whole of the distressing business in which he was innocently involved:--

> SIR,--When the sentence of the law was passed upon me, I received it, I trust, as became a man; and if it had been carried into execution, I should have met my fate, I hope, in a manner becoming a Christian. Your admonition cannot fail to make a lasting impression on my mind. I receive with gratitude my sovereign's mercy, for which my future life shall be faithfully devoted to his service.'[36]

And well did his future conduct fulfil that promise. Notwithstanding the inauspicious manner in which the first five years of his servitude in the navy had been passed, two of which were spent among mutineers and savages, and eighteen months as a close prisoner in irons, in which condition he was shipwrecked, and within an ace of perishing,--notwithstanding this unpromising commencement, he re-entered the naval service under the auspices of his uncle, Commodore Pasley, and Lord Hood, who presided at his trial, and who earnestly recommended him to embark again as a midshipman without delay, offering to take him into the *Victory*, under his own immediate patronage. In the course of his service, to qualify for the commission of lieutenant, he was under the respective commands of three or four distinguished officers, who had sat on his trial, from all of whom he received the most flattering proofs of esteem and approbation. To the application of Sir Thomas Pasley to Lord Spencer for his promotion, that nobleman, with that due regard he was always known to pay to the honour and interests of the navy, while individual claims were never overlooked, gave the following reply, which must have been highly gratifying to the feelings of Mr. Heywood and his family.

Admiralty, Jan. 13th, 1797.

> 'Sir,--I should have returned an earlier answer to your letter of the 6th instant, if I had not been desirous, before I answered it, to look over, with as much attention as was in my power, the proceedings on the Court-Martial held in the year

1792, by which Court Mr. Peter Heywood was condemned for being concerned in the mutiny on board the ***Bounty***. I felt this to be necessary, from having entertained a very strong opinion that it might be detrimental to the interests of his Majesty's service, if a person under such a predicament should be afterwards advanced to the higher and more conspicuous situations of the navy; but having, with great attention, perused the minutes of that Court-Martial, as far as they relate to Mr. Peter Heywood, I have now the satisfaction of being able to inform you, that I think his case was such an one, as, under all its circumstances (though I do not mean to say that the Court were not justified in their sentence), ought not to be considered as a bar to his further progress in his profession; more especially when the gallantry and propriety of his conduct, in his subsequent service, are taken into consideration. I shall, therefore, have no difficulty in mentioning him to the commander-in-chief on the station to which he belongs, as a person from whose promotion, on a proper opportunity, I shall derive much satisfaction, more particularly from his being so nearly connected with you.--I have the honour to be, etc.

(Signed) SPENCER.'

It is not here intended to follow Mr. Heywood through his honourable career of service, during the long and arduous contest with France, and in the several commands with which he was entrusted. In a note of his own writing it is stated, that on paying off the ***Montague***, in July, 1816, he came on shore, after having been actively employed ***at sea*** twenty-seven years, six months, one week, and five days, out of a servitude in the navy of twenty-nine years, seven months, and one day. Having reached nearly the top of the list of captains, he died in this present year, leaving behind him a high and unblemished character in that service, of which he was a most honourable, intelligent, and distinguished member.

CHAPTER VIII
THE LAST OF THE MUTINEERS

Who by repentance is not satisfied,
Is nor of heaven nor earth; for these are pleased;
By penitence th' Eternal's wrath's appeased.

Twenty years had passed away, and the *Bounty*, and Fletcher Christian, and the piratical crew that he had carried off with him in that ship, had long ceased to occupy a thought in the public mind. Throughout the whole of that eventful period, the attention of all Europe had been absorbed in the contemplation of 'enterprises of great pith and moment,'--of the revolutions of empires--the bustle and business of warlike preparations--the movements of hostile armies--battles by sea and land, and of all 'the pomp and circumstance of glorious war.' If the subject of the *Bounty* was accidentally mentioned, it was merely to express an opinion that this vessel, and those within her, had gone down to the bottom, or that some savage islanders had inflicted on the mutineers that measure of retribution so justly due to their crime. It happened, however, some years before the conclusion of this war of unexampled duration, that an accidental discovery, as interesting as it was wholly unexpected, was brought to light, in consequence of an American trading vessel having by mere chance approached one of those numerous islands in the Pacific, against whose steep and iron-bound shores the surf almost everlastingly rolls with such tremendous violence, as to bid defiance to any attempt of boats to land, except at particular times and in very few places.

The first intimation of this extraordinary discovery was transmitted by Sir Sydney Smith from Rio de Janeiro, and received at the Admiralty, 14th May, 1809. It was conveyed to him from Valparaiso by Lieutenant Fitzmaurice, and was as follows:--

'Captain Folger, of the American ship *Topaz*, of Boston, relates that, upon landing on Pitcairn's Island, in lat. 25 deg. 2' S., long. 130 deg. W., he found there an Englishman of the name of Alexander Smith, the only person remaining of nine that escaped in his Majesty's late ship *Bounty*, Captain W. Bligh. Smith relates that, after putting Captain Bligh in the boat, Christian, the leader of the mutiny, took command of the ship and went to Otaheite, where the great part of the crew left her, except Christian, Smith, and seven others, who each took wives and six Otaheitan men-servants, and shortly after arrived at the said island (Pitcairn), where they ran the ship on shore, and broke her up; this event took place in the year 1790.

'About four years after their arrival (a great jealousy existing), the Otaheitans secretly revolted, and killed every Englishman except himself whom they severely wounded in the neck with a pistol ball. The same night, the widows of the deceased Englishmen arose and put to death the whole of the Otaheitans, leaving Smith, the only man alive upon the island, with eight or nine women and several small children. On his recovery, he applied himself to tilling the ground, so that it now produces plenty of yams, cocoa-nuts, bananas, and plantains; hogs and poultry in abundance. There are now some grown-up men and women, children of the mutineers, on the island, the whole population amounting to about thirty-five, who acknowledge Smith as father and commander of them all; they all speak English, and have been educated by him (as Captain Folger represents) in a religious and moral way.

'The second mate of the *Topaz* asserts that Christian, the

ringleader, became insane shortly after their arrival on the island, and threw himself off the rocks into the sea; another died of a fever before the massacre of the remaining six took place. The island is badly supplied with water, sufficient only for the present inhabitants, and no anchorage.

'Smith gave to Captain Folger a chronometer made by Kendall, which was taken from him by the Governor of Juan Fernandez.

'Extracted from the log-book of the *Topaz*, 29th Sept. 1808.

(Signed) 'WM. FITZMAURICE, Lieut. 'Valparaiso, Oct. 10th, 1808.'

This narrative stated two facts that established its general authenticity--the name of Alexander Smith, who was one of the mutineers, and the name of the maker of the chronometer, with which the *Bounty* was actually supplied. Interesting as this discovery was considered to be, it does not appear that any steps were taken in consequence of this authenticated information, the government being at that time probably too much engaged in the events of the war; nor was anything further heard of this interesting little society, until the latter part of 1814, when a letter was transmitted by Rear Admiral Hotham, then cruising off the coast of America, from Mr. Folger himself, to the same effect as the preceding extract from his log, but dated March, 1813.

In the first-mentioned year (1814) we had two frigates cruising in the Pacific,--the *Briton*, commanded by Sir Thomas Staines, and the *Tagus*, by Captain Pipon. The following letter from the former of these officers was received at the Admiralty early in the year 1815.

Briton, Valparaiso, 18th Oct., 1814.

'I have the honour to inform you that on my passage from the Marquesas islands to this port, on the morning of the 17th

September, I fell in with an island where none is laid down in the Admiralty or other charts, according to the several chronometers of the ***Briton*** and ***Tagus***. I therefore hove to, until daylight, and then closed to ascertain whether it was inhabited, which I soon discovered it to be, and, to my great astonishment, found that every individual on the island (forty in number), spoke very good English. They proved to be the descendants of the deluded crew of the ***Bounty***, who, from Otaheite, proceeded to the above-mentioned island, where the ship was burnt.

'Christian appeared to have been the leader and sole cause of the mutiny in that ship. A venerable old man, named John Adams, is the only surviving Englishman of those who last quitted Otaheite in her, and whose exemplary conduct, and fatherly care of the whole of the little colony, could not but command admiration. The pious manner in which all those born on the island have been reared, the correct sense of religion which has been instilled into their young minds by this old man, has given him the pre-eminence over the whole of them, to whom they look up as the father of one and the whole family.

'A son of Christian was the first born on the island, now about twenty-five years of age, named Thursday October Christian; the elder Christian fell a sacrifice to the jealousy of an Otaheitan man, within three or four years after their arrival on the island. The mutineers were accompanied thither by six Otaheitan men and twelve women; the former were all swept away by desperate contentions between them and the Englishmen, and five of the latter died at different periods, leaving at present only one man (Adams) and seven women of the original settlers.

'The island must undoubtedly be that called Pitcairn, although erroneously laid down in the charts. We had the altitude of the meridian sun close to it, which gave us 25 deg. 4' S. latitude, and 130 deg. 25' W. longitude, by the chronometers of the *Briton* and *Tagus*.

'It produces in abundance yams, plantains, hogs, goats, and fowls; but the coast affords no shelter for a ship or vessel of any description; neither could a ship water there without great difficulty.

'I cannot, however, refrain from offering my opinion, that it is well worthy the attention of our laudable religious societies, particularly that for propagating the Christian religion, the whole of the inhabitants speaking the Otaheitan tongue as well as the English.

'During the whole of the time they have been on the island, only one ship has ever communicated with them, which took place about six years since, and this was the American ship *Topaz*, of Boston, Mayhew Folger, master.

'The island is completely iron-bound with rocky shores, and the landing in boats must be at all times difficult, although the island may be safely approached within a short distance by a ship. (Signed) T. STAINES.'

Such was the first official account received of this little colony. As some further particulars of a society so singular, in all respects, were highly desirable, Captain Pipon, on being applied to, had the kindness to draw up the following narrative, which has all the freshness and attraction of a first communication with a new people.

Captain Pipon takes a more extended view, in his private letter,[37] of the condition of this little society. He observes, that when they first saw the island, the latitude, made by the *Tagus*, was 24 deg. 40' S. and longitude 130 deg. 24' W., the ships being then distant from it five or six leagues; and, as in none of the charts in their possession was any land laid down in or near this meridian, they were extremely puzzled to make out what island it could possibly be; for Pitcairn's Island, being the only one known in the neighbourhood, was represented to be in longitude 133 deg. 24' W.[38] If this new discovery as they supposed it to be, awakened their curiosity, it was still more excited when they ran in for the land the next morning, on perceiving a few huts, neatly built, amidst plantations laid out apparently with something like order and regularity; and these appearances confirmed them more than ever that it could not be Pitcairn's Island, because that was described by navigators to be uninhabited. Presently they observed a few natives coming down a steep descent with their canoes on their shoulders; and in a few minutes perceived one of those little vessels darting through a heavy surf, and paddling off towards the ships; but their astonishment was extreme when, on coming alongside, they were hailed in the English language with 'Won't you heave us a rope now?'

The first young man that sprang, with extraordinary alacrity, up the side, and stood before them on the deck, said, in reply to the question, 'Who are you?'--that his name was Thursday October Christian, son of the late Fletcher Christian, by an Otaheitan mother; that he was the first born on the island, and that he was so called because he was brought into the world on a Thursday in October. Singularly strange as all this was to Sir Thomas Staines and Captain Pipon, this youth soon satisfied them that he was no other than the person he represented himself to be, and that he was fully acquainted with the whole history of the ***Bounty***; and, in short, that the island before them was the retreat of the mutineers of that ship. Young Christian was, at this time, about twenty-four years of age, a fine tall youth, full six feet high, with dark, almost black, hair, and a countenance open and extremely interesting. As he wore no clothes except a piece of cloth round his loins, and a straw hat, ornamented with black cocks'-feathers, his fine figure and well-shaped muscular limbs were displayed to great advantage, and attracted general admiration. His body was much tanned by exposure to the weather, and his countenance had a brownish cast, unmixed however with that tinge of red so common among the natives of the Pacific islands.

'Added to a great share of good humour, we were glad to trace,' says Captain Pipon, 'in his benevolent countenance, all the features of an honest English face.' He told them he was married to a woman much older than himself, one of those that accompanied his father from Otaheite. The ingenuous manner in which he answered all questions put to him, and his whole deportment, created a lively interest among the officers of the ship, who, while they admired, could not but regard him with feelings of tenderness and compassion; his manner, too, of speaking English was exceedingly pleasing, and correct both in grammar and pronunciation. His companion was a fine handsome youth of seventeen or eighteen years of age, of the name of George Young, son of Young the midshipman.

If the astonishment of the two captains was great on making, as they thought, this first and extraordinary discovery of a people who had been so long forgotten, and in hearing the offspring of these offenders speaking their language correctly, their surprise and interest were still more highly excited when, on Sir Thomas Staines taking the two youths below, and setting before them something to eat, they both rose up, and one of them, placing his hands together in a posture of devotion, pronounced, distinctly and with emphasis, in a pleasing tone of voice, the words, 'For what we are going to receive the Lord make us truly thankful.'

The youths were themselves greatly surprised at the sight of so many novel objects--the size of the ship--of the guns, and everything around them. Observing a cow, they were at first somewhat alarmed, and expressed a doubt whether it was a huge goat or a horned hog, these being the only two species of quadrupeds they had ever seen. A little dog amused them much. 'Oh! what a pretty little thing it is!' exclaimed Young, 'I know it is a dog, for I have heard of such an animal.'

These young men informed the two captains of many singular events that had taken place among the first settlers, but referred them for further particulars to an old man on shore, whose name, they said, was John Adams, the only surviving Englishman that came away in the ***Bounty***, at which time he was called Alexander Smith.

This information induced the two captains to go on shore, desirous of learning correctly from this old man the fate, not only of Christian, but of the rest of his deluded accomplices, who had adhered to his fortunes. The landing they found to be difficult, and not wholly free from danger; but, with the assistance of their two able conductors, they passed the surf among many rocks, and reached the shore without any other inconvenience than a complete wetting. Old Adams, having ascertained that the two officers alone had landed, and without arms, concluded they had no intention to take him prisoner, and ventured to come down to the beach, from whence he conducted them to his house. He was accompanied by his wife, a very old woman, and nearly blind. It seems they were both at first considerably alarmed; the sight of the king's uniform, after so many years, having no doubt brought fresh to the recollection of Adams the scene that occurred in the *Bounty*, in which he bore so conspicuous a part. Sir Thomas Staines, however, to set his mind at ease, assured him, that so far from having come to the island with any intention to take him away, they were not even aware that such a person as himself existed. Captain Pipon observes, 'that although in the eye of the law they could only consider him in the light of a criminal of the deepest dye, yet that it would have been an act of the greatest cruelty and inhumanity to have taken him away from his little family, who, in such a case, would have been left to experience the greatest misery and distress, and ultimately, in all probability, would have perished of want.'

Adams, however, pretended that he had no great share in the mutiny: said that he was sick in bed when it broke out, and was afterwards compelled to take a musket in his hand; and expressed his readiness to go in one of the ships to England, and seemed rather desirous to do so. On this being made known to the members of the little society, a scene of considerable distress was witnessed; his daughter, a fine young woman, threw her arms about his neck, entreating him not to think of leaving them and all his little children to perish. All the women burst into tears, and the young men stood motionless and absorbed in grief; but on their being assured that he should, on no account, be molested, 'it is impossible,' says Captain Pipon, 'to describe the universal joy that these poor people manifested, and the gratitude they expressed for the kindness and consideration shown to them.'

They now learned from Adams that Fletcher Christian, on finding no good anchorage close to the island, and the *Bounty* being too weakly manned again to entrust themselves in her at sea, determined to run her into a small creek against the cliff, in order the more conveniently to get out of her such articles as might be of use, or necessary, for forming an establishment on the island, and to land the hogs, goats, and poultry, which they had brought from Otaheite; and having accomplished this point he ordered her to be set on fire, with the view, probably, of preventing any escape from the island, and also to remove an object that, if seen, might excite the curiosity of some passing vessel, and thus be the means of discovering his retreat. His plan succeeded, and by Adams's account, everything went on smoothly for a short time; but it was clear enough that this misguided and ill-fated young man was never happy after the rash and criminal step he had taken; that he was always sullen and morose; and committed so many acts of wanton oppression, as very soon incurred the hatred and detestation of his companions in crime, over whom he practised that same overbearing conduct, of which he accused his commander Bligh. The object he had in view when he last left Otaheite had now been accomplished; he had discovered an uninhabited island out of the common track of ships, and established himself and his associates; so far there was a chance that he had escaped all pursuit; but there was no escaping from

> Those rods of scorpions and those whips of steel
> Which conscience shakes.

The fate of this misguided young man, brought on by his ill-treatment both of his associates and the Indians he had carried off with him, was such as might be expected--he was shot by an Otaheitan while digging in his field, about eleven months after they had settled on the island, and his death was only the commencement of feuds and assassinations, which ended in the total destruction of the whole party, except Adams and Young. By the account of the former, the settlers from this time became divided into two parties, and their grievances and quarrels proceeded to such a height, that each took every opportunity of putting the other to death. Old John Adams was himself shot through the neck, but the ball having entered the fleshy part only, he was enabled to make his escape, and avoid the fury of his assailants. The immediate cause of Christian's murder was his having forcibly seized on the wife of one of the Otaheite men, which so exasperated the rest, that they not only sought the life of the offender, but of others also, who might, as they thought, be disposed to pursue the same course.

This interesting little colony was now found to contain about forty-six persons, mostly grown-up young people, with a few infants. The young men all born on the island were finely formed, athletic and handsome--their countenances open and pleasing, indicating much benevolence and goodness of heart, but the young women particularly were objects of attraction, being tall, robust, and beautifully formed, their faces beaming with smiles, and indicating unruffled good humour; while their manners and demeanour exhibited a degree of modesty and bashfulness, that would have done honour to the most virtuous and enlightened people on earth. Their teeth are described as beautifully white, like the finest ivory, and perfectly regular, without a single exception; and all of them, both male and female, had the marked expression of English features, though not exactly the clear red and white, that distinguish English skins, theirs being the colour of what we call brunette. Captain Pipon thinks that from such a race of people, consisting of fine young men and handsome well-formed women, there may be expected to arise hereafter, in this little colony, a race of people possessing in a high degree the physical qualifications of great strength, united with symmetry of form and regularity of feature.

But their personal qualifications, attractive as they were, excited less admiration than the account which Adams gave of their virtuous conduct. He assured his visitors that not one instance of debauchery or immoral conduct had occurred among these young people, since their settlement on the island; nor did he ever hear, or believe, that any one instance had occurred of a young woman having suffered indecent liberties to be taken with her. Their native modesty, assisted by the precepts of religion and morality, instilled into their young minds by John Adams, had hitherto preserved these interesting people from every kind of debauchery. The young women told Captain Pipon, with great simplicity, that they were not married, and that their father, as they called Adams, had told them it was right they should wait with patience till they had acquired sufficient property to bring up a young family, before they thought of marrying; and that they always followed his advice because they knew it to be good.

It appeared that, from the time when Adams was left alone on the island, the sole survivor of all the males that had landed from the **Bounty**, European and Otaheitan, the greatest harmony had prevailed in their little society; they all declared that no serious quarrels ever occurred among them, though a few hasty words might now and then be uttered, but, to make use of their own expression, they were only quarrels of the mouth. Adams assured his visitors that they were all strictly honest in all their dealings, lending or exchanging their various articles of live-stock or produce with each other, in the most friendly manner; and if any little dispute occurred, he never found any difficulty to rectify the mistake or misunderstanding that might have caused it, to the satisfaction of both parties. In their general intercourse they speak the English language commonly; and even the old Otaheitan women have picked up a good deal of this language. The young people, both male and female, speak it with a pleasing accent, and their voices are extremely harmonious.

The little village of Pitcairn is described as forming a pretty square; the house of John Adams, with its out-houses, occupying the upper corner, near a large banyan tree, and that of Thursday October Christian the lower corner opposite to it. The centre space is a fine open lawn, where the poultry wander, and is fenced round so as to prevent the intrusion of the hogs and goats. It was obviously visible, from the manner in which the grounds were laid out, and the plantations formed that, in this little establishment, the labour and ingenuity of European hands had been employed. In their houses they have a good deal of decent furniture, consisting of beds and bedsteads, with coverings. They have also tables and large chests for their clothing; and their linen is made from the bark of a certain tree, and the manufacture of it is the employment of the elderly portion of the women. The bark is first soaked, then beaten with square pieces of wood, of the breadth of one's hand, hollowed out into grooves, and the labour is continued until it is brought to the breadth required, in the same manner as the process is conducted in Otaheite.

The younger part of the females are obliged to attend, with old Adams and their brothers, to the culture of the land, and Captain Pipon thinks this may be one reason why this old director of the work does not countenance too early marriages, for, as he very properly observed, when once they become mothers, they are less capable of hard labour, being obliged to attend to their children; and, judging from appearance, 'one may conclude,' says the Captain, 'they would be prolific'; that 'he did not see how it could be otherwise, considering the regularity of their lives, their simple and excellent though abstemious mode of living, their meals consisting chiefly of a vegetable diet, with now and then good pork and occasionally fish.'

The young girls, although they have only the example of the Otaheitan mothers to follow in their dress, are modestly clothed, having generally a piece of cloth of their own manufacture, reaching from the waist to the knees, and a mantle, or something of that nature, thrown loosely over the shoulders, and hanging sometimes as low as the ankles: this mantle, however, is frequently thrown aside, being used rather as a shelter for their bodies from the heat of the sun, or the severity of the weather, than for the sake of attaching any idea of modesty to the upper part of the person being uncovered; and it is not possible, he says, to behold finer forms than are exhibited by this partial exposure. Captain Pipon observes, 'it was pleasing to see the good taste and quickness with which they form little shades or parasols of green leaves, to place over the head, or bonnets, to keep the sun from their eyes. A young girl made one of these in my presence, with such neatness and alacrity, as to satisfy me that a fashionable dressmaker of London would be delighted with the simplicity and elegant taste of these untaught females.' The same young girl, he says, accompanied them to the boat, carrying on her shoulders, as a present, a large basket of yams, 'over such roads and down such precipices, as were scarcely passable by any creatures except goats, and over which we could scarcely scramble with the help of our hands. Yet with this load on her shoulders, she skipped from rock to rock like a young roe.'

'But,' says Captain Pipon, 'what delighted us most, was the conviction which John Adams had impressed on the minds of these young people, of the propriety and necessity of returning thanks to the Almighty for the many blessings they enjoy. They never omit saying grace before and after meals, and never think of touching food without asking a blessing from Him who gave it. The Lord's Prayer and the Creed they repeat morning and evening.'

Captain Pipon imagines the island to be about six miles long, and perhaps three or four miles broad, covered with wood; the soil apparently very rich, and the variety of products great and valuable, but much labour would seem to be required to clear away the woods. The dimensions here given, however, are much greater than they have subsequently been found to be.

The visitors having supplied these poor people with some tools, kettles, and other articles, such as the high surf would allow them, with the assistance of the natives, to land, but to no great extent, the two officers again passed through the surf, with the same assistance, and took leave of these interesting people--satisfied that the island is so well fortified by nature, as to oppose an invincible barrier to an invading enemy; that there was no spot apparently where a boat could land with safety, and perhaps not more than one where it could land at all; an everlasting swell of the ocean, rolling in on every side, is dashed into foam against its rocky and iron-bound shores.

Such were the first details that were received respecting this young settlement. It may here be remarked that, at the time when Folger visited the island, Alexander Smith went by his proper name, and that he had changed it to John Adams in the intermediate time between his visit and that of Sir Thomas Staines; but it does not appear, in any of the accounts which have been given of this interesting little colony, when or for what reason he assumed the latter name. It could not be with any view to concealment, for he freely communicated his history to Folger, and equally so to every subsequent visitor.

The interesting account of Captains Sir Thomas Stairies and Pipon, in 1814, produced as little effect on the government as that of Folger; and nothing more was heard of Adams and his family for twelve years nearly, when, in 1825, Captain Beechey, in the *Blossom*, bound on a voyage of discovery, paid a visit to Pitcairn's Island. Some whale-fishing ship, however, had touched there in the intermediate time, and left on the island a person of the name of John Buffet. 'In this man,' says Captain Beechey, 'they have very fortunately found an able and willing schoolmaster; he had belonged to a ship which visited the island, and was so infatuated with the behaviour of the people, being himself naturally of a devout and serious turn of mind, that he resolved to remain among them; and, in addition to the instruction of the children, has taken upon himself the duty of clergyman, and is the oracle of the community.'

On the approach of the *Blossom* towards the island, a boat was observed, under all sail, hastening towards the ship, which they considered to be the boat of some whaler, but were soon agreeably undeceived by the singular appearance of her crew, which consisted of old Adams and many of the young men belonging to the island. They did not venture at once to lay hold of the ship till they had first inquired if they might come on board; and on permission being granted, they sprang up the side and shook every officer by the hand with undisguised feelings of gratification.

The activity of the young men, ten in number, outstripped that of old Adams, who was in his sixty-fifth year, and somewhat corpulent. He was dressed in a sailor's shirt and trousers, and a low-crowned hat, which he held in his hand until desired to put it on. He still retained his sailor's manners, doffing his hat and smoothing down his bald forehead whenever he was addressed by the officers of the *Blossom*.

The young men were tall, robust, and healthy, with good-natured countenances, and a simplicity of manner, and a fear of doing something that might be wrong, which at once prevented the possibility of giving offence. Their dresses were whimsical enough; some had long coats without trousers, and others trousers without coats, and others again waistcoats without either. None of them had either shoes or stockings, and there were only two hats among them, 'neither of which,' Captain Beechey says, 'seemed likely to hang long together.'

Captain Beechey procured from Adams a narrative of the whole transaction of the mutiny, which however is incorrect in many parts; and also a history of the broils and disputes which led to the violent death of all these misguided men (with the exception of Young and Adams), who accompanied Christian in the *Bounty* to Pitcairn's Island.

It may be recollected that the *Bounty* was carried away from Otaheite by nine of the mutineers. Their names were:--

1. FLETCHER CHRISTIAN, Acting Lieutenant.
2. EDWARD YOUNG, Midshipman.
3. ALEXANDER SMITH (*alias* JOHN ADAMS), Seaman.
4. WILLIAM M'KOY, Seaman.
5. MATTHEW QUINTAL, Seaman.
6. JOHN WILLIAMS, Seaman.
7. ISAAC MARTIN, Seaman.
8. JOHN MILLS, Gunner's Mate.
9. WILLIAM BROWN, Botanist's Assistant.

They brought with them six men and twelve women, natives of Tabouai and Otaheite. The first step after their arrival was to divide the whole island into nine equal portions, to the exclusion of those poor people whom they had seduced to accompany them, and some of whom are stated to have been carried off against their inclination. At first they were considered as the friends of the white men, but very soon became their slaves. They assisted in the cultivation of the soil, in building houses, and in fetching wood and water, without murmuring or complaining; and things went on peaceably and prosperously for about two years, when Williams, who had lost his wife about a month after their arrival, by a fall from a rock while collecting bird's eggs, became dissatisfied, and insisted on having another wife, or threatened to leave the island in one of the ***Bounty's*** boats. Being useful as an armourer, the Europeans were unwilling to part with him, and he, still persisting in his unreasonable demand, had the injustice to compel one of the Otaheitans to give up his wife to him.

By this act of flagrant oppression his countrymen made common cause with their injured companion, and laid a plan for the extermination of the Europeans; but the women gave a hint of what was going forward in a song, the burden of which was, 'Why does black man sharpen axe?--to kill white man.' The plot being thus discovered, the husband who had his wife taken from him, another whom Christian had shot at (though, it is stated, with powder only), fled into the woods, and were treacherously murdered by their countrymen, on the promise of pardon for the perpetration of this foul deed.

Tranquillity being thus restored, matters went on tolerably well for a year or two longer; but the oppression and ill-treatment which the Otaheitans received, more particularly from Quintal and M'Koy, the most active and determined of the mutineers, drove them to the formation of another plot for the destruction of their oppressors, which but too successfully succeeded. A day was fixed for attacking and putting to death all the Englishmen while at work in their respective plantations. Williams was the first man that was shot. They next proceeded to Christian, who was working at his yam-plot, and shot him. Mills, confiding in the fidelity of his Otaheitan friend, stood his ground, and was murdered by him and another. Martin and Brown were separately attacked and slain, one with a maul, the other with a musket. Adams was wounded in the shoulder, but succeeded in making terms with the Otaheitans; and was conducted by them to Christian's house, where he was kindly treated. Young, who was a great favourite of the women, was secreted by them during the attack, and afterwards carried to Christian's house. M'Koy and Quintal, the worst of the gang, escaped to the mountains. 'Here,' says Captain Beechey, 'this day of bloodshed ended, leaving only four Englishmen alive out of nine. It was a day of emancipation to the blacks, who were now masters of the island, and of humiliation and retribution to the whites.'

The men of colour now began to quarrel about choosing the women whose European husbands had been murdered; the result of which was the destruction of the whole of the former, some falling by the hands of the women, and one of them by Young, who it would seem coolly and deliberately shot him. Adams now proceeded into the mountains to communicate the fatal intelligence to the two Europeans, M'Koy and Quintal, and to solicit their return to the village. All these events are stated to have happened so early as October, 1793.

From this time to 1798, the remnant of the colonists would appear to have gone on quietly with the exception of some quarrels these four men had with the women, and the latter among themselves; ten of them were still remaining, who lived promiscuously with the men, frequently changing their abode from one house to another. Young, being a man of some education, kept a kind of journal, but it is a document of very little interest, containing scarcely anything more than the ordinary occupations of the settlers, the loan or exchange of provisions, the dates when the sows farrowed, the number of fish caught, etc., and it begins only at the time when Adams and he were sole masters of the island; and the truth, therefore, of all that has been told rests solely on the degree of credit that is due to Adams.

M'Koy, it appears, had formerly been employed in a Scotch distillery, and being much addicted to ardent spirits, set about making experiments on the **tee-root** (***Dracaena terminalis***), and at length unfortunately succeeded in producing an intoxicating liquor. This success induced his companion Quintal to turn his kettle into a still. The consequence was, that these two men were in a constant state of drunkenness, particularly M'Koy, on whom, it seems, it had the effect of producing fits of delirium; and in one of these he threw himself from a cliff and was killed on the spot. Captain Beechey says, 'the melancholy fate of this man created so forcible an impression on the remaining few, that they resolved never again to touch spirits; and Adams has, I believe, to this day kept his vow.'

Some time in the following year, that is, about 1799, 'we learned from Adams,' says Captain Beechey, 'that Quintal lost his wife by a fall from the cliff, while in search of birds' eggs; that he grew discontented, and, though there were several disposable women on the island, and he had already experienced the fatal effects of a similar demand, nothing would satisfy him but the wife of one of his companions. Of course neither of them felt inclined to accede to this unreasonable demand; and he sought an opportunity of putting them both to death. He was fortunately foiled in his first attempt, but swore openly he would speedily repeat it. Adams and Young having no doubt he would follow up his intention, and fearing he might be more successful in the next attempt, came to the resolution that, as their own lives were not safe while he was in existence, they were justified in putting him to death, which they did by felling him, as they would an ox, with a hatchet.

'Such was the melancholy fate of seven of the leading mutineers, who escaped from justice only to add murder to their former crimes'; and such, it may be added, was the polluted source, thus stained with the guilt of mutiny, piracy, and murder, from which the present simple and innocent race of islanders has proceeded; and what is most of all extraordinary, the very man, from whom they have received their moral and religious instruction, is one who was among the first and foremost in the mutiny, and deeply implicated in all the deplorable consequences that were the results of it. This man and Young were now the sole survivors out of the fifteen males that had landed upon the island. Young, as has been stated, was a man of some education, and of a serious turn of mind, and, as Beechey says, it would have been wonderful, after the many dreadful scenes at which they had assisted, if the solitude and tranquillity that ensued had not disposed them to repentance. They had a Bible and a Prayer Book, which were found in the ***Bounty***, and they read the Church Service regularly every Sunday. They now resolved to have morning and evening family prayers, and to instruct the children, who amounted to nineteen, many of them between the ages of seven and nine years. Young, however, was not long suffered to survive his repentance. An asthmatic complaint terminated his existence about a year after the death of Quintal; and Adams was now left the sole survivor of the guilty and misguided mutineers of the ***Bounty***. It is remarkable that the name of Young should never once occur in any shape as connected with the mutiny, except in the evidence of Lieutenant Hayward, who includes his name in a mass of others. He neither appears among the armed nor the unarmed; he is not stated to be among those who were on deck, and was probably therefore one of those who were confined below. Bligh, nevertheless, has not omitted to give him a character. 'Young was an able and stout seaman; he, however, always proved a worthless wretch.'

If the sincere repentance of Adams, and the most successful exertions to train up the rising generation in piety and virtue, can be considered as expiating in some degree his former offences, this survivor is fully entitled to every indulgence that frail humanity so often requires, and which indeed has been extended to him, by all the officers of the navy who have visited the island, and witnessed the simple manners, and the settled habits of morality and piety which prevail in this happy and well-regulated society. They have all strongly felt that the merits and redeeming qualities of the latter years of his life have so far atoned for his former guilt, that he ought not to be molested, but rather encouraged, in his meritorious efforts, if not for his own sake, at least for that of the innocent young people dependent on him.

Still it ought never to be forgotten that he was one of the first and most daring in the atrocious act of mutiny and piracy, and that, had he remained in Otaheite, and been taken home in the *Pandora*, nothing could have saved him from an ignominious death. His pretending to say that he was in his cot, and that he was forced to take arms, may perhaps be palliated under his peculiar circumstances, wishing to stand as fair before his countrymen as his case would admit--but it is not strictly true; for he was the third upon deck armed, and stood sentry over Bligh with a loaded musket and fixed bayonet. The story he told to Beechey respecting the advice stated to have been given by Mr. Stewart to Christian, 'to take possession of the ship,' is, as has been shown, wholly false; but here his memory may have failed him. If any such advice was given, it is much more likely to have proceeded from Young. He also told two different stories with regard to the conduct of Christian. To Sir Thomas Staines and Captain Pipon, he represented this ill-fated young man as never happy, after the rash and criminal step he had taken, and that he was always sullen and morose, and committed so many acts of cruelty, as to incur the hatred and detestation of his associates in crime. Whereas he told Captain Beechey, that Christian was always cheerful; that his example was of the greatest service in exciting his companions to labour; that he was naturally of a happy, ingenuous disposition, and won the good opinion and respect of all who served under him: which cannot be better exemplified, he says, than by his maintaining, under circumstances of great perplexity, the respect and regard of all who were associated with him, up to the hour of his death; and that, even at the present moment, Adams, in speaking of him, never omits to say *Mr*. Christian. Why indeed should he? Christian was a gentleman by birth, and an officer in his Majesty's service, and was of course always so addressed. But why was he murdered within two years (one account says nine months) after the party reached the island? Captain Beechey has answered the question--for oppression and ill-treatment of the Otaheitans.[39]

That Christian, so far from being cheerful, was, on the contrary, always uneasy in his mind about his own safety, is proved by his having selected a cave at the extremity of the high ridge of craggy hills that runs across the island, as his intended place of refuge, in the event of any ship of war discovering the retreat of the mutineers, in which cave he resolved to sell his life as dearly as he could. In this recess he always kept a store of provisions, and near it erected a small hut, well concealed by trees, which served the purpose of a watch-house. 'So difficult,' says Captain Beechey, 'was the approach to this cave, that even if a party were successful in crossing the ridge, he might have bid defiance, as long as his ammunition lasted, to any force.' The reflection alone of his having sent adrift, to perish on the wide ocean, for he could entertain no other idea, no less than nineteen persons, all of whom, one only excepted, were innocent of any offence towards him, must have constantly haunted his mind, and left him little disposed to be happy and cheerful.

The truth is, as appears in Morrison's journal, that during the short time they remained at Tabouai, and till the separation of the mutineers at Otaheite, when sixteen forsook him, and eight only, of the very worst, accompanied him in quest of some retreat, he acted the part of a tyrant to a much greater extent than the man who, he says, drove him to the act of mutiny. After giving an account of the manner of his death, Captain Beechey says, 'Thus fell a man who, from being the reputed ringleader of the mutiny, has obtained an unenviable celebrity, and whose crime may perhaps be considered as in some degree palliated by the tyranny which led to its commission.' It is to be hoped, such an act as he was guilty of will never be so considered.

If mutiny could be supposed to admit of palliation, a fatal blow would be struck not only at the discipline, but at the very existence, of the navy; any relaxation in bringing to condign punishment persons guilty of mutiny, would weaken and ultimately destroy the efficiency of this great and powerful machine. Nor, indeed, is it at all necessary that the punishment for mutiny should admit of any palliation. Whenever an act of tyranny, or an unnecessary degree of severity, is exercised by a commanding officer, let the fact only be proved, and he is certain to be visited with all the rigour that the degree of his oppressive conduct will warrant. Had Christian but waited patiently the arrival of the *Bounty* in England, and the alleged conduct of Bligh towards his officers and crew had been proved, he would, unquestionably, have been dismissed from his Majesty's service.

With regard to Adams, though his subsequent conduct was highly meritorious, and to him alone it might be said is owing the present happy state of the little community on Pitcairn's Island, his crime like that of Christian's can never be considered as wiped away. Sir Thomas Staines, the first British officer who called at the island, it may well be supposed, had to struggle, on this trying occasion, between duty and feeling. It was his imperative duty to have seized and brought him a prisoner to England, where he must have been tried, and would no doubt have been convicted of a crime for which several of his less active accomplices had suffered the penalty of death; though he might, and probably would, from length of time and circumstances in his favour, have received the king's pardon. Perhaps, however, on the whole, it was fortunate, that in balancing, as it is known this gallant officer did, between the sense of duty and the sense of feeling, the latter prevailed, and justice yielded to mercy. Had a Bligh or an Edwards been placed in his situation it is to be feared that, judging from their former conduct, passion in the one, and frigidity in the other, would most likely have consigned the criminal to captivity in irons, and the innocent and helpless family, solely dependent on him, to misery and destruction--and yet, in so doing, they would not have deviated from their strict line of duty,-- ***Dis aliter visum***.

The ***Blossom*** was the first ship of war that John Adams had been on board of since the mutiny; and, as Captain Beechey observes, his mind would naturally revert to scenes that could not fail to produce a temporary embarrassment, but no apprehension for his safety appeared to form any part of his thoughts; and as every person endeavoured to set his mind at rest, he soon found himself at ease and at home. It was several hours before the ship approached the shore, and the boats put off before she came to an anchor.

On account of the rocks and formidable breakers, the party who went on shore were landed by the young men, two at a time, in their whale boat. 'The difficulty of landing,' says Captain Beechey, 'was more than repaid by the friendly reception we met with on the beach from Hannah Young, a very interesting young woman, the daughter of Adams. In her eagerness to greet her father, she had outrun her female companions, for whose delay she thought it necessary, in the first place, to apologize, by saying they had all been over the hill in company with John Buffet to look at the ship, and were not yet returned. It appeared that John Buffet, who was a seafaring man, had ascertained that the ship was a man of war, and, without knowing exactly why, became so alarmed for the safety of Adams, that he either could not or would not answer any of the interrogatories which were put to him. This mysterious silence set all the party in tears, as they feared he had discovered something adverse to their patriarch. At length his obduracy yielded to their entreaties; but before he explained the cause of his conduct, the boats were seen to put off from the ship, and Hannah immediately hurried to the beach to kiss the old man's cheek, which she did with a fervency demonstrative of the warmest affection. Her apology for her companions was rendered unnecessary by their appearance on the steep and circuitous path down the mountain, who, as they arrived on the beach, successively welcomed us to their island, with a simplicity and sincerity which left no doubt of the truth of their professions.' The whole group simultaneously expressed a wish that the visitors would stay with them several days; and on their signifying a desire to get to the village before dark and to pitch the observatory, every article and instrument found a bearer, along a steep path which led to the village, concealed by groups of cocoa-nut trees; the females bearing their burthens over the most difficult parts without inconvenience. The village consisted of five houses, on a cleared piece of ground sloping toward the sea. While the men assisted in pitching the tent, the women employed themselves in preparing the supper. The mode of cooking was precisely that of Otaheite, by heated stones in a hole made in the ground. At young Christian's, the table was spread with plates, knives and forks. John Buffet said grace in an emphatic manner, and this is repeated every time a fresh guest sits down while the meal is going on. So strict are they in this respect, that it is not deemed proper to touch a bit of bread without saying grace before and after it. 'On one occasion,' says Captain Beechey, 'I had engaged Adams in conversation, and he incautiously took the first mouthful without having said grace; but before he had swallowed it, he recollected himself, and feeling as if he had committed a crime, immediately put away what he had in his mouth, and commenced his prayer.' Their rooms and table are lighted up by torches made of ***doodoe*** nuts (Aleurites triloba), strung upon the fibres of a palm-leaf, which form a good substitute for candles.

It is remarkable enough, that although the female part of the society is highly respected, yet, in one instance, a distinction is kept up, which in civilized countries would be deemed degrading. It is that which is rigidly observed in all the South Sea Islands, and indeed throughout almost the whole eastern world, that no woman shall eat in the presence of her husband; and though this distinction between man and wife is not carried quite so far in Pitcairn's Island, it is observed to the extent of excluding all women from table, when there is a deficiency of seats. It seems they defended the custom on the ground that man was made before woman, and is entitled, therefore, to be first served--a conclusion, observes Beechey, 'that deprived us of the company of the women at table, during the whole of our stay at the island, Far, however, from considering themselves neglected, they very good-naturedly chatted with us behind our seats, and flapped away the flies, and by a gentle tap, accidentally or playfully delivered, reminded us occasionally of the honour that was done us.' The women, when the men had finished, sat down to what remained.

The beds were next prepared. A mattress composed of palm-leaves was covered with native cloth made of the paper mulberry-tree, in the same manner as in Otaheite; the sheets were of the same material; and it appeared, from their crackling, that they were quite new from the loom, or rather the beater. The whole arrangement is stated to have been comfortable, and inviting to repose; one interruption only disturbed their first sleep; this was the melody of the evening hymn, which, after the lights were put out, was chanted by the whole family in the middle of the room. At early dawn they were also awaked by their morning hymn and the family devotion; after which the islanders all set out to their several occupations. Some of the women had taken the linen of their visitors to wash; others were preparing for the next meal; and others were employed in the manufacture of cloth.

The innocence and simplicity of these interesting young creatures are strongly exemplified in the following description. 'By our bedside had already been placed some ripe fruits; and our hats were crowned with chaplets of the fresh blossom of the ***nono*** or flower-tree (***Morinda citrifolia***), which the women had gathered in the freshness of the morning dew. On looking round the apartment, though it contained several beds, we found no partition, curtain, or screens; they had not yet been considered necessary. So far, indeed, from concealment being thought of, when we were about to get up, the women, anxious to show their attention, assembled to wish us good morning, and to inquire in what way they could best contribute to our comforts, and to present us with some little gift, which the produce of the island afforded. Many persons would have felt awkward at rising and dressing before so many pretty black-eyed damsels, assembled in the centre of a spacious room; but by a little habit we overcame this embarrassment, and from the benefit of their services in fetching water as we required it, and in substituting clean linen for such as we pulled off.'

Their cottages are spacious, and strongly built of wood, in an oblong form, and thatched with the leaves of the palm-tree bent round the stem of a branch from the same, and laced horizontally to rafters, so placed as to give a proper pitch to the roof. An upper story is appropriated to sleeping, and has four beds, one in each angle of the room, and large enough for three or four persons to sleep on. The lower is the eating room, having a broad table with several stools placed round it. The lower room communicates with the upper, by a stout ladder in the centre. Immediately round the village are small enclosures for fattening pigs, goats, and poultry; and beyond them are the cultivated grounds producing the banana, plantain, melon, yam, taro, sweet potatoes, ***tee***-tree, cloth-plant, with other useful roots, fruits, and a variety of shrubs. Every cottage has its out-house for making cloth, its baking-place, its pig-sty, and its poultry-house.

During the stay of the strangers on the island, they dined sometimes with one person, and sometimes with another, their meals being always the same, and consisting of baked pig, yams, and taro, and sometimes sweet potatoes. Goats are numerous on the island, but neither their flesh nor their milk is relished by the natives. Yams constitute their principal food, either boiled, baked, or mixed with cocoa-nut, made into cakes, and eaten with molasses extracted from the tee-root. Taro-root is no bad substitute for bread; and bananas, plantains, and ***appoi***, are wholesome and nutritive fruits. The common beverage is water, but they make tea from the tee-plant, flavoured with ginger, and sweetened with the juice of the sugar-cane. They but seldom kill a pig, living mostly on fruit and vegetables. With this simple diet, early rising, and taking a great deal of exercise, they are subject to few diseases; and Captain Beechey says, 'they are certainly a finer and more athletic race than is usually found among the families of mankind.'

The young children are punctual in their attendance at school, and are instructed by John Buffet in reading, writing, and arithmetic; to which are added, precepts of religion and morality, drawn chiefly from the Bible and Prayer Book; than which, fortunately, they possess no others that might mystify and perplex their understandings on religious subjects. They seldom indulge in jokes or other kinds of levity; and Beechey says, they are so accustomed to take what is said in its literal meaning, that irony was always considered a falsehood in spite of explanation; and that they could not see the propriety of uttering what was not strictly true, for any purpose whatever. The Sabbath is wholly devoted to the church service, to prayer, reading, and serious meditation; no work of any kind is done on that day, not even cooking, which is prepared on the preceding evening.

'I attended,' says Beechey, 'their church on this day, and found the service well conducted; the prayers were read by Adams, and the lessons by Buffet, the service being preceded by hymns. The greatest devotion was apparent in every individual; and in the children there was a seriousness unknown in the younger part of our communities at home. In the course of the Litany, they prayed for their sovereign and all the royal family, with much apparent loyalty and sincerity. Some family prayers, which were thought appropriate to their own particular case, were added to the usual service; and Adams, fearful of leaving out any essential part, read in addition all those prayers which are intended only as substitutes for others. A sermon followed, which was very well delivered by Buffet; and lest any part of it should be forgotten or escape attention, it was read three times. The whole concluded with hymns, which were first sung by the grown people, and afterwards by the children. The service thus performed was very long; but the neat and cleanly appearance of the congregation, the devotion that animated every countenance, and the innocence and simplicity of the little children, prevented the attendance from becoming wearisome. In about half an hour afterwards we again assembled to prayers, and at sunset service was repeated; so that, with their morning and evening prayers, they may be said to have church five times on a Sunday.'

Perhaps it will be thought by some that they carry their seriousness too far, and that the younger people are not allowed a sufficient quantity of recreation. The exercise and amusement of dancing, once so much resorted to in most of the islands of the Pacific, is here almost excluded. With great difficulty and much entreaty, the visitors prevailed on three grown-up ladies to stand up to perform the Otaheitan dance, which they consented to with a reluctance that showed it was done only to oblige them. It was little more than a shuffling of the feet, sliding past each other, and snapping their fingers. They did not long continue this diversion, considering it as too great a levity, and only the three beforementioned ladies could be prevailed on to exhibit their skill. They appeared to have little taste for music either instrumental or vocal. Adams, when on board the ***Blossom*** for two or three days, made no difficulty of joining in the dance and was remarkably cheerful, but on no occasion neglected his usual devotions. Captain Beechey has no doubt of the sincerity of his piety. He slept in the same cabin, but would never get into his cot until the captain was in bed, and supposed to be asleep, when, in a retired corner of the cabin, he fell on his knees and performed his devotions; and he was always up first in the morning for the same purpose.

This good old man told Beechey one day, that it would add much to his happiness if he would read the marriage ceremony to him and his wife, as he could not bear the idea of living with her without its being done, when a proper opportunity should offer, as was now the case. Though Adams was aged, and the old woman had been blind and bedridden for several years, Beechey says he made such a point of it, that it would have been cruel to refuse him. They were accordingly, the following day, duly united, and the event noted in a register by John Buffet. The marriages that take place among the young people are, however, performed by Adams, who makes use of a ring for such occasions, which has united every couple on the island since its first settlement; the regulated age under which no man is allowed to marry is twenty, and that of the woman eighteen. The restrictions with regard to relationship are the same as with us, and are strictly put in force when parties are about to marry. Adams also officiates at christenings.

Captain Beechey observes, that these amiable people rigidly adhere to their word and promise, even in cases where the most scrupulous among Europeans might think themselves justified in some relaxation of them. Thus, George Adams, in his early days, had fallen in love with Polly Young, a girl somewhat older than himself; but Polly, for some reason or other, had incautiously declared, she **never would** give her hand to George Adams; who, however, still hoped she would one day relent, and of course was unremitting in his endeavours to please her; nor was he mistaken; his constancy and his handsome form, which George took every opportunity of displaying before her, softened Polly's heart, and she would willingly have given him her hand. But the vow of her youth was not to be got over, and the lovesick couple languished on from day to day, victims to the folly of early resolutions. This weighty case was referred to the British officers, who decided that it would be much better to marry than to continue unhappy in consequence of a hasty resolution made before the judgement was matured; but Polly's scruples still remained, and those who gave their decision left them unmarried. Captain Beechey, however, has recently received a letter, stating that George Adams and Polly Young had joined hands and were happy; but the same letter announced the death of John Adams, which took place in March 1829.

The demise of this old patriarch is the most serious loss that could have befallen this infant colony. The perfect harmony and contentment in which they appear to live together, the innocence and simplicity of their manners, their conjugal and parental affection, their moral, religious, and virtuous conduct, and their exemption from any serious vice, are all to be ascribed to the exemplary conduct and instructions of old John Adams; and it is gratifying to know, that five years after the visit of the ***Blossom***, and one year subsequent to Adams's death, the little colony continued to enjoy the same uninterrupted state of harmony and contentment as before.

In consequence of a representation, made by Captain Beechey when there, of the distressed state of this little society, with regard to the want of certain necessary articles, his Majesty's government sent out to Valparaiso, to be conveyed from thence for their use, a proportion for sixty persons of the following articles: sailors' blue jackets and trousers, flannel waistcoats, pairs of stockings and shoes, women's dresses, spades, mattocks, shovels, pickaxes, trowels, rakes; all of which were taken in his Majesty's ship ***Seringapatam,*** commanded by Captain the Hon. William Waldegrave, who arrived there in March 1830.

The ship had scarcely anchored when George Young was alongside in his canoe, which he guided by a paddle; and soon after Thursday October Christian, in a jolly-boat, with several others, who, having come on board, were invited to breakfast, and one of them said grace as usual both before and after it. The captain, the chaplain, and some other officers accompanied these natives on shore, and having reached the summit of the first level or plain, which is surrounded by a grove or screen of cocoa-nut trees, they found the wives and mothers assembled to receive them. 'I have brought you a clergyman,' says the captain. 'God bless you,' issued from every mouth; 'but is he come to stay with us?'--'No.' 'You bad man, why not?'--'I cannot spare him, he is the chaplain of my ship; but I have brought you clothes and other articles, which King George has sent you.' 'But,' says Kitty Quintal, 'we want food for our souls.'

'Our reception,' says Captain Waldegrave, 'was most cordial, particularly that of Mr. Watson, the chaplain; and the meeting of the wives and husbands most affecting, exchanging expressions of joy that could not have been exceeded had they just returned from a long absence. The men sprang up to the trees, throwing down cocoa-nuts, the husks of which were torn off by others with their teeth, and offering us the milk. As soon as we had rested ourselves, they took us to their cottages, where we dined and slept.'

Captain Waldegrave says it was highly gratifying to observe their native simplicity of manners, apparently without guile: their hospitality was unbounded, their cottages being open to all, and all were welcome to such food as they possessed; pigs and fowls were immediately killed and dressed, and when the guests were seated, one of the islanders, in the attitude of prayer, and his eyes raised towards heaven, repeated a simple grace for the present food they were about to partake of, beseeching, at the same time, spiritual nourishment; at the end of which each responded *amen*. On the arrival of any one during the repast, they all paused until the new guest had said grace.

At night they all assembled in one of the cottages to hear the afternoon church service performed by Mr. Watson, and Captain Waldegrave describes it as a most striking scene. The place chosen was the bedroom of one of the double cottages, or one with an upper story. The ascent was by a broad ladder from the lower room through a trap-door. The clergyman took his station between two beds, with a lamp burning close behind him. In the bed on his right were three infants sound asleep; at the foot of that on his left were three men sitting. On each side and in front were the men, some wearing only the simple mara, displaying their gigantic figures; others in jackets and trousers, their necks and feet bare; behind stood the women, in their modest home-made cloth dresses, which entirely covered the form, leaving only the head and feet bare. The girls wore, in addition, a sheet knotted in the manner of a Roman senator's *toga*, thrown over the right shoulder and under the left arm. When the general confession commenced, they all knelt down facing the clergyman, with their hands raised to the breast in the attitude of prayer, slowly and distinctly repeating the confession after the clergyman. They prayed for the King of England, whom they consider as their sovereign. A sermon followed from a text which Captain Waldegrave thinks was most happily chosen: 'Fear not, little flock, for it is your Father's good pleasure to give you the kingdom.' At the conclusion of the service they requested permission to sing their parting hymn, when the whole congregation, in good time, sang 'Depart in peace.'

Captain Waldegrave, like all former visitors, bears testimony to the kind disposition and active benevolence of these simple islanders. The children, he says, are fond and obedient, the parents affectionate and kind towards their children. None of the party ever heard a harsh word made use of by one towards another. They never slander or speak ill of one another. If any question was asked as to the character or conduct of a particular individual, the answer would probably be something of this kind, 'If it could do any good, I would answer you; but as it cannot, it would be wrong to tell tales'; or if the question applied to one who had committed a fault, they would say, 'It would be wrong to tell my neighbour's shame.' The kind and benevolent feeling of these amiable people is extended to the surviving widows of the Otaheite men who were slain on the island, and who would be left in a helpless and destitute state, were it not for the humane consideration of the younger part of the society, by whom they are supported and regarded with every mark of attention.

The women are clothed in white cloth made from the paper mulberry, the dress extending from the shoulders to the feet, in double folds, and so loose as entirely to conceal the shape of the person. The mothers, while nursing, carry the infant within their dress; as the child advances in growth it sits across the hip of the parent with its little hands clinging to the shoulder, while the mother's arm passing round it keeps it in safety. The men and boys, except on Sunday, when they appear in English dresses, generally wear only the *mara*, or waist-cloth, which, passing over the hips, and between the legs, is knotted behind; the climate is in fact too hot for cumbersome clothing. The women, when working, use only a petticoat, with a jacket.

The men are stated to be from five feet eight inches to six feet high, of great muscular strength and excellent figures. 'We did not see,' says Captain Waldegrave, 'one cripple or defective person, except one boy, whom, in the most good-humoured way, and laughing heartily, they brought to me, observing, "You ought to be brothers, you have each lost the right eye." I acknowledged the connexion, and no doubt for the future he will be called the Captain.'

Captain Beechey has given a more detailed account of the physical qualities of the Pitcairn Islanders. He says they are tall, robust, and healthy; their average height five feet ten inches; the tallest man measured six feet and one quarter of an inch, and the shortest of the adults five feet nine inches and one-eighth; their limbs well proportioned, round and straight; their feet turning a little inwards. A boy of eight years measured four feet and one inch; another of nine years, four feet three inches. Their simple food and early habits of exercise give them a muscular power and activity not often surpassed. It is recorded on the island that George Young and Edward Quintal have each carried, at one time, a kedge anchor, two sledge hammers, and an armourer's anvil, weighing together upwards of six hundred pounds; and that Quintal once carried a boat twenty-eight feet in length. In the water they are almost as much at home as on land, and can remain almost a whole day in the sea. They frequently swim round their little island, the circuit of which is at the least seven miles; and the women are nearly as expert swimmers as the men.

The female descendants of the Otaheite women are almost as muscular as the males, and taller than the generality of the sex. Polly Young, who is not the tallest on the island, measured five feet nine inches and a half. The features of both men and women are regular and well-formed; eyes bright and generally hazel, though in a few instances blue; the eyebrows thin and rarely meeting; the nose a little flattened, and being rather extended at the nostrils, partakes of the Otaheitan character, as do the lips, which are broad and strongly sulcated; their ears moderately large, and the lobes are invariably united with the cheek; they are generally perforated, when young, for the reception of flowers, a very common custom among the natives of the South Sea Islands; hair black, sometimes curling, sometimes straight;

teeth regular and white. On the whole they are a well-looking people.

Captain Beechey says, the women have all learned the art of midwifery; that parturition generally takes place during the night-time; that the duration of labour is seldom longer than five hours, and has not yet in any case proved fatal; but there is no instance of twins, nor of a single miscarriage, except from accident. Infants are generally bathed three times a day in cold water, and are sometimes not weaned for three or four years; but when that does take place, they are fed upon 'popoe,' made of ripe plantains and boiled taro-root rubbed into a paste. Mr. Collie, the surgeon of the *Blossom*, remarks that nothing is more extraordinary, in the history of the island, than the uniform good health of the children; the teething is easily got over, they have no bowel complaints, and are exempt from those contagious diseases which affect children in large communities. He offered to vaccinate the children as well as all the grown persons; but they deemed the risk of infection of small-pox to be too small to render that operation necessary.

As a proof how very much simple diet and constant exercise tend to the healthful state of the body, the skin of these people, though in such robust health, compared with that of the Europeans, always felt cold, and their pulses always considerably lower. The doctor examined several of them: in the forenoon he found George Young's only sixty; three others, in the afternoon, after dinner, were sixty-eight, seventy-two, and seventy-six, while those of the officers who stood the heat of the climate best were above eighty.

It is impossible not to feel a deep interest in the welfare of this little society, and at the same time an apprehension that something may happen to disturb that harmony and destroy that simplicity of manners which have hitherto characterized it. It is to be feared, indeed, that the seeds of discord are already sown. It appears from Captain Waldegrave's statement, that no less than three Englishmen have found their way into this happy society. One of them, John Buffet, mentioned by Beechey, is a harmless man, and, as it has been stated, of great use to the islanders in his capacity of clergyman and schoolmaster; he is also a clever and useful mechanic, as a ship-wright and joiner, and is much beloved by the community. Two others have since been left on the island, one of them, by name John Evans, son of a coachmaker in the employ of Long of St. Martin's Lane, who has married a daughter of John Adams, through whom he possesses and cultivates a certain portion of land;

the third is George Hunn Nobbs, who calls himself pastor, registrar, and schoolmaster, thus infringing on the privileges of John Buffet; and being a person of superior talents, and of exceeding great impudence, has deprived Buffet of a great number of his scholars; and hence a sufficient cause exists of division and dissension among the members of the little society, which were never known before. Buffet and Evans support themselves by their industry, but this Nobbs not only claims exemption from labour as being their pastor, but also as being entitled to a maintenance at the expense of the community. He has married a daughter of Charles, and granddaughter to the late Fletcher Christian, whose descendants, as captain of the gang, might be induced to claim superiority, and which, probably, might be allowed by general consent, had they but possessed a moderate share of talent; but it is stated that Thursday October and Charles Christian, the sons of the chief mutineer, are ignorant, uneducated men. The only chance for the continuance of peace is the general dislike in which this Nobbs is held, and the gradual intellectual improvement of the rising generation.[40]

It seems that Adams on his death-bed called all the heads of families together, and urged them to appoint a chief;--this, however, they have not done, which makes it the more to be apprehended that Nobbs, by his superior talent or cunning, will force himself upon them into that situation. Captain Waldegrave thinks, however, that Edward Quintal, who possesses the best understanding of any on the island, will in time arrive at that honour; his only book is the Bible, but it is quite astonishing, he observes, what a fund of knowledge he has derived from it. His wife, too, is stated to be a woman of excellent understanding; and their eldest boy, William, has been so carefully educated, that he excels greatly all the others. The descendants of Young are also said to be persons generally of promising abilities.

How the patriarch Adams contrived to instil into the minds of these people the true principles of religion and morality is quite surprising. He was able to read, but only learnt to write in his latter days; and having accomplished this point, he made a scheme of laws by which he succeeded to govern his little community in the way we have seen. The celebration of marriage and baptism were strictly observed, according to the rites of the Church of England, but he never ventured on confirmation and the sacrament of the Lord's Supper. He taught the children the Church catechism, the ten commandments, the Lord's prayer, and the Creed, and he satisfied himself, that in these were comprised all the Christian duties. By the instrumentality of these precepts, drawn from the Book of Common Prayer and the Bible,[41] he was enabled, after the slaughter of all his associates, to rear up all the children in the principles and precepts of Christianity, in purity of morals, and in a simplicity of manners, that have surprised and delighted every stranger that has visited the island.

Captain Waldegrave says they are so strongly attached to those beautiful prayers that are found in the liturgy of the Church of England, that there is no danger of a dissenting minister being received among them. It is to be hoped this may be the case; but it may be asked, will they escape from the snares of George Hunn Nobbs? It would seem, indeed, that this man has already thrust upon them what he calls a code of laws, in which he enumerates crimes, such as murder and adultery, unknown and unheard of among these simple people since the time that Adams was sole legislator and patriarch. The punishment of adultery, to give a specimen of Nobbs's legislation, is whipping for the first offence to both parties, and marriage within three months; for the second, if the parties refuse to marry, the penalties are, forfeiture of lands, property, and banishment from the island. Offenders are to be tried before three elders, who pronounce sentence. It is quite clear this silly person does not understand what is meant by adultery. As to the tenure of land, it is fortunately provided for previous to his arrival on the island. The whole island, it seems, was partitioned out by Adams among the families of the original settlers, so that a foreigner cannot obtain any, except by purchase or marriage. Captain Waldegrave reckons, that eleven-twelfths are uncultivated, and that population is increasing so rapidly, that in the course of a century the island will be fully peopled, and that the limit may be taken at one thousand souls.

The rate at which population is likely to increase may, perhaps, be determined by political economists from the following data.

In 1790 the island was first settled by fifteen men and twelve women, making a total of twenty-seven. Of these were remaining in 1800, one man and five women, with nineteen children, the eldest nine years of age, making in the whole twenty-five. In 1808, Mr. Folger makes the population amount to thirty-five, being an increase of ten in eight years. In 1814, six years afterwards, Sir Thomas Staines states the ***adult*** population at forty, which must be a mistake, as fourteen years before, nineteen of the twenty-five then existing were children. In 1825, Captain Beechey states the whole population at sixty-six, of whom thirty-six were males, and thirty females. And in 1830, Captain Waldegrave makes it amount to seventy-nine; being an increase of thirteen in five years, or twenty per cent, which is a less rapid increase than might be expected; but there can be little doubt it will go on with an accelerated ratio, provided the means of subsistence should not fail them.

Captain Waldegrave's assumption, that this island is sufficiently large for the maintenance of one thousand souls, is grounded on incorrect data; it does not follow, that because one-twelfth of the island will maintain eighty persons, the whole must support nine hundred and sixty persons. The island is not more than four square miles, or two thousand five hundred and sixty acres; and as a ridge of rocky hills runs from north to south, having two peaks exceeding one thousand feet in height, it is more than probable that not one half of it is capable of cultivation. It would seem, indeed, from several ancient morais being discovered among these hills; some stone axes or hatchets of compact basaltic lava, very hard and capable of a fine polish; four stone images, about six feet high, placed on a platform, not unlike those on Easter Island, one of which has been preserved, and is the rude representation of the human figure to the hips, hewn out of a piece of red lava:--these remains would seem to indicate a former population, that had found it expedient to abandon the island from its insufficiency to support it. Captain Beechey observes, that 'from these images and the large piles of stones, on heights to which they must have been dragged with great labour, it may be concluded that the island was inhabited for a considerable time; and from bones being found, always buried under these piles, and never upon the surface, we may presume that those who survived, quitted the island in their canoes to seek an asylum elsewhere.'

It appears from Beechey, that Adams had contemplated the prospect of an increasing population with the limited means of supporting it, and requested that he would communicate with the British Government upon the subject, which he says he did, and that, through the interference of the Admiralty and Colonial Office, means have been taken for removing them to any place they may choose for themselves. It is to be hoped, however, that no such interference will take place; for half a century, at least, there is no danger of any want of food. The attempt, however, was made through the means of a Mr. Nott, a missionary of Otaheite, who, being on a visit to this country, was authorized, on his return, to make arrangements for their removal to Otaheite, if they wished it, and if Pomarre, the king of the island, should not object to receive them; and he carried a letter to this chief from Lord Bathurst, acquainting him with the intention of the British Government, and expressing the hope that he would be induced to receive under his protection a people whose moral and religious character had created so lively an interest in their favour; but it fortunately happened that this missionary passed the island without stopping. A Mr. Joshua Hill subsequently proposed their removal to New South Wales, but his vessel was considered too small for the purpose.

Two years after this, as difficulties had occurred to prevent the above-mentioned intentions from being carried into effect, Sir George Murray deemed it desirable that no time should be lost in affording such assistance to these islanders as might, at all events, render their present abode as comfortable as circumstances would allow, *until* arrangements could be made for their future disposal, either in one of the Society Islands, as originally proposed, or at one of our settlements on New Holland. The assistance here alluded to has been afforded, as above mentioned, by his Majesty's ship **Seringapatam**.

It is sincerely to be hoped that such removal will be no longer thought of. No complaint was made, no apprehension of want expressed to Captain Waldegrave, who left them contented and happy; and Captain Beechey, since his return, has received a letter from John Buffet, who informs him of a notification made by Nott the missionary at Otaheite, that the king was willing to receive them, and that measures would be taken for their removal; but, he adds, the people are so much attached to, and satisfied with, their native island, as not to have a wish to leave it. The breaking up of this happy, innocent, and simple-minded little society, by some summary process, and consigning them to those sinks of infamy on New Holland or Van Diemen's Land, or to mix them up with the dram-drinkers, the psalmsingers, and the languid and lazy Otaheitans, would, in either case, be a subject of deep regret to all who take an interest in their welfare; and to themselves would be the inevitable loss of all those amiable qualities which have obtained for them the kind and generous sympathy of their countrymen at home. We have a person who acts as consul at Otaheite, and it is to be hoped he will receive instructions, on no account to sanction, but on the contrary to interdict, any measure that maybe attempted on the part of the missionaries for their removal;--perhaps, however, as money would be required for such a purpose, they may be considered safe from that quarter.

The time must come when they will emigrate on their own accord. When the hive is full, they will send out their swarms. Captain Beechey tells us that the reading of some books of voyages and travels, belonging to Bligh and left in the ***Bounty***, had created a desire in some of them to leave it; but that family ties and an ardent affection for each other, and for their native soil, had always interposed, on the few occasions that offered, to prevent individuals going away singly. George Adams, however, who had failed when the ***Blossom*** was there to soften the heart of Polly Young, and had no wife to detain him, was very anxious to embark in that ship, that he might see something of the world beyond the narrow limits of his own little island; and Beechey would have taken him, had not his mother wept bitterly at the idea of parting from him, and wished to impose terms touching his return to the island, that could not be acceded to.

Pitcairn Island lies at the south-eastern extremity of a chain of islands, which, including the Society and Friendly Islands, exceed a hundred in number, many of them wholly uninhabited, and the rest but thinly peopled, all speaking the same or nearly the same language, which is also spoken by the natives of Pitcairn Island; and all of the two groups are richly clothed with the spontaneous products of nature fit for the use of man. To all these they will have, when necessity prompts them, easy means of access. No large vessels are required for an emigration of this kind; the frailest barks and single canoes have been driven hundreds of miles over the Pacific. The Pitcairners have already proceeded from the simple canoe to row-boats, and the progress from this to small decked vessels is simple and natural. They may thus at some future period, which is not at all improbable, be the means of spreading Christianity and consequently civilization throughout the numerous groups of islands in the Southern Pacific; whereas to remove them, as has been imprudently suggested, would be to devote them at once to misery and destruction.

That there is no deficiency in the number and variety of plants, producing food and clothing for the use of man, will appear from the following list, which is far from being complete:

INDIGENOUS

Cocos nucifera	Cocoa-nut.
Musa Paradisiaca	Plantains.
Musa sapientum	Bananas.
Dioscorea sativum	Yams.
Convolvulus batatas	Sweet potatoes.
Arum, esculentum	Taro Root.
Arum costatum	Yappa.
Broussonetia papyrifera	Cloth-tree.
Dracaena terminalis	*Tee*-plant.
Aleurites triloba	Doodoe.
Morinda citrifolia	Nono.
----	Toonena, a large timber tree.
Ficus indica	Banyan-tree.
Morus chinensis	Mulberry.
Pandanus odoratissimus	(?)

And a great number of other indigenous plants, some of which are useful and others ornamental.

INTRODUCED

Artocarpus incisa	Bread-fruit.
Cucurbita citrullus	Water-melons
Cucurbita pepo	Pumpkins.
Solanum esculenlum	Potatoes.
Nicotiana tabaccum	Tobacco.
Citrus lemoneum	Lemon.
---- *aurantium*	Orange.

Besides these they have European peas, beans, and onions; sugar-canes, ginger, pepper, and turmeric. In fact, situated as the island is, in a temperate climate just without the tropic, and enjoying abundance of rain, there is scarcely any vegetable, with the exception of a few of the equinoxial plants, that may not be cultivated here. The zea maize, or Indian corn, would be infinitely useful both for themselves, their poultry, and their pigs.

As a great part of the island is at present covered with trees, which would necessarily give way to an extended cultivation, and as trees attract rain, Captain Waldegrave seems to think that when these are removed showers will be less frequent; but there is little fear of this being the case; the central ridge, with points that exceed eleven hundred feet in height, will more effectually attract and condense the clouds than any quantity of trees growing at a less elevation; and there can be little doubt that plenty of water will be found by digging at the foot of the hills or close to the sea-coast.

The climate appears to be unexceptionable. During the sixteen days of December (the height of summer) that the ***Blossom*** remained there, the range of the thermometer on the island, from nine in the morning till three in the afternoon, was from 76 deg. to 80 deg.; on board ship from 74 deg. to 76 deg.; from whence Captain Beechey places the mean temperature during that time at 76-1/2 deg.. In winter he says the southwesterly winds blow very cold, and even snow has been known to fall.

Not one visitor to this happy island has taken leave of its amiable inhabitants without a feeling of regret. Captain Beechey says, 'When we were about to take leave, our friends assembled to express their regret at our departure. All brought some little present for our acceptance, which they wished us to keep in remembrance of them; after which they accompanied us to the beach, where we took our leave of the female part of the inhabitants. Adams and the young men pushed off in their own boat to the ship, determined to accompany us to sea, as far as they could with safety. They continued on board, unwilling to leave us, until we were a considerable distance from land, when they shook each of us feelingly by the hand, and, amidst expressions of the deepest concern at our departure, wished us a prosperous voyage, and hoped that we might one day meet again. As soon as they were clear of the ship, they all stood up in their boat, and gave us three hearty cheers, which were as heartily returned. As the weather became foggy, the barge towed them towards the shore, and we took a final leave of them, unconscious, until the moment of separation, of the warm interest their situation and good conduct had created in us.'

Happy, thrice happy people! May no improper intruders thrust themselves into your peaceful and contented society! May that Providence which has hitherto protected you, still continue to pour down those blessings upon you, of which you appear to be so truly sensible, and for which you are justly thankful! May it throw round the shores of your enviable little Eden, 'cherubim and a flaming sword,' to guard its approaches from those who would endanger your peace; and above all, shield you from those, who would perplex and confuse your unsophisticated minds, by mysterious doctrines which they do not themselves comprehend! Remain steadfast to the faith, which your late father and benefactor has instilled into your minds, culled from the precepts of your Bible, and be content for the present to observe those simple rules for your religious and moral conduct, which he has taught you, and which he drew pure and undefiled from that sacred source; and be assured that, so long as you shall adhere to the line of conduct you have hitherto pursued, and be contented with your present lot, your happiness is secure; but once admit ignorant or false teachers among you, and from that period you may date the commencement of misfortunes and misery!

CONCLUSION

Many useful and salutary lessons of conduct may be drawn from this eventful history, more especially by officers of the navy, both old and young, as well as by those subordinate to them. In the first place, it most strongly points out the dreadful consequences that are almost certain to ensue from a state of insubordination and mutiny on board a ship of war; and the equally certain fate that, at one time or other, awaits all those who have the misfortune to be concerned in a transaction of this revolting nature. In the present instance, the dreadful retribution which overtook them, and which was evinced in a most extraordinary manner, affords an awful and instructive lesson to seamen, by which they may learn, that although the guilty may be secured for a time in evading the punishment due to the offended laws of society, yet they must not hope to escape the pursuit of Divine vengeance. It will be recollected that the number of persons who remained in the *Bounty*, after her piratical seizure, and of course charged with the crime of mutiny, was twenty-five; that these subsequently separated into two parties, sixteen having landed at Otaheite, and afterwards taken from thence in the *Pandora*, as prisoners, and nine having gone with the *Bounty* to Pitcairn's Island.

Of the sixteen taken in the *Pandora*:--

1. Mr PETER HEYWOOD, midshipman,   } sentenced to death, but pardoned.
2. JAMES MORBISON, boatswain's mate,   }   do.
3. WILLIAM MUSPRATT, commander's steward,} do.
4. THOS. BURKITT, seaman   } condemned and executed.

5. JOHN MILLWARD, do.   } do.
6. THOS. ELLISON, do.   } do.
7. JOSEPH COLEMAN, armourer   } do.
8. CHARLES NORMAN, carpenter's mate } tried and acquitted.
9. THOS. M'INTOSH, carpenter's crew } do.
10. MICHAEL BYRNE, seaman   } do
11. Mr. GEORGE STEWART, midshipman} drowned in irons
12. JOHN SUMNER, seaman   } when the
13. RICHARD SKINNER, seaman   } *Pandora*
14. HENRY HILLBRANT, cooper   } was wrecked.
15. CHAS. CHURCHILL, master-at-arms, murdered by Matthew Thompson.
16. MATTHEW THOMPSON, seaman,   murdered by Churchill's friends in Otaheite.

Of the nine who landed on Pitcairn's Island:

1. Mr. FLETCHER CHRISTIAN,
   acting-lieut.   } murdered by the Otaheitans.
2. JOHN WILLIAMS, seaman   } do.
3. ISAAC MARTIN,   do.   } do.
4. JOHN MILLS, gunner's mate   } do.
5. WILLM. BROWN, botanist's assistant } do.
6. MATTHEW QUINTAL, seaman,   put to death by Young and Adams in self-defence.
7. WILLIAM M'KOY, seaman,   became insane, and killed by throwing himself from a rock.
8. Mr. EDWAKD YOUNG, midshipman,   died of asthma.
9. ALEX. SMITH, *alias* John Adams, seaman, died in 1829.

Young officers of the navy, as well as the common seamen, may also derive some useful lessons from the events of this history. They will see the melancholy results of affording the least encouragement for seamen to depart from their strict line of duty, and to relax in that obedience to the orders of superiors, by which alone the discipline of the service can be preserved; they will learn how dangerous it is to show themselves careless and indifferent in executing those orders, by thus setting a bad example to the men. It ought also to enforce on their minds, how necessary it is to avoid even the appearance of acting in any way that can be considered as repugnant to, or subversive of, the rules and regulations of the service; and most particularly to guard against any conduct that may have the appearance of lowering the authority of their superiors, either by their words or actions.

No doubt can remain on the minds of unprejudiced persons, or such as are capable of weighing evidence, that the two young midshipmen, Stewart and Heywood, were perfectly innocent of any share in the transaction in question; and yet, because they happened to be left in the ship, not only contrary to their wish and intention, but kept down below by force, the one lost his life, by being drowned in chains, and the other was condemned to die, and only escaped from suffering the last penalty of the law by a recommendation to the royal mercy. The only point in which these two officers failed, was, that they did not at once demand permission to accompany their commander, while they were allowed to remain on deck and had the opportunity of doing so. The manly conduct of young Heywood, throughout his long and unmerited sufferings, affords an example of firmness, fortitude, and resignation to the Divine will, that is above all praise; in fact, nothing short of conscious innocence could have supported him in the severe trials he had to undergo.

The melancholy effects which tyrannical conduct, harsh and opprobrious language, ungovernable passion, and a worrying and harassing temper, on the part of naval commanders, seldom fail to produce on the minds of those who are subject to their capricious and arbitrary command, are strongly exemplified in the cause and consequences of the mutiny in the **Bounty**, as described in the course of this history. Conduct of this kind, by making the inferior officers of a ship discontented and unhappy, has the dangerous tendency, as in the case of Christian, to incite the crew to partake in their discontent, and be ready to assist in any plan to get rid of the tyrant. We may see in it, also, how very little credit a commander is likely to gain, either with the service or the public at large, when the duties of a ship are carried on, as they would appear to have been in the *Pandora*, in a cold, phlegmatic, and unfeeling manner, and with an indifference to the comfort of all around him,--subjecting offenders of whatever description to unnecessary restraint, and a severity of punishment, which, though strictly within the letter of the law, contributes in no way to the ends of discipline or of justice.

The conduct of Bligh, however mistaken he may have been in his mode of carrying on the duties of the ship, was most exemplary throughout the long and perilous voyage he performed in an open boat, on the wide ocean, with the most scanty supply of provisions and water, and in the worst weather. The result of such meritorious conduct holds out every encouragement to both officers and men, by showing them that, by firmness and perseverance, and the adoption of well-digested measures, steadily ursued in spite of opposition, the most hopeless undertaking, to all appearance, may be successfully accomplished.

And lastly--The fate that has attended almost every one of those concerned in the mutiny and piracy of his Majesty's ship **Bounty** ought to operate as a warning to, and make a deep impression on the minds of, our brave seamen, not to suffer themselves to be led astray from the straightforward line of their duty, either by order or persuasion of some hot-brained, thoughtless, or designing person, whether their superior or equal, but to remain faithful, under all circumstances, to their commanding officer, as any mutinous proceedings or disobedience of his orders are sure to be visited upon them in the long run, either by loss of life, or by a forfeiture of that liberal provision which the British government has bestowed on its seamen for long and faithful services.

P.S.--Just as this last sheet came from the press, the editor has noticed, with a feeling of deep and sincere regret, a paragraph in the newspapers, said to be extracted from an American paper, stating that a vessel sent to Pitcairn's Island by the missionaries of Otaheite has carried off the whole of the settlers to the latter island. If this be true--and the mention of the name of Nott gives a colour to the transaction--the 'cherubim' must have slept, the 'flaming sword' have been sheathed, and another Eden has been lost: and, what is worse than all, that native simplicity of manners, that purity of morals, and that singleness of heart, which so peculiarly distinguished this little interesting society, are all lost. They will now be dispersed among the missionary stations as humble dependents, where Kitty Quintal and the rest of them may get 'food for their souls,' such as it is, in exchange for the substantial blessings they enjoyed on Pitcairn's Island.

ADDITIONAL NOTE

In reference to the subject of extraordinary passages made in open boats on the wide ocean, and the note thereon at page 127, the following may be added as another instance, the most painfully interesting, and the most calamitous, perhaps, ever recorded. It was related to Mr. Bennet, a gentleman deputed by the Missionary Society of London, together with the Rev. Daniel Tyerman, to visit their several stations in the South Sea Islands, by Captain George Pollard, the unfortunate sufferer, whom these gentlemen met with at Raiatea, then a passenger in an American vessel, having a second time lost his ship near the Sandwich Islands. The narrative is extracted from *The Journal of Voyages and Travels*, just published, of the two gentlemen above-mentioned, and is as follows:--

'My first shipwreck was in open sea, on the 20th of November, 1820, near the equator, about 118 degrees W. long. The vessel, a South Sea whaler, was called the ***Essex***. On that day, as we were on the look-out for sperm whales, and had actually struck two, which the boats' crews were following to secure, I perceived a very large one--it might be eighty or ninety feet long--rushing with great swiftness through the water, right towards the ship. We hoped that she would turn aside, and dive under, when she perceived such a baulk in her way. But no! the animal came full force against our stern-post: had any quarter less firm been struck, the vessel must have been burst; as it was, every plank and timber trembled, throughout her whole bulk.

'The whale, as though hurt by a severe and unexpected concussion, shook its enormous head, and sheered off to so considerable a distance that for some time we had lost sight of her from the starboard quarter; of which we were very glad, hoping that the worst was over. Nearly an hour afterwards, we saw the same fish--we had no doubt of this, from her size, and the direction in which she came--making again towards us. We were at once aware of our danger, but escape was impossible. She dashed her head this time against the ship's side, and so broke it in that the vessel filled rapidly, and soon became water-logged. At the second shock, expecting her to go down, we lowered our three boats with the utmost expedition, and all hands, twenty in the whole, got into them--seven, and seven, and six. In a little while, as she did not sink, we ventured on board again, and, by scuttling the deck, were enabled to get out some biscuit, beef, water, rum, two sextants, a quadrant, and three compasses. These, together with some rigging, a few muskets, powder, etc., we brought away; and, dividing the stores among our three small crews, rigged the boats as well as we could; there being a compass for each, and a sextant for two, and a quadrant for one, but neither sextant nor quadrant for the third.[42] Then, instead of pushing away for some port, so amazed and bewildered were we that we continued sitting in our places gazing upon the ship, as though she had been an object of the tenderest affection. Our eyes could not leave her, till, at the end of many hours, she gave a slight reel, then down she sank. No words can tell our feelings. We looked at each other--we looked at the place where she had so lately been afloat--and we did not cease to look, till the terrible conviction of our abandoned and perilous situation roused us to exertion, if deliverance were yet possible.

'We now consulted about the course which it might be best to take--westward to India, eastward to South America, or south-westward to the Society Isles. We knew that we were at no great distance from Tahiti, but were so ignorant of the state and temper of the inhabitants, that we feared we should be devoured by cannibals, if we cast ourselves on their mercy. It was determined, therefore, to make for South America, which we computed to be more than two thousand miles distant. Accordingly we steered eastward, and though for several days harassed with squalls, we contrived to keep together. It was not long before we found that one of the boats had started a plank, which was no wonder, for whale-boats are all clinker-built, and very slight, being made of half-inch plank only, before planing. To remedy this alarming defect we all turned to, and having emptied the damaged boat into the two others, we raised her side as well as we could, and succeeded in restoring the plank at the bottom. Through this accident, some of our biscuit had become injured by the salt-water. This was equally divided among the several boats' crews. Food and water, meanwhile, with our utmost economy, rapidly failed. Our strength was exhausted, not by abstinence only, but by the labours which we were obliged to employ to keep our little vessels afloat amidst the storms which repeatedly assailed us. One night we were parted in rough weather; but though the next day we fell in with one of our companion-boats, we never saw or heard any more of the other, which probably perished at sea, being without either sextant or quadrant.[43]

'When we were reduced to the last pinch, and out of everything, having been more than three weeks abroad, we were cheered with the sight of a low, uninhabited island, which we reached in hope, but were bitterly disappointed. There were some barren bushes and many rocks on this forlorn spot. The only provision that we could procure were a few birds and their eggs: this supply was soon reduced; the sea-fowls appeared to have been frightened away, and their nests were left empty after we had once or twice plundered them. What distressed us most was the utter want of fresh water; we could not find a drop anywhere, till, at the extreme verge of ebb tide, a small spring was discovered in the sand; but even that was too scanty to afford us sufficient to quench our thirst before it was covered by the waves at their turn.

'There being no prospect but that of starvation here, we determined to put to sea again. Three of our comrades, however, chose to remain, and we pledged ourselves to send a vessel to bring them off, if we ourselves should ever escape to a Christian port. With a very small morsel of biscuit for each, and a little water, we again ventured out on the wide ocean. In the course of a few days our provisions were consumed. Two men died; we had no other alternative than to live upon their remains. These we roasted to dryness by means of fires kindled on the ballast-sand at the bottom of the boats.[44] When this supply was spent, what could we do? We looked at each other with horrid thoughts in our minds, but we held our tongues. I am sure that we loved one another as brothers all the time; and yet our looks told plainly what must be done. We cast lots, and the fatal one fell on my poor cabin-boy. I started forward instantly, and cried out, "My lad, my lad, *if you don't like your lot*, I'll shoot the first man that touches you." The poor emaciated boy hesitated a moment or two; then, quietly laying his head down upon the gunnel of the boat, he said, "*I like it as well as any other.*" He was soon despatched, and nothing of him left. I think, then, another man died of himself, and him, too, we ate. But I can tell you no more--my head is on fire at the recollection; I hardly know what I say. I forgot to say that we had parted company with the second boat before now. After some more days of horror and despair, when some were lying down at the bottom of the boat not able to rise, and scarcely one of us could move a limb, a vessel hove in sight. We were taken on board, and treated with extreme kindness. The second last boat was also picked up at sea, and the survivors saved. A ship afterwards sailed in search of our companions on the desolate island, and brought them away.'

Captain Pollard closed his dreary narrative with saying, in a tone of despondency never to be forgotten by him who heard it, 'After a time I found my way to the United States, to which I belonged, and got another ship. That, too, I have lost by a second wreck off the Sandwich Islands, and now I am utterly ruined. No owner will ever trust me with a whaler again, for all will say I am an *unlucky* man.'

The following account respecting the three men that were left on the uninhabited island, is given in a note of the same work, and said to be extracted from a religious tract, No. 579, issued by the Society in Paternoster Row.

'On the 26th of December the boats left the island: this was, indeed, a trying moment to all: they separated with mutual prayers and good wishes, seventeen[45] venturing to sea with almost certain death before them, while three remained on a rocky isle, destitute of water, and affording hardly anything to support life. The prospects of these three poor men were gloomy: they again tried to dig a well, but without success, and all hope seemed at an end, when providentially they were relieved by a shower of rain. They were thus delivered from the immediate apprehension of perishing by thirst. Their next care was to procure food, and their difficulties herein were also very great; their principal resource was small birds, about the size of a blackbird, which they caught while at roost. Every night they climbed the trees in search of them, and obtained, by severe exertions, a scanty supply, hardly enough to support life. Some of the trees bore a small berry which gave them a little relief, but these they found only in small quantities. Shell-fish they searched for in vain; and although from the rocks they saw at times a number of sharks, and also other sorts of fish, they were unable to catch any, as they had no fishing tackle. Once they saw several turtles, and succeeded in taking five, but they were then without water: at those times they had little inclination to eat, and before one of them was quite finished the others were become unfit for food.

'Their sufferings from want of water were the most severe, their only supply being from what remained in holes among the rocks after the showers which fell at intervals; and sometimes they were five or six days without any; on these occasions they were compelled to suck the blood of the birds they caught, which allayed their thirst in some degree; but they did so very unwillingly, as they found themselves much disordered thereby.

'Among the rocks were several caves formed by nature, which afforded shelter from the wind and rain. In one of these caves they found eight human skeletons, in all probability the remains of some poor mariners who had been shipwrecked on the isle, and perished for want of food and water. They were side by side, as if they had laid down and died together! This sight deeply affected the mate and his companions; their case was similar, and they had every reason to expect ere long the same end: for many times they lay down at night, with their tongues swollen and their lips parched with thirst, scarcely hoping to see the morning sun; and it is impossible to form an idea of their feelings when the morning dawned, and they found their prayers had been heard and answered by a providential supply of rain.

'In this state they continued till the 5th of April following. On the morning of that day they were in the woods as usual, searching for food and water, as well as their weakness permitted, when their attention was aroused by a sound which they thought was distant thunder; but looking towards the sea, they saw a ship in the offing, which had just fired a gun. Their joy at this sight may be more easily imagined than described; they immediately fell on their knees, and thanked God for His goodness, in thus sending deliverance when least expected; then, hastening to the shore, they saw a boat coming towards them. As the boat could not approach the shore without great danger, the mate, being a good swimmer, and stronger than his companions, plunged into the sea, and providentially escaped a watery grave at the moment when deliverance was at hand. His companions crawled out further on the rocks, and, by the great exertions of the crew, were taken into the boat, and soon found themselves on board the **Surrey**, commanded by Captain Raine, by whom they were treated in the kindest manner, and their health and strength were speedily restored.'

Mr. Montgomery, the editor, observes, 'there is some incongruity in these two narratives, which more minute particulars might reconcile.' We have noticed them.

Mr. Bennet received the account verbally, and may be mistaken in some points, but there is little doubt of its being substantially correct.

This melancholy history supplies an additional and complete answer to Bligh's doubts of men feeding on each other to preserve existence.

NOTES:

[1] The discovery of this island is owing to Fernandez de Quiros in 1606, which he named *La Sagittaria*, Some doubts were at first entertained of its identity with Otaheite, but the small difference of a few miles in latitude, and about two degrees of longitude, the description as to size, the low isthmus, the distance from it of any other island at all similar, and above all, the geographical position--all prove its identity--although Quiros calls it, what it certainly is not, a low island.

[2] *A Missionary Voyage to the Southern Pacific Ocean*, Appendix, pp. 336, 342.

[3] Cook appears not to have exercised his usual judgement in estimating the population of this island. After stating the number of war-canoes at seventeen hundred and twenty, and able men to man them, at sixty-eight thousand eight hundred, he comes to the conclusion that the population must consist of two hundred and four thousand souls; and reflecting on the vast swarms which everywhere appeared, 'I was convinced,' he says, 'that this estimate was not much, if at all, too great.'

[4] The words within brackets are in the original despatch.

[5] He was born in the Isle of Man, his father being Deemster of Man, and Seneschal to the Duke of Athol.

[6] *United Service Journal*, April, 1831.

[7] Hayward and Hallet, who may thus be considered as the ***passive*** cause of the mutiny.

[8] ***Quarterly Review***, No. 89.

[9] One person turns his back on the object that is to be divided; another then points separately to the portions, at each of them asking aloud, 'Who shall have this?' to which the first answers by naming somebody. This impartial method of distribution gives every man an equal chance of the best share. Bligh used to speak of the great amusement the poor people had at the beak and claws falling to his share.

[10] If Bligh here meant to deny the fact of men, in extreme cases, destroying each other for the sake of appeasing hunger, he is greatly mistaken. The fact was

but too well established, and to a great extent, on the raft of the French frigate *Meduse*, when wrecked on the coast of Africa, and also on the rock in the Mediterranean, when the *Nautilus* frigate was lost. There may be a difference between men, in danger of perishing by famine, when in robust health, and men like those of the *Bounty*, worn by degrees to skeletons, by protracted famine, who may thus have become equally indifferent to life or death.

[11] The escape of the *Centaur's* boat, perhaps, comes nearest to it. When the *Centaur* was sinking, Captain Inglefield and eleven others, in a small leaky boat, five feet broad, with one of the gunwales stove, nearly in the middle of the Western Ocean, without compass, without quadrant, without sail, without greatcoat or cloak, all very thinly clothed, in a gale of wind, with a great sea running, and the winter fast approaching,--the sun and stars, by which alone they could shape their course, sometimes hidden for twenty-four hours;--these unhappy men, in this destitute and hopeless condition, had to brave the billows of the stormy Atlantic, for nearly a thousand miles. A blanket, which was by accident in the boat, served as a sail, and with this they scudded before the wind, in expectation of being swallowed up by every wave; with great difficulty the boat was cleared of water before the return of the next great sea; all of the people were half drowned, and sitting, except the balers, at the bottom of the boat. On quitting the ship the distance of Fayal was two hundred and sixty leagues, or about nine hundred English miles.

Their provisions were a bag of bread, a small ham, a single piece of pork, two quart bottles of water, and a few of French cordials. One biscuit, divided into twelve morsels, was served for breakfast, and the same for dinner; the neck of a bottle broken off, with the cork in, supplied the place of a glass; and this filled with water was the allowance for twenty-four hours for each man.

On the fifteenth day, they had only one day's bread, and one bottle of water remaining of a second supply of rain; on this day Matthews, a quarter-master, the stoutest man in the boat, perished of hunger and cold. This poor man, on the day before, had complained of want of strength in his throat, as he expressed it, to swallow his morsel; and, in the night, drank salt-water, grew delirious, and died without a groan. Hitherto despair and gloom had been successfully prevented, the men, when the evenings closed in, having been encouraged by turns to sing a song, or relate a story, instead of a supper: 'but,' says the Captain, 'this evening I found it impossible to raise either.' The Captain had directed the clothes to be taken from the corpse of Matthews and given to some of the men, who were perishing with, cold; but the shocking skeleton-like appearance of his remains made such an impression on the people, that all efforts to raise their spirits were ineffectual. On the following day, the sixteenth, their last breakfast was served with the bread and water remaining, when John Gregory, the quarter-master, declared with much confidence that he saw land in the south-east, which turned out to be Fayal.

But the most extraordinary ***feat of navigation*** is that which is related (on good authority) in a note of the ***Quarterly Review***, vol. xviii. pp. 337-339:--

Of all the feats of navigation on record, however, that of Diogo Botelho Perreira, in the early period of 1536-37, stands pre-eminent; it is extracted from the voluminous Decades of Diogo de Couto, whose work, though abounding with much curious matter, like those of most of the old Portuguese writers, has not been fortunate enough to obtain an English translation. We are indebted to a friend for pointing it out to us, and we conceive it will be read with interest.

> 'In the time of the vice-royalty of Don Francisco de Almeyda there was a young gentleman in India of the name of Diogo Botelho Perreira, son of the commander of Cochin, who educated him with great care, so that he soon became skilled in the art of navigation, and an adept in the construction of marine charts. As he grew up, he felt anxious to visit Portugal, where, on his arrival, he was well received at court, and the king took pleasure in conversing with him on those subjects which had been the particular objects of his studies. Confident of his own talents, and presuming on the favour with which the king always treated him, he ventured one day to request his Majesty to appoint him commander of the fortress of Chaul. The king smiled at his request, and replied, that "the command of the fortress was not for pilots." Botelho was piqued at this answer, and, on returning into the ante-chamber, was met by Don Antonio Noronha, second son of the Marquis of Villa Real, who asked him if his suit had been granted: he answered, "Sir, I

will apply where my suit will not be neglected." When this answer came to the ears of the king, he immediately ordered Botelho to be confined in the castle of Lisbon, lest he should follow the example of Megalhaens, and go over to Spain. There he remained a prisoner until the admiral viceroy Don Vasco da Gama, solicited his release, and was permitted to take him to India; but on the express condition that he should not return to Portugal, except by special permission. Under these unpleasant circumstances this gentleman proceeded to India, anxious for an opportunity of distinguishing himself, that he might be permitted again to visit Portugal.

'It happened about this time that the Sultan Badur, sovereign of Cambaya, gave the governor, Nuno da Cunha, permission to erect a fortress on the island of Diu, an object long and anxiously wished for, as being of the greatest importance to the security of the Portuguese possessions in India. Botelho was aware how acceptable this information would be to the king, and therefore deemed this a favourable opportunity of regaining his favour, by conveying such important intelligence; and he resolved to perform the voyage in a vessel so small, and so unlike what had ever appeared in Portugal, that it should not fail to excite astonishment, how any man could undertake so long and perilous a navigation, in such a frail and diminutive bottom.

'Without communicating his scheme to any person, he procured a *fusta*, put a deck on it from head to stern, furnished it with spare sails and spars, and every other necessary, and constructed two small tanks for water.

'As soon as the monsoon served, he embarked with some men in his service, giving out that he was going to Melinde; and, to give colour to this story, he proceeded to Baticala, where he purchased some cloths and beads for that market, and laid in provisions; some native merchants also embarked with a few articles on board for the Melinde market, to which he did not choose to object, lest it should alarm his sailors.

'He set sail with the eastern monsoon, in the beginning of October, and arrived safely at Melinde, where he landed the native merchants, took in wood, water, and refreshments, and again put to sea, informing his crew that he was going to Quiloa. When he had got to a distance from the land, it would appear that some of his crew had mutinied; but this he had foreseen and provided for; putting some of them in irons, and promising at the same time amply to reward the services of the rest, and giving them to understand that he was going to Sofala on account of the trade in gold. Thus he proceeded, touching at various places for refreshments, which he met with in great plenty and very cheap.

'From Sofala he proceeded along the coast till he had passed the Cabo dos Correntes, and from thence along the shore, without ever venturing to a distance from the land, and touching at the different rivers, until he passed the Cape of Good Hope, which he did in January 1537.

'From thence he stretched into the ocean with gentle breezes, steering for St. Helena; where, on arriving, he drew his little vessel ashore, to clean her bottom and repair her, and also to give a few days' rest to his crew, of whom some had perished of cold, notwithstanding his having provided warm clothing for them.

'Departing from St. Helena, he boldly steered his little bark across the wide ocean, directing his career to St. Thome, where he took in provisions, wood, and water; and from thence he proceeded to the bar of Lisbon, where he arrived in May, when the king was at Almeyrin. He entered the river with his oars, his little vessel being dressed with flags and pendants, and anchored at Point Leira opposite to Salvaterra, not being able to get farther up the river. This novelty produced such a sensation in Lisbon that the Tagus was covered with boats to see the *fusta* Diogo Botelho Perreira landed in a boat, and proceeded to Almeyrin, to give the king an account of his voyage, and solicit a gratification for the good news which he brought, of his Majesty now being possessed of a fortress on the island of Diu.

'The king was highly pleased with this intelligence, but, as Botelho brought no letters from the governor, he did not give him the kind of reception which he had expected. On the contrary, the king treated him with coldness and distance; his Majesty, however, embarked to see the *fusta*, on board of which he examined every thing with much attention, and was gratified in viewing a vessel of such a peculiar form, and ordered money and clothes to be given to the sailors--nor could he help considering Diogo Botelho as a man of extraordinary enterprise and courage, on whose firmness implicit reliance might be placed.

'The little vessel was ordered to be drawn ashore at Sacabem, where it remained many years (until it fell to pieces), and was visited by people from all parts of Europe, who beheld it with astonishment. The king subsequently received letters from the governor of Nuno da Cunha, confirming the news brought by Botelho; the bearer of these letters, a Jew, was immediately rewarded with a pension of a hundred and forty milreas; but

Botelho was neglected for many years, and at last appointed commander of St. Thome, and finally made captain of Cananor in India, that he might be at a distance from Portugal.'

The vessel named *fusta* is a long, shallow, Indian-built row-boat, which uses latine sails in fine weather. These boats are usually open, but Botelho covered his with a deck: its dimensions, according to Lavanha, in his edition of De Barros' unfinished Decade, are as follows:--length, twenty-two palmos, or sixteen feet six inches. Breadth, twelve palmos, or nine feet. Depth, six palmos, or four feet six inches. Bligh's boat was twenty-three feet long, six feet nine inches broad, and two feet nine inches deep. From the circumstance mentioned of some of his crew having perished with cold, it is probable that they were natives of India, whom the Portuguese were in the habit of bringing home as part of their crew.

[12] Previous to the writing of this letter, the following copy of verses shows how anxiously this young lady's mind was engaged on the unhappy circumstances under which her brother was placed.

>   Tell me, thou busy flatt'ring Telltale, why--
>   Why flow these tears--why heaves this deep-felt sigh,--
>   Why is all joy from my sad bosom flown,
>   Why lost that cheerfulness I thought my own;
>   Why seek I now in solitude for ease.
>   Which once was centred in a wish to please,
>   When ev'ry hour in joy and gladness past,
>   And each new day shone brighter than the last;
>   When in society I loved to join;
>   When to enjoy, and give delight, was mine?--
>   Now--sad reverse! in sorrow wakes each day,
>   And griefs sad tones inspire each plaintive lay:
>   Alas! too plain these mournful tears can tell
>   The pangs of woe my lab'ring bosom swell!
>   Thou best of brothers--friend, companion, guide,
>   Joy of my youth, my honour, and my pride!
>   Lost is all peace--all happiness to me,

And fled all comfort, since deprived of thee.
In vain, my Lycidas, thy loss I mourn,
In vain indulge a hope of thy return;
Still years roll on and still I vainly sigh,
Still tears of anguish drown each gushing eye.
Ah I cruel Time I how slow thy ling'ring pace,
Which keeps me from his tender, loved embrace.
At home to see him, or to know him near,
How much I wish--and yet how much I fear!
Oh I fatal voyage! which robb'd my soul of peace
And wreck'd my happiness in stormy seas!
Why, my loved Lycidas, why did'st thou stay,
Why waste thy life from friendship far away?
Though guiltless thou of mutiny or blame,
And free from aught which could disgrace thy name;
Though thy pure soul, in honour's footsteps train'd,
Was never yet by disobedience stain'd;
Yet is thy fame exposed to slander's wound,
And fell suspicion whispering around.
In vain--to those who knew thy worth and truth,
Who watch'd each op'ning virtue of thy youth;
When noblest principles inform'd thy mind,
Where sense and sensibility were join'd;
Love to inspire, to charm, to win each heart,
And ev'ry tender sentiment impart;
Thy outward form adorn'd with ev'ry grace;
With beauty's softest charms thy heav'nly face,
Where sweet expression beaming ever proved
The index of that soul, by all beloved;
Thy wit so keen, thy genius form'd to soar,
By fancy wing'd, new science to explore;
Thy temper, ever gentle, good, and kind,
Where all but guilt an advocate could find:

To those who know this character was thine,
(And in this truth assenting numbers join)
How vain th' attempt to fix a crime on thee,
Which thou disdain'st--from which each thought is free!
No, my loved brother, ne'er will I believe
Thy seeming worth was meant but to deceive;
Still will I think (each circumstance though strange)
That thy firm principles could never change;
That hopes of preservation urged thy stay,
Or force, which those resistless must obey.
If this is error, let me still remain
In error wrapp'd--nor wake to truth again!
Come then, sweet Hope, with all thy train of joy
Nor let Despair each rapt'rous thought destroy;
Indulgent Heav'n, in pity to our tears,
At length will bless a parent's sinking years;
Again shall I behold thy lovely face,
By manhood form'd, and ripen'd ev'ry grace,
Again I'll press thee to my anxious breast,
And ev'ry sorrow shall be hush'd to rest.
Thy presence only can each comfort give.
Come then, my Lycidas, and let me live;
Life without thee is but a wretched load,
Thy love alone can smooth its thorny road;
But blest with thee, how light were every woe;
How would my soul with joy and rapture glow!
Kind Heav'n! thou hast my happiness in store,
Restore him *innocent*--I ask no more!

Isle of Man, Feb. 25, 1792. NESSY HEYWOOD.

[13] This interesting letter is given in the following Chapter, to which it appropriately belongs.

[14] His orders run thus: 'You are to keep the mutineers as closely confined as may preclude all possibility of their escaping, having, however, proper regard to the

preservation of their lives, that they may be brought home, to undergo the punishment due to their demerits.'

[15] *Voyage round the World*, by Mr. George Hamilton, p. 84.

[16] *A Missionary Voyage to the Southern Pacific*, p. 360.

[17] *United Service Journal*.

[18] The Phoceans, on account of the sterility of their country, were in the habit of practising piracy, which, according to Justin, was held to be an honourable profession.

[19] These laws are contained in an ancient authentic book, called 'The Black Book of the Admiralty,' in which all things therein comprehended are engrossed on vellum, in an ancient character; which hath been from time to time kept in the registry of the High Court of Admiralty, for the use of the Judges. When Mr. Luders made enquiry at the office in Doctors' Commons, in 1808, he was informed by the proper officers there, that they had never seen such book, and knew nothing of it, nor where to find it. The fact is, the book in question was put into Lord Thurlow's hands when Attorney-General, and never returned. There is a copy of it in the Admiralty.

[20] Morrison mentions, in his *Journal*, a plan to this effect, contrived by Heywood, Stewart, and himself, but observes, 'it was a foolish attempt, as, had we met with bad weather, our crazy boat would certainly have made us a coffin.'

[21] The following shows how much her fond mind was fixed on her unfortunate brother:--

On the Arrival of my dearly-beloved Brother, Peter Heywood, in England, written while a Prisoner, and waiting the Event of his Trial on board his Majesty's Ship 'Hector.'

> Come, gentle Muse, I woo thee once again,
> Nor woo thee now in melancholy strain;
> Assist my verse in cheerful mood to flow,
> Nor let this tender bosom Anguish know;
> Fill all my soul with notes of Love and Joy,
> No more let Grief each anxious thought employ:
> With Rapture now alone this heart shall burn,
> And Joy, my Lycidas, for thy return!

> Return'd with every charm, accomplish'd youth,
> Adorn'd with Virtue, Innocence, and Truth;
> Wrapp'd in thy conscious merit still remain,
> Till I behold thy lovely form again.
> Protect him, Heav'n, from dangers and alarms,
> And oh! restore him to a sister's arms;
> Support his fortitude in that dread hour
> When he must brave Suspicion's cruel pow'r;
> Grant him to plead with Eloquence divine,
> In ev'ry word let Truth and Honour shine;
> Through each sweet accent let Persuasion flow,
> With manly Firmness let his bosom glow,
> Till strong Conviction, in each face exprest,
> Grants a reward by Honour's self confest.
> Let thy Omnipotence preserve him still,
> And all his future days with Pleasure fill;
> And oh! kind Heav'n, though now in chains he be,
> Restore him soon to Friendship, Love, and me.

[22] The late Aaron Graham, Esq., the highly respected police magistrate in London.

[23] Till the moment of the trial, it will readily be supposed that every thought of this amiable young lady was absorbed in her brother's fate. In this interval the following lines appear to have been written:--

On receiving information by a letter from my ever dearly loved brother Peter Heywood, that his trial was soon to take place.

Isle of Man, August 22, 1792. NESSY HEYWOOD.

[24] The minutes being very long, a brief abstract only, containing the principal points of evidence, is here given.

[25] This Journal, it is presumed, must have been lost when the ***Pandora*** was wrecked.

[26] It was in this state of mind, while in momentary expectation of receiving an account of the termination of the court-martial, that Heywood's charming sister Nessy wrote the following lines:--

ANXIETY.
Doubting, dreading, fretful guest,
Quit, oh I quit this mortal breast.
Why wilt thou my peace invade,
And each brighter prospect shade?
Pain me not with needless Fear,
But let Hope my bosom cheer;
While I court her gentle charms,
Woo the flatterer to my arms;
While each moment she beguiles
With her sweet enliv'ning smiles,
While she softly whispers me,
'Lycidas again is free,'
While I gaze on Pleasure's gleam,
Say not thou 'Tis all a dream.'
Hence--nor darken Joy's soft bloom
With thy pale and sickly gloom:
Nought have I to do with thee--
Hence--begone--Anxiety.

Isle of Man, September 10th. NESSY HEYWOOD.

[27] This is supposed to allude to the evidence given by Hallet.

[28] This refers to a very kind and encouraging letter written to him by the Rev. Dr. Scott, of the Isle of Man, who knew him from a boy, and had the highest opinion of his character.

[29] Captain Bligh states in his journal, that none of his officers were suffered to come near him while held a prisoner by Christian; and Hallet was, no doubt, mistaken, but he had probably said it in the boat, and thought it right to be consistent on the trial.

It has been said that Hallet, when in the *Penelope*, in which frigate he died, expressed great regret at the evidence he had given at the court-martial, and frequently alluded to it, admitting that he might have been mistaken. There can be very little doubt that he was so. But the Editor has ascertained, from personal inquiry of one of the most distinguished flag-officers in the service, who was then first lieutenant of the *Penelope*, that Hallet frequently expressed to him his deep contrition for having given in evidence what, on subsequent reflection, he was convinced to be incorrect; that he ascribed it to the state of confusion in which his mind was when under examination before the Court; and that he had since satisfied himself that, owing to the general alarm and confusion during the mutiny, he must have confounded Heywood with some other person.

[30] Vol. ii. p. 778.

[31] Some few captains were in the habit of turning over a delinquent to be tried by their messmates, and when found guilty, it invariably happened that the punishment inflicted was doubly severe to what it would have been in the ordinary way. This practice,--which, as giving a deliberative voice to the ship's company, was highly reprehensible,--it is to be hoped has entirely ceased.

[32] Information that the pardon was gone down to Portsmouth.

[33] She had received, previous to this, information of what the event would be, and thus gives vent to her feelings.

On receiving certain Intelligence that my most amiable and beloved Brother, Peter Heywood, would soon be restored to Freedom.

>Oh, blissful hour!--oh moment of delight!
>Replete with happiness, with rapture bright!
>An age of pain is sure repaid by this,
>'Tis joy too great--'tis ecstasy of bliss!
>Ye sweet sensations crowding on my soul,
>Which following each other swiftly roll,--
>Ye dear ideas which unceasing press,
>And pain this bosom by your wild excess,
>Ah! kindly cease--for pity's sake subside,
>Nor thus o'erwhelm me with joy's rapid tide:
>My beating heart, oppress'd with woe and care,
>Has yet to learn such happiness to bear:
>From grief, distracting grief, thus high to soar,
>To know dull pain and misery no more,
>To hail each op'ning morn with new delight,
>To rest in peace and joy each happy night,

To see my Lycidas from bondage free,
Restored to life, to pleasure, and to me,
To see him thus--adorn'd with virtue's charms,
To give him to a longing mother's arms,
To know him by surrounding friends caress'd,
Of honour, fame, of life's best gifts possess'd,
Oh, my full heart! 'tis joy--'tis bliss supreme,
And though 'tis real--yet, how like a dream!
Teach me then, Heav'n, to bear it as I ought,
Inspire each rapt'rous, each transporting thought;
Teach me to bend beneath Thy bounteous hand,
With gratitude my willing heart expand:
To Thy omnipotence I humbly bow,
Afflicted once--but ah! how happy now!
Restored in peace, submissive to Thy will,
Oh! bless his days to come--protect him still;
Prolong his life, Thy goodness to adore,
And oh! let sorrow's shafts ne'er wound him more.

NESSY HEYWOOD. *London, October 15th, 1792, Midnight*.

[34] Mr. Graham's daughter.

[35] Several elegiac stanzas were written on the death of this accomplished young lady. The following are dated from her native place, the Isle of Man, where her virtues and accomplishments could best be appreciated.

How soon, sweet maid! how like a fleeting dream
The winning graces, all thy virtues seem!
How soon arrested in thy early bloom
Has fate decreed thee to the joyless tomb!
Nor beauty, genius, nor the Muse's care,
Nor aught could move the tyrant Death to spare:
Ah! could their power revoke the stern decree,
The fatal shaft had past, unfelt by thee!
But vain thy wit, thy sentiment refined,
Thy charms external, and accomplish'd mind;

Thy artless smiles, that seized the willing heart,
Thy converse, that could pure delight impart;
The melting music of thy skilful tongue,
While judgement listen'd, ravish'd with thy song:
Not all the gifts that art and nature gave,
Could save thee, lovely Nessy! from the grave.
Too early lost! from friendship's bosom torn,
Oh might I tune *thy* lyre, and sweetly mourn
In strains like thine, when beauteous Margaret's[A] fate
Oppress'd thy friendly heart with sorrow's weight;
Then should my numbers flow, and laurels bloom
In endless spring around fair Nessy's tomb.

[A] Alluding to some elegant lines, by the deceased, on the death of a female friend.

[36] The following appears to have been written by Mr. P. Heywood on the day that the sentence of condemnation was passed on him.

----Silence then
The whispers of complaint,--low in the dust
Dissatisfaction's daemon's growl unheard.
All--all is good, all excellent below;
Pain is a blessing--sorrow leads to joy--
Joy, permanent and solid! ev'ry ill,
Grim death itself, in all its horrors clad,
Is man's supremest privilege! it frees
The soul from prison, from foul sin, from woe,
And gives it back to glory, rest, and God!
Cheerly, my friends,--oh, cheerly! look not thus
With Pity's melting softness!--that alone
Can shake my fortitude---all is not lost.
Lo! I have gain'd on this important day
A victory consummate o'er myself,
And o'er this life a victory,--on this day.
My birthday to eternity, I've gain'd

>   Dismission from a world, where for a while,
>   Like you, like all, a pilgrim, passing poor,
>   A traveller, a stranger, I have met
>   Still stranger treatment, rude and harsh! I so much
>   The dearer, more desired, the home I seek,
>   Eternal of my Father, and my God!
>   Then pious Resignation, meek-ey'd pow'r,
>   Sustain me still! Composure still be mine.
>   Where rests it? Oh, mysterious Providence
>   I Silence the wild idea.--I have found
>   No mercy yet--no mild humanity,
>   With cruel, unrelenting rigour torn,
>   And lost in prison--lost to all below!

And the following appears to have been written on the day of the king's pardon being received.

>   --Oh deem it not
>   Presumptuous, that my soul grateful thus rates
>   The present high deliv'rance it hath found;--
>   Sole effort of Thy wisdom, sov'reign Pow'r,
>   Without whose knowledge, not a sparrow fells!
>   Oh I may I cease to live, ere cease to bless
>   That interposing hand, which turn'd aside--
>   Nay, to my life and preservation turn'd,--
>   The fatal blow precipitate, ordain'd
>   To level all my little hopes in dust,
>   And give me--to the grave.

[37] With which the Editor, at his request, was favoured at the time.

[38] The only authority that then existed for laying down this island was that of Captain Carteret, who first saw it in 1767. 'It is so high,' he says, 'that we saw it at the distance of more than fifteen leagues, and it having been discovered by a young gentleman, son to Major Pitcairn of the marines, who was unfortunately lost in the *Aurora*, we called it **Pitcairn's Island**.' He makes it in lat. 25 deg. 2' S. and long. 133 deg. 30' W., no less than **three degrees** out of its true longitude! **Three**

minutes would ***now*** be thought a considerable error:--such are the superior advantages conferred by lunar observations and improvements in chronometers.

Pitcairn's Island has been supposed to be the '***Encarnacion***' of Quiros, by whom it is stated to be in lat. 24 deg. 30', and one thousand leagues from the coast of Peru; but as he describes it as 'a low, sandy island, almost level with the sea, having a few trees on it,' we must look for '***Encarnacion***' somewhere else; and ***Ducies*** Island, nearly in that latitude, very low, and within 5 deg. of longitude from Pitcairn's Island, answers precisely to it.

[39] As the manner of Christian's death has been differently reported to each different visitor, by Adams, the only evidence in existence, with the exception of three or four Otaheitan women, and a few infants, some singular circumstances may here be mentioned that happened at home, just at the time of Folder's visit, and which might render his death on Pitcairn's Island almost a matter of doubt.

About the years 1808 and 1809, a very general opinion was prevalent in the neighbourhood of the lakes of Cumberland and Westmoreland, that Christian was in that part of the country, and made frequent private visits to an aunt who was living there. Being the near relative of Mr. Christian Curwen, long member of Parliament for Carlisle, and himself a native, he was well known in the neighbourhood. This, however, might be passed over as mere gossip, had not another circumstance happened just about the same time, for the truth of which the Editor does not hesitate to avouch. In Fore Street, Plymouth Dock, Captain Heywood found himself one day walking behind a man, whose shape had so much the appearance of Christian's, that he involuntarily quickened his pace. Both were walking very fast, and the rapid steps behind him having roused the stranger's attention, he suddenly turned his face, looked at Heywood, and immediately ran off. But the face was as much like Christian's as the back, and Heywood, exceedingly excited, ran also. Both ran as fast as they were able, but the stranger had the advantage, and, after making several short turns, disappeared.

That Christian should be in England, Heywood considered as highly improbable, though not out of the scope of possibility; for at this time no account of him whatsoever had been received since they parted at Otaheite; at any rate the resemblance, the agitation, and the efforts of the stranger to elude him, were circumstances too strong not to make a deep impression on his mind. At the moment, his first thought was to set about making some further inquiries, but on recollection of the pain and trouble such a discovery must occasion him, he considered it more prudent to let the matter drop; but the circumstance was frequently called to his memory for the remainder of his life.

[40] This Nobbs is probably one of those half-witted persons who fancy they have received a *call* to preach nonsense--some cobbler escaped from his stall, or tailor from his shopboard. Kitty Quintal's cant phrase--'we want food for our souls,' and praying at meals for 'spiritual nourishment,' smack not a little of the jargon of the inferior caste of evangelicals. Whoever this pastoral drone may be, it is but too evident that the preservation of the innocence, simplicity, and happiness of these amiable people, is intimately connected with his speedy removal from the island.

[41] Well may Adams have sought for rules for his little society in a book, which contains the foundation of the civil and religious policy of two-thirds of the human race,--in that wonderful book, into whose inspired pages the afflicted never seek for consolation in vain. Millions of examples attest this truth. 'There is no incident in *Robinson Crusoe*,' observes a writer in a critical journal, 'told in language more natural and affecting, than Robert Knox's accidental discovery of a Bible, in the midst of the Candian dominions of Ceylon. His previous despondency from the death of his father, his only friend and companion, whose grave he had but just dug with his own hands, "being now," as he says, "left desolate, sick, and in captivity,"--his agitation, joy, and even terror, on meeting with a book he had for such a length of time not seen, nor hoped to see--his anxiety lest he should fail to procure it--and the comfort, when procured, which it afforded him in his affliction--all are told in Buch a strain of true piety and genuine simplicity as cannot fail to interest and affect every reader of sensibility.'

[42] If there were *three* instruments and *three* boats, there must have been *one* for *each*, for the quadrant was just as good as a sextant.--ED.

[43] The mistake is here again repeated; it would be absurd to suppose that one boat had both quadrant and sextant.

[44] It is not explained with what kind of fuel they performed this distressing operation.

[45] Here, again, is another mistake; the number must have been *eleven* at most, one of the boats having parted before the others reached the island.--ED.

www.bookjungle.com *email: sales@bookjungle.com fax: 630-214-0564 mail: Book Jungle PO Box 2226 Champaign, IL 61825*

The Codes Of Hammurabi And Moses
W. W. Davies

QTY

The discovery of the Hammurabi Code is one of the greatest achievements of archaeology, and is of paramount interest, not only to the student of the Bible, but also to all those interested in ancient history...

Religion   **ISBN:** *1-59462-338-4*   **Pages:** 132
                                                MSRP $12.95

The Theory of Moral Sentiments
Adam Smith

QTY

This work from 1749. contains original theories of conscience amd moral judgment and it is the foundation for systemof morals.

Philosophy **ISBN:** *1-59462-777-0*   **Pages:** 536
                                                MSRP $19.95

Jessica's First Prayer
Hesba Stretton

QTY

In a screened and secluded corner of one of the many railway-bridges which span the streets of London there could be seen a few years ago, from five o'clock every morning until half past eight, a tidily set-out coffee-stall, consisting of a trestle and board, upon which stood two large tin cans, with a small fire of charcoal burning under each so as to keep the coffee boiling during the early hours of the morning when the work-people were thronging into the city on their way to their daily toil...

Childrens   **ISBN:** *1-59462-373-2*   **Pages:** 84
                                                MSRP $9.95

My Life and Work
Henry Ford

QTY

Henry Ford revolutionized the world with his implementation of mass production for the Model T automobile. Gain valuable business insight into his life and work with his own auto-biography... "We have only started on our development of our country we have not as yet, with all our talk of wonderful progress, done more than scratch the surface. The progress has been wonderful enough but..."

Biographies/ **ISBN:** *1-59462-198-5*   **Pages:** 300
                                                MSRP $21.95

www.bookjungle.com email: sales@bookjungle.com fax: 630-214-0564 mail: Book Jungle PO Box 2226 Champaign, IL 61825

The Art of Cross-Examination
Francis Wellman

QTY

I presume it is the experience of every author, after his first book is published upon an important subject, to be almost overwhelmed with a wealth of ideas and illustrations which could readily have been included in his book, and which to his own mind, at least, seem to make a second edition inevitable. Such certainly was the case with me; and when the first edition had reached its sixth impression in five months, I rejoiced to learn that it seemed to my publishers that the book had met with a sufficiently favorable reception to justify a second and considerably enlarged edition. ..

Reference   ISBN: *1-59462-647-2*   **Pages:412**
                                      MSRP $19.95

On the Duty of Civil Disobedience
Henry David Thoreau

QTY

Thoreau wrote his famous essay, On the Duty of Civil Disobedience, as a protest against an unjust but popular war and the immoral but popular institution of slave-owning. He did more than write—he declined to pay his taxes, and was hauled off to gaol in consequence. Who can say how much this refusal of his hastened the end of the war and of slavery ?

Law   ISBN: *1-59462-747-9*   **Pages:48**
                                       MSRP $7.45

Dream Psychology Psychoanalysis for Beginners
Sigmund Freud

QTY

Sigmund Freud, born Sigismund Schlomo Freud (May 6, 1856 - September 23, 1939), was a Jewish-Austrian neurologist and psychiatrist who co-founded the psychoanalytic school of psychology. Freud is best known for his theories of the unconscious mind, especially involving the mechanism of repression; his redefinition of sexual desire as mobile and directed towards a wide variety of objects; and his therapeutic techniques, especially his understanding of transference in the therapeutic relationship and the presumed value of dreams as sources of insight into unconscious desires.

Psychology   ISBN: *1-59462-905-6*   **Pages:196**
                                      MSRP $15.45

The Miracle of Right Thought
Orison Swett Marden

QTY

Believe with all of your heart that you will do what you were made to do. When the mind has once formed the habit of holding cheerful, happy, prosperous pictures, it will not be easy to form the opposite habit. It does not matter how improbable or how far away this realization may see, or how dark the prospects may be, if we visualize them as best we can, as vividly as possible, hold tenaciously to them and vigorously struggle to attain them, they will gradually become actualized, realized in the life. But a desire, a longing without endeavor, a yearning abandoned or held indifferently will vanish without realization.

Self Help   ISBN: *1-59462-644-8*   **Pages:360**
                                      MSRP $25.45

www.bookjungle.com email: sales@bookjungle.com fax: 630-214-0564 mail: Book Jungle PO Box 2226 Champaign, IL 61825

QTY

	Title	ISBN	Price
☐	**The Rosicrucian Cosmo-Conception Mystic Christianity** by *Max Heindel*	ISBN: *1-59462-188-8*	**$38.95**
	The Rosicrucian Cosmo-conception is not dogmatic, neither does it appeal to any other authority than the reason of the student. It is: not controversial, but is: sent forth in the, hope that it may help to clear...		New Age/Religion Pages 646
☐	**Abandonment To Divine Providence** by *Jean-Pierre de Caussade*	ISBN: *1-59462-228-0*	**$25.95**
	"The Rev. Jean Pierre de Caussade was one of the most remarkable spiritual writers of the Society of Jesus in France in the 18th Century. His death took place at Toulouse in 1751. His works have gone through many editions and have been republished...		Inspirational/Religion Pages 400
☐	**Mental Chemistry** by *Charles Haanel*	ISBN: *1-59462-192-6*	**$23.95**
	Mental Chemistry allows the change of material conditions by combining and appropriately utilizing the power of the mind. Much like applied chemistry creates something new and unique out of careful combinations of chemicals the mastery of mental chemistry...		New Age Pages 354
☐	**The Letters of Robert Browning and Elizabeth Barret Barrett 1845-1846 vol II** by *Robert Browning* and *Elizabeth Barrett*	ISBN: *1-59462-193-4*	**$35.95**
			Biographies Pages 596
☐	**Gleanings In Genesis (volume I)** by *Arthur W. Pink*	ISBN: *1-59462-130-6*	**$27.45**
	Appropriately has Genesis been termed "the seed plot of the Bible" for in it we have, in germ form, almost all of the great doctrines which are afterwards fully developed in the books of Scripture which follow...		Religion/Inspirational Pages 420
☐	**The Master Key** by *L. W. de Laurence*	ISBN: *1-59462-001-6*	**$30.95**
	In no branch of human knowledge has there been a more lively increase of the spirit of research during the past few years than in the study of Psychology, Concentration and Mental Discipline. The requests for authentic lessons in Thought Control, Mental Discipline and...		New Age/Business Pages 422
☐	**The Lesser Key Of Solomon Goetia** by *L. W. de Laurence*	ISBN: *1-59462-092-X*	**$9.95**
	This translation of the first book of the "Lernegton" which is now for the first time made accessible to students of Talismanic Magic was done, after careful collation and edition, from numerous Ancient Manuscripts in Hebrew, Latin, and French...		New Age/Occult Pages 92
☐	**Rubaiyat Of Omar Khayyam** by *Edward Fitzgerald*	ISBN: *1-59462-332-5*	**$13.95**
	Edward Fitzgerald, whom the world has already learned, in spite of his own efforts to remain within the shadow of anonymity, to look upon as one of the rarest poets of the century, was born at Bredfield, in Suffolk, on the 31st of March, 1809. He was the third son of John Purcell...		Music Pages 172
☐	**Ancient Law** by *Henry Maine*	ISBN: *1-59462-128-4*	**$29.95**
	The chief object of the following pages is to indicate some of the earliest ideas of mankind, as they are reflected in Ancient Law, and to point out the relation of those ideas to modern thought.		Religion/History Pages 452
☐	**Far-Away Stories** by *William J. Locke*	ISBN: *1-59462-129-2*	**$19.45**
	"Good wine needs no bush, but a collection of mixed vintages does. And this book is just such a collection. Some of the stories I do not want to remain buried for ever in the museum files of dead magazine-numbers an author's not unpardonable vanity..."		Fiction Pages 272
☐	**Life of David Crockett** by *David Crockett*	ISBN: *1-59462-250-7*	**$27.45**
	"Colonel David Crockett was one of the most remarkable men of the times in which he lived. Born in humble life, but gifted with a strong will, an indomitable courage, and unremitting perseverance...		Biographies/New Age Pages 424
☐	**Lip-Reading** by *Edward Nitchie*	ISBN: *1-59462-206-X*	**$25.95**
	Edward B. Nitchie, founder of the New York School for the Hard of Hearing, now the Nitchie School of Lip-Reading, Inc, wrote "LIP-READING Principles and Practice". The development and perfecting of this meritorious work on lip-reading was an undertaking...		How-to Pages 400
☐	**A Handbook of Suggestive Therapeutics, Applied Hypnotism, Psychic Science** by *Henry Munro*	ISBN: *1-59462-214-0*	**$24.95**
			Health/New Age/Health/Self-help Pages 376
☐	**A Doll's House: and Two Other Plays** by *Henrik Ibsen*	ISBN: *1-59462-112-8*	**$19.95**
	Henrik Ibsen created this classic when in revolutionary 1848 Rome. Introducing some striking concepts in playwriting for the realist genre, this play has been studied the world over.		Fiction/Classics/Plays 308
☐	**The Light of Asia** by *sir Edwin Arnold*	ISBN: *1-59462-204-3*	**$13.95**
	In this poetic masterpiece, Edwin Arnold describes the life and teachings of Buddha. The man who was to become known as Buddha to the world was born as Prince Gautama of India but he rejected the worldly riches and abandoned the reigns of power when...		Religion/History/Biographies Pages 170
☐	**The Complete Works of Guy de Maupassant** by *Guy de Maupassant*	ISBN: *1-59462-157-8*	**$16.95**
	"For days and days, nights and nights, I had dreamed of that first kiss which was to consecrate our engagement, and I knew not on what spot I should put my lips..."		Fiction/Classics Pages 240
☐	**The Art of Cross-Examination** by *Francis L. Wellman*	ISBN: *1-59462-309-0*	**$26.95**
	Written by a renowned trial lawyer, Wellman imparts his experience and uses case studies to explain how to use psychology to extract desired information through questioning.		How-to/Science/Reference Pages 408
☐	**Answered or Unanswered?** by *Louisa Vaughan* Miracles of Faith in China	ISBN: *1-59462-248-5*	**$10.95**
			Religion Pages 112
☐	**The Edinburgh Lectures on Mental Science (1909)** by *Thomas*	ISBN: *1-59462-008-3*	**$11.95**
	This book contains the substance of a course of lectures recently given by the writer in the Queen Street Hall, Edinburgh. Its purpose is to indicate the Natural Principles governing the relation between Mental Action and Material Conditions...		New Age/Psychology Pages 148
☐	**Ayesha** by *H. Rider Haggard*	ISBN: *1-59462-301-5*	**$24.95**
	Verily and indeed it is the unexpected that happens! Probably if there was one person upon the earth from whom the Editor of this, and of a certain previous history, did not expect to hear again...		Classics Pages 380
☐	**Ayala's Angel** by *Anthony Trollope*	ISBN: *1-59462-352-X*	**$29.95**
	The two girls were both pretty, but Lucy who was twenty-one who supposed to be simple and comparatively unattractive, whereas Ayala was credited, as her Bombwhat romantic name might show, with poetic charm and a taste for romance. Ayala when her father died was nineteen...		Fiction Pages 484
☐	**The American Commonwealth** by *James Bryce*	ISBN: *1-59462-286-8*	**$34.45**
	An interpretation of American democratic political theory. It examines political mechanics and society from the perspective of Scotsman James Bryce		Politics Pages 572
☐	**Stories of the Pilgrims** by *Margaret P. Pumphrey*	ISBN: *1-59462-116-0*	**$17.95**
	This book explores pilgrims religious oppression in England as well as their escape to Holland and eventual crossing to America on the Mayflower, and their early days in New England...		History Pages 268

www.bookjungle.com *email: sales@bookjungle.com fax:* 630-214-0564 *mail:* Book Jungle PO Box 2226 Champaign, IL 61825

QTY

The Fasting Cure *by Sinclair Upton* ISBN: *1-59462-222-1* $13.95
In the Cosmopolitan Magazine for May, 1910, and in the Contemporary Review (London) for April, 1910, I published an article dealing with my experiences in fasting. I have written a great many magazine articles, but never one which attracted so much attention... *New Age/Self Help/Health Pages 164*

Hebrew Astrology *by Sepharial* ISBN: *1-59462-308-2* $13.45
In these days of advanced thinking it is a matter of common observation that we have left many of the old landmarks behind and that we are now pressing forward to greater heights and to a wider horizon than that which represented the mind-content of our progenitors... *Astrology Pages 144*

Thought Vibration or The Law of Attraction in the Thought World ISBN: *1-59462-127-6* $12.95
by William Walker Atkinson *Psychology/Religion Pages 144*

Optimism *by Helen Keller* ISBN: *1-59462-108-X* $15.95
Helen Keller was blind, deaf, and mute since 19 months old, yet famously learned how to overcome these handicaps, communicate with the world, and spread her lectures promoting optimism. An inspiring read for everyone... *Biographies/Inspirational Pages 84*

Sara Crewe *by Frances Burnett* ISBN: *1-59462-360-0* $9.45
In the first place, Miss Minchin lived in London. Her home was a large, dull, tall one, in a large, dull square, where all the houses were alike, and all the sparrows were alike, and where all the door-knockers made the same heavy sound... *Childrens/Classic Pages 88*

The Autobiography of Benjamin Franklin *by Benjamin Franklin* ISBN: *1-59462-135-7* $24.95
The Autobiography of Benjamin Franklin has probably been more extensively read than any other American historical work, and no other book of its kind has had such ups and downs of fortune. Franklin lived for many years in England, where he was agent... *Biographies/History Pages 332*

Name

Email

Telephone

Address

City, State ZIP

☐ **Credit Card**   ☐ **Check / Money Order**

Credit Card Number

Expiration Date

Signature

Please Mail to: Book Jungle
PO Box 2226
Champaign, IL 61825
or Fax to: 630-214-0564

ORDERING INFORMATION
web: *www.bookjungle.com*
email: *sales@bookjungle.com*
fax: *630-214-0564*
mail: *Book Jungle PO Box 2226 Champaign, IL 61825*
or PayPal *to sales@bookjungle.com*

Please contact us for bulk discounts

DIRECT-ORDER TERMS

**20% Discount if You Order
Two or More Books**
Free Domestic Shipping!
Accepted: Master Card, Visa,
Discover, American Express

www.ingramcontent.com/pod-product-compliance
Lightning Source LLC
Chambersburg PA
CBHW080240170426
43192CB00014BA/2515